LEFT OUT

Saskatchewan's NDP
and the Relentless
Pursuit of Mediocrity

JOHN GORMLEY

indie ink
PUBLISHING

Cover Design: Caroline Dinter, Freelance Graphic Designer, Saskatoon
Cover Photo: Trevor Owen, Trevor Owen Photography (trevorowen.com)
Book Layout and Typography: Jacqueline Germin Graphic Design (jgermin.com)
Editor: Suzanne Paschall

©2010 by John Gormley
johngormley.ca and leftout.ca

Published by Indie Ink Publishing
610 Rusholme Road
Saskatoon, SK, Canada S7L 0G7
T 306.280.6578
info@indieinkpublishing.com

Printed in Canada by Friesens Book Division

First edition: October, 2010

ISBN 978-0-9866936-0-1

Library and Archives Canada Cataloguing in Publication

Gormley, John
Left out: Saskatchewan's NDP and the relentless pursuit of mediocrity/John Gormley.

Includes bibliography and index.
ISBN 978-0-9866936-0-1

1. Saskatchewan New Democratic Party.
2. Saskatchewan–Politics and government–20th century.
3. Saskatchewan–Politics and government–21st century. I. Title.

JL319.A545G67 2010   324.27124'07   C2010-905201-3

Mixed Sources
Cert no. SW-COC-001271
© 1996 FSC

To the four women who mean so much in my life:
Helen, my Mum, who defined it
Deirdre and Jill, who gave it meaning and purpose
And Marie, who changed it forever

Acknowledgments

I wish to sincerely thank the many people who made this inaugural book possible. Some have left us, like my Dad who stoked the fires of politics early; and Lise, who tirelessly supported and tolerated a young guy's political dreams.

To others, like my friend, Mike Couros—one of the smartest political people I know—thanks for the encouragement, tough questions and proofreads. To Professor Joe Garcea and Senator Pamela Wallin, who agreed to review early copies, your observations and kind words were much appreciated. Also, to the several other readers who shall remain nameless and whose wisdom and sage advice were so welcomed, many thanks. You know who you are. Thanks, too, to my friend Ezra Levant for his always sound advice; to Kate McMillan, the world-renowned Saskatchewan blogger (your title prevailed!), and to Trent Lalonde...keep up the good work.

I owe a great debt to the people responsible for the finished product, including Suzanne Paschall and Jaime Nicklas for their editing prowess and the artistic flair and creativity of cover designer Caroline Dinter and book designer Jacqueline Germin, who makes the written word look so good. Special thanks to Suzanne not only for managing every stage of this project but also in her capacity as publisher. Congratulations on the launch of her publishing company, Indie Ink, an exciting and creative venture for Saskatchewan writers.

To Bernard Lau and the team at Numa Corp, thanks for the terrific website, www.leftout.ca.

After years of dining out on my radio show with "Saskatchewinners and Saskatchewhiners" I wish I could take credit; but that's to Al Logue. Thanks. Ditto for "lion at the waterhole" which I swiped from Ken Gryschuk. You have finally been acknowledged!

To Pam Leyland, Gordon and Doug Rawlinson and many of the finest people that I know and am honoured and fortunate to work with in Rawlco Radio—thanks for the inspiration and commitment to being better everyday at what we do, on the radio and in life.

And, mostly to my beloved Marie, who spent many winter nights gently saying "back to your book", thanks for your support, encouragement and love. I am a blessed and truly lucky man and this book would not have been possible without you.

Table of contents

Introduction

SASKATCHEWAN LIFE, RADIO AND THE RANT

I grew up in small town Saskatchewan. It was like living in a Norman Rockwell print, only better. Our street teemed with kids. We were all the same—or thought we were. It was only later we'd learn that some of our friends never did have dads and some families had less than others. But at the time, none of this mattered. Anyone's mom had the right to yell "smarten up!" out the window at you; we drank water from neighbours' garden hoses and played until we dropped.

I don't remember when my attraction to politics began but for as long as I can remember, I have been a political junkie. It's who I am.

I also couldn't tell you why we called the basement the "rumpus room." Our rumpus room had a provincial electoral map on the wall, each constituency marked by a coloured stick pin—red ones for New Democratic Party (NDP) ridings, green ones for Liberal. My Irish immigrant dad thought it a good idea to learn Saskatchewan politics. Next to his life-long passion for opera and the Saskatchewan Roughriders, politics was big in our house. While normal kids traded baseball and hockey cards, I could pull out the pins on that map and replace them by memory. It didn't do a thing for me on the ice or the baseball diamond, but it helped later.

This book is about a lifetime interest in politics that finally erupted in a rant I could no longer hold back. The rant had been building for a while.

In the late 1990s, I returned to Saskatchewan to host a radio talk show and help launch Rawlco Radio's news talk franchise. I'd been living in Alberta for six years practicing law. I loved Alberta and thought I'd spend the rest of my days there as a management labour lawyer. But the pull home was irresistible.

Just so you know the entire story, my first life—the one before politics and law—was in broadcast journalism, reading newscasts and hosting a current affairs talk show, not the opinionated stuff I do today. I left the media in my 20s when I was elected as a Progressive Conservative MP from Saskatchewan. After just one term in Ottawa, I left politics because of ill health—the voters got sick of me.

After politics, I studied law at the University of Saskatchewan in Saskatoon, graduated and left for Alberta. Living there, I followed from afar Roy Romanow's NDP and the tough decisions taken to balance Saskatchewan's budget. The same thing was happening in Alberta with Ralph Klein. In Saskatchewan, where the debt was deeper, much of Romanow's work in restoring the province's finances transcended partisan politics—it was the right thing and had to be done.

Within months of returning to Saskatchewan in 1998, the closer I looked at politics the more disappointing it was. Was it my faltering memory? Had I remembered the NDP better than they really were? Had immersion in the positive Alberta attitude of hope and perseverance skewed my perception? Whatever the reason, it was abundantly clear that my province was being governed by people without a plan—many of them chronic under-achievers, always ready to keep expectations low and spread the fear of change.

As the 1990s yielded to the 21st century and we all somehow survived Y2K, it was a hopeful time of anticipation, new challenges and boundless optimism. In the early 2000s the tech bubble was bursting, some economies would go into a minor recession and the events of a terrible day in September, 2001 would change all of us forever. But in Western Canada, as the new millennium dawned, it was a time of incredible opportunity. Commodity and energy prices were strengthening and new markets in Asia opened to the West.

In the early 2000s, a red-hot economy enveloped Alberta, BC and the Western United States. Particularly next door, fuelled by energy, finance and immigration, Alberta's economy (especially the corridor along Highway 2 from Edmonton to Calgary) was the strongest in North America.

But here in Saskatchewan, even as our economy expanded, there was a sense of ennui, an unsettled feeling that we were falling short, and always would. Talk still centered on what we *could be* rather than what we were. And underneath it all, there was a lingering sense that, after all, this *was* Saskatchewan and things weren't really ever going to change, were they?

I've always believed that elections, in addition to being the vital instruments in a democracy, are useful social barometers.

Like a Beethoven symphony, an Angus Young guitar solo or Oscar Peterson gliding through improvised jazz, the subtexts of an election flow like the melodies and dynamics of a great musical work. The election messages rise and fall and disappear like motifs within the music but they are always there, teasing at the edges of our consciousness or hitting us head on. The best way to watch an election is the same way we appreciate great music—close your eyes and listen past the policies, noise and rhetoric. Listen carefully and then, ever so subtly, the hidden and critical themes will emerge where the political parties really tell you about them-selves and, more importantly, what they think of you.

In every NDP campaign, including Roy Romanow's 1999 near loss and the two later elections of 2003 and 2007, there was an underlying and consistent theme about change. It was to be feared and resisted. The melody was the same in every election: "Change is about the unknown; it will take away what you have; it will hurt you; it will not be good; and you should be afraid. Don't even think about change."

Like much of Saskatchewan's collective psyche for the 70 years since the Great Depression, the election talk revolved around potential and future opportunity rather than results. And if change resistance and fear didn't work, the NDP fallback message was clear: "Things here are as good as they're going to get." But were they, really?

As the Romanow government transformed into the Lorne Calvert NDP, the political fabric seemed to fray; the once rigid and controlled Romanow agenda became more relaxed, more lackadaisical. Partly it was the Calvert style; but part of it was a more entitled sense of governing—the NDP had ruled for 10 years and was confident, sometimes arrogant. And with

Calvert's regime came scandals—more scandals than any government in Saskatchewan history, often borne out of weak management and a governing style that had lost a connection with real people.

> "Socialism—the philosophy of failure, the creed of ignorance and the gospel of envy. Its inherent virtue is the equal sharing of misery."
>
> *Sir Winston Churchill*

Then came the tipping point.

Late one night, while researching a talk show segment on a former Saskatchewan NDP senior advisor and strategist charged with murder, I surfed the Net looking for a court date for Mark Stobbe who was accused of killing his wife in Manitoba five months after he'd left a high powered political job in Saskatchewan as Romanow's communications guru. Every query on Stobbe turned up a book that he had edited years earlier on the Progressive Conservative government of Grant Devine.

Stobbe is a huge, hulking and socially awkward left-wing introvert whose book was released just before the 1991 election when Devine's Tories were crushed at the polls. An edgy writer who uses words to skewer his opponents, Stobbe wrote the book while he was employed by the NDP as a researcher and political assistant. *Devine Rule in Saskatchewan: A Decade of Hope and Hardship* was a compilation of essays by left-wing academics and polemicists, more hatchet job than magnum opus. But for many, it is the definitive record of everything that went on during the Devine years, although it omits anything remotely positive about nearly a decade of Saskatchewan history.

Stobbe's book was just one small cog in the well-oiled Saskatchewan NDP political machine—large, powerful, all present and always able to rely on its supporters for even an approved version of political history.

From the end of the Romanow years into the clumsy and embarrassing Calvert era, with each passing NDP misstep and scandal, Saskatchewan continued to lose confidence and people, as our population plummeted to lows not seen since the early 1980s. Witnessing this, I lamented that our Saskatchewan, the one place which should be the envy of Canada, was slipping further away. The NDP seemed to have no plan beyond the relentless pursuit of mediocrity and driving our kids away to Alberta. At the same time, sympathetic academics and pundits consistently justified weak left-wing policies and even defended them as "the Saskatchewan way."

Watching this bleak landscape, I grumbled that if the usual pattern held, it wouldn't be long before someone from the University of Regina or the NDP caucus wrote a book extolling the Calvert years as another high watermark in Saskatchewan political history. And this couldn't be further from the truth.

I get paid to rant, which I do often and sometimes well. It's one of the benefits of hosting a radio talk show. One day, in the middle of a rant about Saskatchewan's NDP—inept, arrogant, scandal-plagued and slowly killing our province—I muttered "someone ought to write this stuff down."

So I did.

Chapter 1

Just my luck: there's a natural governing party that runs the place...but I don't think they're very good

Naturally Saskatchewan

The NDP is Saskatchewan's natural governing party. Since first being elected in 1944, they've ruled for all but 19 years. Like the sports dynasties of childhood—the Canadiens, Oilers, Yankees, Bulls or Packers—the NDP is a winning machine. Every NDP leader from Tommy Douglas to Lorne Calvert has become premier. In Saskatchewan, you're either an NDPer or you're not.

But, despite the party's long run, most people actually don't vote for the NDP. Only twice in the last 50 years has the party captured more than 50% of the popular vote. Usually, the NDP wins majority governments with just over 40% of the vote because their opponents split the remaining 60%. The NDP's impressive batting average, winning 12 of the last 17 elections, stands for the proposition that you can govern when most people don't agree with you—as long as your opponents spend their time fighting one another.

In those rare times when non-New Democrats unite behind one party, the NDP loses. In 2007, Saskatchewan Party leader Brad Wall became only the third person ever to break the NDP stranglehold on Saskatchewan. In the 1960s, Liberal Ross Thatcher had 7 years in government but his party virtually disappeared within a decade of his defeat in 1971. In 1982, Progressive Conservative Grant Devine rolled into office with a huge landslide. Nine years later, with criminal charges pending, the Tories became an embarrassing political footnote in Saskatchewan history.

Notice a trend here? The party that unseats the NDP usually lasts two terms and then disappears. And while this is partially self-inflicted, it is also the genius of the NDP in literally destroying its opponents, often ruthlessly. Other parties come and go, but the NDP lives on.

Microsoft founder Bill Gates attributes much of his success to competitors who were very poorly run, unable to combine business and engineering and unwilling to renew their product "to get it to the next generation." The NDP is the Microsoft of politics—knowing the business of running government and the engineering of successful election campaigns with the added benefit of facing poorly run competitors unable to sustain their political product long enough to get it to the next generation.

For Saskatchewan's NDP there's more to being the natural governing party than merely dividing the opposition and being lucky. The party has a broad reach, a coalition extending from the radical left loons who oppose capitalism, war and development, to their Birkenstock-wearing, latte-sipping Earth Muffin cousins all the way to accountants working in office jobs, a handful of small businesspeople and social workers, teachers, civil servants and trade union leaders who see the NDP as the only party that "cares" for people.

The NDP has a strong connection to the past, evoking heroes and history; getting the organizational fundamentals right and, like Microsoft, constantly evolving and adapting to meet new challenges and getting the next generation of party workers and Members of the Legislative Assembly (MLAs) ready for roll-out. Like Alberta's Progressive Conservative party which has governed non-stop since 1971, the NDP has been able to convince some important players in Saskatchewan that they're the only game in town. And although they can't match the Alberta Tories for an uninterrupted run, there is the Alberta-like perception in Saskatchewan; that nagging suspicion in the minds of civil servants, businesspeople and the media that the NDP always matters and will always bounce back. And when it does, the party has a long memory for those who opposed them.

Even though the NDP has proudly boasted throughout history that it is a socialist party, the "s" word upsets many NDPers. Suggest that some of them are Marxists (which they are) and you'll be called a red baiter or worse. As recently as late 2009 when a critic referred to the NDP as "socialists," Leader Post/Star Phoenix newspaper columnist Murray Mandryk harrumphed "ridiculous." It's never been entirely clear from observing Mandryk's world if he doesn't really believe a socialist party is socialist or if hearing the word simply makes him cranky.

> "Socialism is simply Communism for people without the testosterone to man the barricades."
>
> *Dr. Gary North, Libertarian historian and philosopher*

Historically, NDP governments are cautious, not usually flashy or exciting and prefer to manage expectations downward—no point in getting the citizens too encouraged. The governing style prefers carefully balanced budgets, which is a good thing, except for the borrowing done by Crown corporations which then pay "dividends" back to the government. The NDP views government as an instrument for change—particularly social change at the expense of capitalism. And, because of a belief in collectivist policies, the NDP embraces the idea of government directly participating in the economy and sometimes competing against private business.

During my political coming of age in the 1970s, senior Allan Blakeney Cabinet minister Wes Robbins explained to me the success of the NDP. Speaking simply and slowly, as if lecturing a child (no wonder; after all, I was both a journalist and a teenager at the time) Robbins painstakingly explained that "as Tommy Douglas told us 'from each according to his abilities, to each according to his needs'." I don't know if Douglas actually said this but if he did, he'd lifted it from Karl Marx who used those words in 1875 to explain the "higher phase" of communist society.

The craziness of the "from each/to each" stuff has been debunked by history, economics and the collapse of the Soviet Union. But even today, gently scratch many ardent NDPers and you'll find someone all too ready to judge who should get and who should pay (hint: it's usually not them paying).

Non-NDP governments, like the current SaskParty, tend to place greater reliance on the individual and on community-based organizations, businesses, churches and institutions beyond government. They also prefer less direct government intervention in the economy. Evolved modern voters (and their political parties) know that government has an important and accepted role in social policy and that no party in today's Saskatchewan has the exclusive franchise on compassion. It is an acknowledged role of modern government, regardless of party affiliation, to provide for citizens in need.

It was telling when Wall's SaskParty government, within a year of being elected, brought in the largest tax cut in history and pulled off a huge social policy coup by raising the basic personal tax exemption, which moved 80,000 lower income people off the tax rolls entirely. The government also announced a pay down of the provincial debt by 40% and added a half-billion dollars to one-time infrastructure spending. Wall's government followed up with commitments to a variety of social programs.

In response, the only reaction from the NDP was "this is what we would have done." Beyond sour grapes, this points to a more problematic issue in Saskatchewan's political culture. Instead of using their defeat as a message for renewal and a new policy direction, many in the NDP regard their rare loss as an aberration and a mere time-out, like kids being sent to their room. For some in the inner circle of the NDP, like a long-time party communications specialist who confided to a friend, the voters made a big mistake by rejecting the NDP and electing the SaskParty. When things go wrong, as they inevitably will when anyone but the NDP governs, he warned, the people will pay for their mistake and the NDP will have to come back to save them.

In the Beginning, God Created the NDP...

To truly understand the NDP and its political effectiveness we have to go back to its creation in the early 1930s when it was called the Cooperative Commonwealth Federation (CCF). More like a religious movement than a political party, the CCF was born of the Great Depression when farmer, labour and socialist groups merged. The social gospel played a strong role, promoted by preachers turned politicians like the party's first leader, Oxford-educated social activist and Methodist minister J.S. Woodsworth, and later Baptist minister T.C. (Tommy) Douglas.

Both Woodsworth and Douglas would often speak of their hope for the "New Jerusalem," a place referred to in the Book of Revelations as the dwelling place of the saints. This place of universal love and peace is also mentioned in William Blake's 1808 poem And Did Those Feet in Ancient Time. Ironically, in the 2000s, NDP Premier Lorne Calvert, an ordained United Church minister, would also refer to the New Jerusalem which, besides confirming the old joke that the United Church is the NDP at prayer, illustrates how even today a strong social gospel underlies the NDP.

The CCF's first party convention in the summer of 1933 unveiled its founding document, the *Regina Manifesto*, which featured 14 sections and a strong streak of Fabian socialism and Marxism at their most enthusiastic and naive.

> "No CCF Government will rest content until it has eradicated capitalism."
>
> *Regina Manifesto*

From its promise to eliminate capitalism, the utopian *Regina Manifesto* pledged a social order committed to "supplying human needs and not the making of profits." The CCF's 140 delegates at the founding convention actually did not write the *Manifesto*. It had been written in advance because, as Woodsworth lectured the group, "the untrained masses are incompetent to pass judgment upon the complicated problems of capitalism."

The CCF also promised to replace the "inherent injustice and inhumanity" of capitalism by having the government own banks, insurance companies and "other industries essential to social planning." Government would first take over "transportation, communications and electrical power" with "mining, pulp and paper and the distribution of milk, bread, coal and gasoline" being next.

The *Regina Manifesto*, which Woodsworth saw as part of his search for "a distinctive type of socialism" was distinctive alright—distinctively nutty. Astonishingly out of touch with what would later happen across the world (post-War economic expansion, a growing middle class and finally the death of the Soviet Union) the *Manifesto* is a quaint throwback to a different time. As a footnote—which has cost our province greatly in low levels of private investment and historically weak population numbers—the only place in North America to actually try extensive government ownership and a "socialized economic order" was Saskatchewan.

The only single principle of the *Manifesto* that still endures in Canada —or anywhere else for that matter—is socialized health care and the "publicly organized health, hospital and medical services" envisioned all those years ago.

Both capitalism and our modern pluralist liberal democracy turned out to be more robust and resilient than socialism. The *Regina Manifesto*— quaint and disjointed as it is—hasn't aged well and, through modern eyes, looks just plain bizarre.

In practice, the NDP long ago abandoned the *Manifesto* and evolved to a more modern social democratic party. But stubbornly refusing to remove the *Regina Manifesto* from the NDP website, it still sends a tingle of delight through ardent NDP supporters who surf by for an occasional shot of old time socialism in the digital world.

The CCF was re-named the "New" Democratic Party in a 1961 when it entered a formal alliance with the Canadian Labour Congress designed to "save democratic socialism" in Canada. Like the CCF, the NDP is long on tradition, putting party first and running a formidable political machine.

Fire Up the Party Machine...

Bill Safire, the New York Times columnist, long time Washington insider and one-time Nixon speechwriter, described a political machine in his book "Safire's Political Dictionary" as "a strict organization with rewards going to those who observe its disciplines and traditions." He cited a Bronx Democrat in the Teddy Roosevelt era who observed that beyond goodwill and patronage a political machine is "an army and in any organization, as in any army, there must be discipline."

With tangible, winning results over the years, lots of experience and loyalty to the party, the NDP is a true political machine and well disciplined to its core. Before the 2007 election, a friend of mine who works as a political consultant most recently supporting the Green Party told of attending a government workshop and being asked for advice by a young Aboriginal woman working in an NDP Cabinet minister's office. The woman's minister had asked that she buy an NDP membership, attend a weekend NDP election training seminar, pay the party for the training and bank her holidays and then use them during the coming election as an NDP campaign worker. My friend indignantly called this "the corrupting of First Nations youth, forced to toe the NDP line all the way to disillusionment." Sure. But I call it the way the NDP gets the job done.

I often compare Saskatchewan's left-wing NDP to America's right-wing Republicans. It's not as odd as you think. Obama-mania aside, the Republican Party of Reagan, Lincoln and Washington, like Saskatchewan's NewDems, is historically the best organized party, able to mobilize the vote and, as a result, the party that most often governs the U.S.

Although more Americans identify themselves as being Republicans than Saskatchewanians do NDP, there's an old saying that "Democrats fall in love, but Republicans fall in line." This speaks to the kind of "party first" discipline that natural governing parties have. And, as President Ronald Reagan used to say, "You've got to preach to the choir first"—a message well understood by NDPers who always refine the message first to their core supporters and then move it outward to the public.

For the NDP, from talking points regularly circulated in their official newspaper, the *Commonwealth*, to carefully orchestrated letter writing campaigns to the editor, a highly motivated and disciplined group of true believers at its core is invaluable for disseminating the broader party message.

The night before the 2007 election, an NDP loyalist named "Mark" took to CBC's Saskatchewan website to implore people to re-elect the NDP, which he described as the "moral conscience of Canada." Then he went all daft, describing Saskatchewan as the "home of Tommy Douglas with no foreign-induced daylight saving time" and arguing that the re-election of Saskatchewan's NDP would help "end the unjust occupation of Afghanistan, the climate crisis and poverty." As well, wrote the zealot, re-electing the Calvert government would end "the housing, transit, social and ecological woes and the erosion of our sovereignty because of covert and deep integration with the US." He exhorted, "we need the people of Saskatchewan to help save our nation—please vote NDP." With supporters this loyal who needs religious cults?

Most NDP loyalists aren't as over the top as this guy. But they are relentless. From the retired NDPers who congregate for coffee every morning at the local co-op to the party members who religiously read every word of the NDP's *Commonwealth*, there is a core group that never strays whether the NDP is in government or not. Like Orcs coming over the walls in *Lord of the Rings*, they never stop, wave after wave of them storming the castle. Whether the NDP is governing or in opposition, the battle is on until they take their last breath.

A good example is a relatively anonymous Saskatoon letter writer and retired school teacher Randy Nelson, whose often caustic letters to the editor have echoed the NDP party line for over 25 years, effusively praising the NDP in government and taking a hatchet to their opponents. The fact that Nelson was an NDP youth executive in the 1960s and later the NDP MLA in Yorkton until his defeat in 1982 seems to escape many people, except those of us with long memories (and that election map in the family basement…thanks, Dad).

For years, frequent letters to the editor in both the Leader Post and Star Phoenix—as well as in weeklies around the province—have echoed the NDP party line, almost to the word, whether in government or opposition. Even a cursory look at the letter writers' names usually reveals local union leaders, Saskatchewan Federation of Labour executives, NDP riding presidents or past party candidates. For some reason these "concerned citizens" never identify their deep involvement in the party.

The discipline, loyalty and hard work of NDP foot soldiers are impressive, at times awe inspiring. Like any well-organized club or church, the sense of belonging within the NDP embraces history, personality and a perception of shared values and interests. This is obvious when reading the *Commonwealth*. Created by Tommy Douglas in the 1930s and published every two months, the magazine is full of ads from NDP lawyers, accountants, insurance agents and unions, and brims with chatty updates of party events, fundraisers, meetings and people of interest.

The *Commonwealth* has regular columns and frequent articles of interest to the left, including essays on the evils of corporations, oil, genetically modified crops, globalization and free trade. There was even a piece from perennially failed NDP candidate Nettie Wiebe explaining why higher taxes are actually good for us. And for loyal supporters there is "NDP Coffee Row" which contains talking points supportive of the NDP and critical of their opponents intended to be repeated by party supporters in social encounters with friends and colleagues. There is also "Labour Briefs," updating party members on the latest union organizing drives, strikes and labour conferences.

Amidst the glowing biographies of federal and provincial NDP candidates and new executive members in the party, the *Commonwealth* frequently features tributes to NDP old-timers and lifelong party workers who usually trace their activism back to the campaigns of Tommy Douglas. In one case, an 80-year-old describes his "most memorable experience" as attending a Vancouver meeting of Socialist International in the 1970s. Socialist International—most memorable? How about falling in love, the birth of your kids or a great vacation?

Days after Brad Wall became leader of the SaskParty, the spring issue of the *Commonwealth* in 2004 provided insight into how NDP loyalists load up on attack politics. In a scathing and defamatory personal profile of Wall written by the radical and vituperative University of Regina professor John Conway, the article ends with dictionary excerpts mocking Wall's name, as in "Wall: enclosing, dividing, separating, blocking, closing… and 'stonewall', 'off the wall', 'up the wall' and 'handwriting on the wall'." For a party that likes to believe it attracts the intelligentsia, this juvenile stuff is telling.

In addition to the party newsletter, many NDPers—particularly on the left edge of the party—subscribe to the *Briarpatch*, a radical left-wing magazine from Regina dating to the early 1970s. Published every two months, and sometimes sharing authors with the *Commonwealth*, the *Briarpatch* is occasionally critical of NDP governments for being not left-wing enough in reining in capitalism, redistributing wealth and setting up more Crown corporations. In the rare times when non-NDP governments are in office (like now) the Briarpatch is often over the top in its vitriol.

Throughout its history in Saskatchewan, the NDP reached into every facet of life. And it had deep bench strength. In every town and city there was a devout following of small business owners, members of the Legion and farmers who embraced the party's populist message of people before profits. And the NDP had official proxies: members of the local labour council, Crown corporation employees, Saskatchewan Wheat Pool delegates,and directors of the vast network of credit unions and co-ops —most, card-carrying NDP members.

Hitting up farmers, too, was Joe Phelps, who sat in Douglas' first Cabinet in 1944 and, when defeated, created the Saskatchewan Farmers Union, which later became the National Farmers Union, led by "Red" Roy Atkinson—father of MLA Pat Atkinson. The NDP was everywhere, all the time.

The party's grip on Saskatchewan was philosophic but not so much on the tenets of Marxism and socialism as the principles learned from painful experience during the Great Depression of the 1930s. Big insurance companies, banks and grain companies, as well as the free market, were the enemy. They were the outsiders, the external forces designed to undermine and attack "the Saskatchewan way" by promoting self-reliance based on greed.

This also dovetailed with an attitude based on fear—fear of the outside, unknown world and the change that would bring external threats to hurt Saskatchewan. People here needed security, opportunity mediated by government—which would not hurt you like greedy outsiders would —and protection. The NDP would do all of this.

The NDP historically cut a wide swath through teachers. From the earliest days of CCF co-founder MJ Coldwell, a teacher, to 1960s NDP Premier Woodrow Lloyd—an executive of the Saskatchewan Teachers' Federation (STF)—there have been dozens of NDP MLAs and party activists whose first lives were in the classroom. Even today, while teachers have become as politically diverse as any other professionals, still within the bowels of the powerful STF, a loyal core of NDP activists rules with an iron hand.

Today's NDP still has many academics and civil servants well-ensconced within the party but, like teachers and co-op/credit union people, employees in universities and government have become increasingly diverse in their political choices.

The one entity that remains as committed to the NDP today as it was in 1933 is organized labour. The NDP is the exclusive party of trade unions. Unions still hold seats on the NDP executive and vote at party conventions. Finding a union leader in Saskatchewan who is not an NDPer is like finding a gay guy who doesn't like Judy Garland, Liza Minnelli or Cher. No group works as hard or receives as much gratitude from the NDP as organized labour, which donates money to campaigns, recruits door-knockers and election volunteers and even brings in highly trained political consultants on the payroll of large unions to run individual NDP election campaigns.

The structure of the NDP for many years was breathtaking in scope —broad-based local, well organized and mainstream. That hardworking and decent family next door who went to your church, whose kids played with you, whose dad coached hockey and mom led the Brownies were NDPers. Every election, the dad would be out hammering in lawn signs while his wife scrutineered at the polls for the NDP. They were part of an expansive network of local committees and grassroots members with a shared sense of mission that stretched from every street in small-town Saskatchewan to the halls of the Legislature in Regina.

The NDP's broad reach began to narrow in 1969 when a hard-core leftist crowd called "the Waffle" emerged within the party. Mainly rooted in universities and Marxism, the Waffle was aptly called "Trotskyites and goofballs" by one annoyed Saskatchewan NDP MP. With policies that made the *Regina Manifesto* look moderate and reasonable, the Waffle was finally tossed from the NDP by the early 1970s but not without causing far reaching shifts in the party.

While many in the old NDP base of farmers and trade unions thought they'd cut out this ingrown toenail of radicalism, just a few years later in 1975 Saskatchewan's decision to nationalize the potash industry by expropriating potash mines from American companies was a direct salute to the Waffle—put away your hammers and sickles and join the "mainstream" NDP, if there is such a thing.

Even by the 1980s, the NDP was a party with more a past than a future. As an MP in the mid-80s, I remember looking at polling data that suggested if elections were limited to people over the age of 65, the NDP would sweep every seat provincially and federally. While today's seniors are more independent, diverse and less homogenous, there are still many who connect to the NDP message of protecting us, resisting the unknowns of change and auguring back to past victories.

Today's NDP loyalists are less grassroots and more likely to be committed left-wingers or labour organizers. But they're a highly motivated and skilled group that knows the fundamentals of election campaigning.

If You Don't ID, You'll Never GOTV

They are the most important initials in every election and the most basic of political commandments: ID, which stands for "identify the vote" and GOTV, "get out the vote."

In the months before an election and during the entire campaign, an effective party organization will identify the vote—not the "kinda-sorta, I might vote for you" vote—but the actual people who will cast a ballot for the party. And when the ID is confirmed, names, phone numbers, e-mail and home addresses are recorded. This information is needed in the critical final days of GOTV when campaign strategists and party workers ensure that every single identified voter gets to the polls. All the hope and good intentions in the world mean nothing until someone actually puts an "x" on the ballot.

Seasoned political strategists know that in elections, unlike nominations or leadership conventions, the campaign starts first with the strongest and most likely supporters, who are identified, confirmed and then gotten out to vote. Campaigning where your opponent is dominant and you're weaker is a waste of time, effort and resources. Only when the most supportive voter base is covered then are weaker zones done.

NDP campaigns are notoriously successful at the ID/GOTV principles. Computerized voters lists from past provincial and federal elections are collected, collated and ready for each new election. With professional, paid party organizers, union staff and government employees who take holidays or conveniently timed leaves of absence during elections, it's impressive to see how effective the operational part of the NDP machine is. These rules weren't invented by the NDP. Every effective campaign uses them, except the NDP usually does it better.

With this in mind, pretend that you are a political candidate and do the math. As the Office of Saskatchewan's Chief Electoral Officer indicates, the average provincial constituency in Saskatchewan has about 10,500 eligible voters. Voter turnout is rarely higher than 75%. So, usually no more than 7,900 people will vote in your riding. If there are no other candidates beyond you and just one opponent (which is unlikely) you'll need 50% of the votes plus one to win. So, plan on recruiting one-half of the people who will come out to vote. That's 3,950 people. Your entire campaign is focused on finding 3,950 people whose names you will catalogue on data bases and whose every political whim you will answer.

Unlike the time you were elected as Grade 8 class president, the election is not about throwing out nice speeches and brochures to a mass audience and then hoping something clicks. Election campaigns are all about getting your message to stick to 3, 950 people and then knowing who those people are and where to find them on Election Day. Assume that you have identified the necessary votes. Then you must consider the "conversion rate"—the proportion of identified supporters and "friendlies" that will actually get out to vote for you and your party. Even though supporters will tell you that they're going to vote for you, there are many reasons they simply do not show up on Election Day. So your challenge is to find more than 3,950 people as confirmed "IDs," and use a conversion rate that delivers the highest number to vote when you GOTV.

Most Saskatchewan seats are won with between 3,500 and 4,000 votes. So, to get 4,000 people to vote for you (assuming your conversion rate is 80%, where eight out of 10 people who say they'll vote for you actually turn out to vote and cast their ballots for you) then you will need 5,000 people on your confirmed ID list. These are the people that you and your campaign team will persuade, cajole, phone and even drive to the polls. If you can actually get the full 5,000 people to vote for you, you will be a rare and very successful politician.

Winning by Numbers

240 Candidates in 2007 Saskatchewan election

58 Number of provincial ridings

17 Number of candidates with over 5,000 votes

17 Number of candidates with 5,000 votes elected as MLAs

1 NDP Candidate with over 5,000 votes (Harry Van Mulligen)

3 Candidates with over 6,000 votes
(Premier Brad Wall, Ken Cheveldayoff and Don Morgan)

For ease of voting and organization, each constituency is broken into polls, which are groupings of approximately 300 voters. So, in every single poll—voter by voter, house by house—the hunt is on for supporters to identify and put on your ID list. Then the GOTV team takes over to ensure that your ID'd voters get out and cast their ballot for you on Election Day.

Every time a candidate or door knocker shows up at your house or your phone rings, campaigns are deliberately asking questions to determine how you're voting or at least, if you're "leaning." It is far more scientific than you think it is, as every encounter is usually put on a voter ID list which builds up to Election Day when the voters are "gotten out."

Just days after being elected in my own brief political career—which, by the way, was an honour I never felt truly worthy of—a wise Ottawa political veteran took me out for lunch one day just a few blocks from Parliament Hill and explained a valuable principle called the "16 percent rule."

Give or take a few percentage points, only about 16 percent of the people who vote for you are actually voting for you as a person or candidate. The remaining 84% of your votes are for your leader, your party or a policy. Or they're votes cast *against* some other party, leader or policy. It is humbling for the healthy ego of a new politician to learn that less than 20% of people who voted for them actually voted *for them*! This rule changes the longer an MLA serves, as the power of incumbency results in voters actually getting to know, respect and choose the individual MLA over his or her party.

NDP campaigns know the 16% principle well: It's all about party and leader first. The individual MLA or candidate—like the member of a union executive or co-op delegate—is part of a larger team or, for socialists, a collective. Unfortunately for many non-NDPers from the business community or other individual endeavors, their campaigns are lost before they start because they focus on the "I and me" rather than on the strength and effectiveness of party, leader and team.

Sophisticated NDP campaigns often run on two rails. Mindful of the 16% rule, the main and most visible campaign emphasizes party, leader and policy—positive for one's own, while often viciously attacking and undermining the opposing leader and party. A small part of this will deal with the individual candidate. But inside the main campaign—at the doors, in coffee shops and in person to person contact—there will often be a specific local wedge issue or whisper campaign that questions or discredits the individual opposing candidate within the riding, often in very harsh terms. This is designed for the 16% of voters who focus on the individual candidate.

From issues during a campaign—positive, negative, planned and improvised—to the profile of leaders and then the use of paid media and targeted campaigning, the election campaign is all about nudging voters to where they can be identified by the local campaign organization. Historically, the NDP is best at this and boasts the highest conversion rate on Election Day where the test is who can mobilize best and GOTV.

The NDP's Seven Rules for Getting & Keeping Power in Saskatchewan

I marvel at the NDP—their discipline, their capacity to focus, their ability to win at all costs. I'd likely worship at their feet and want to sign up…if they weren't socialists holding back my province.

In a lifetime of observing Saskatchewan politics, election campaigns and knowing many NDP MLAs, I've observed certain characteristics that distinguish every successful NDP MLA. From the brilliant ones like Premier and Rhodes Scholar Allan Blakeney to others so dumb they can't work a spoon, every NDP MLA that keeps getting elected follows these seven rules. It explains a long winning record and the NDP's tenacious grip on power:

1. Strive to win at any cost. Maintaining political power is everything. Nothing matters unless your party gets elected;

2. Always stay publicly humble and honoured to have the job;

3. Campaign relentlessly like you are always 10 points behind;

4. Always come to the aid of the party because it is cohesive, publicly unified and more important than any individual within it;

5. Maintain power with a fiercely loyal, small and dedicated group that is prepared to work harder than your opponents. Even though your opponents, between elections, may have broader public support, at

election time you will beat them when they are less organized and at a shallower depth of party loyalty;

6. Always put a positive face on your own accomplishments and promises while swearing to all that is holy that your opponent has a hidden agenda—about which you'll be witheringly negative—and which will terrorize old folks, the vulnerable and upset people who fear change; and

7. Always defend your core vote, don't waste time where you're weak and focus laser-like on any pressure point that can bring an opponent down, including hot button issues and local polls and ridings where your opponent hasn't been keeping their support shored up.

Just to show that I'm not making up this stuff, one day on my radio show I called Emory University's Drew Westen, a neuro-psychologist and author of *The Political Brain* to ask him about what really matters in elections.

Westen analyzes campaign messaging by examining brain physiology and its role in emotions. He argues that our brain is "an emotional compass crafted by millions of years of evolution" and, as with so many other decision-making processes, we vote with our emotions. He identifies four main political objectives that follow in this order:

- **Party:** Even transcending the party leader, the party must define itself and its principles in an emotionally compelling way, including defining the opposing party in ways that undermine its emotional resonance with voters;
- **Leader:** Maximize positive and minimize negative feelings toward the party leader and encourage the opposite feelings toward the opponent;
- **Personal Characteristics of the Leader:** Manage feelings toward a leader's personal characteristics like trustworthiness, competence and empathy. The opposite should also be done to one's opponent; and
- **Policies:** Well down the list is the need to manage feelings toward policies and positions or "to present voters with cogent arguments for a set of policies."

It's not that policies are unimportant, according to Westen; they're just less important than a voter asking "does this leader share the values that matter most to me and does he or she care about people like me?"

Voters will also ask whether they trust the leader to represent them faithfully and whether the leader has the necessary personal qualities like integrity, leadership and competence.

If you are embarking on a political career, apply Drew Westen's *Political Brain* to the NDP's Seven Rules for Getting and Keeping Power and you'll be in good shape.

Q: Are NDP Supporters Really Better Than Everyone Else? A: No. Just More Self-Righteous.

"If I could press a button tonight and bring a million people into this party but knew that those people were coming in for some ulterior motive and they didn't understand the kind of society we were trying to build… I wouldn't press the button because we don't want those kind of people."

Tommy Douglas, NDP Convention, early 1980s

The religious origins and zeal of the social gospel often make the NDP different from any other political party. Their political opinions are often bound up in morality, which means they're not just right but morally right. And this makes New Dems good people—in fact, in their view, the best kind of people. In the logic of many on the political left, if you disagree with their opinions you are not only incorrect but morally wrong. And, therefore, this makes you a bad person.

This self-righteousness rolled off old-time NDPers from the Tommy Douglas years as easily as a seven-second sound bite from the new generation of young leftists like ex-NDP president and leadership candidate Yens

Pedersen who earnestly intoned that "this has always been the party of integrity and morality."

This approach is as puzzling as it is pious and arrogant. Politics is a complex and intimately human endeavor involving personal experience, philosophy, psychology and judgment. And then it's woven into the necessary trade-offs between the practical and the philosophic, the greater good and the expedient, the necessary and what it takes to get elected. There are many good, principled and fine people within the NDP, just as there are in the SaskParty, Liberals, Conservatives, Communists, Green Party and Libertarians. No party—least of all the NDP—has a greater or lesser percentage of good people. No party or individuals within it has the franchise on goodness sewn up. Similarly, there are hypocrites, fools, sleaze balls and dishonest people in every party.

When holding yourself out as "the party of integrity and morality" and therefore full of better and more worthy people, a couple of unfortunate things occur. First, it gives permission to paint those who disagree with you as being less moral and of less integrity, which debases political debate and then gives you permission to attack people rather than ideas because these are "bad" people—after all, they disagree with your "moral" point of view.

It's also self-destructive to be so sanctimonious. When bad things happen—as they always will in anything involving human beings—it hurts the NDP more than it has to. Rather than acknowledge the problem and repair it, difficulties are internalized and often denied because if they are talked about it might have to be conceded that the NDP is not perfect. The evil twin of this is the cover-up. Once human failings are denied internally, they are concealed in case someone thinks the party of integrity and morality isn't. Many of the NDP's most damaging scandals during the uncomfortable Calvert years didn't come from immoral and wrong acts but from trying so hard to either hide them or whitewash them.

Laborious efforts were made to avoid, deflect and even deny that a Cabinet minister lied in the Spudco scandal, that a well connected NDP civil servant had harassed women, that the police had been misled over a theft years earlier in the NDP caucus office and even that a Dwain Lingenfelter campaign worker had fraudulently obtained memberships during the NDP leadership campaign. Had these wrongful acts been openly and quickly dealt with, the harm would have been far less than the cover ups. Ironically, when the self-professed party of morality and integrity engages in conceal-ment, it actually publicly casts the party as being the party of dishonesty and immorality. Talk about standing in front of your own dartboard.

It is also human nature to want to watch the self-righteous stumble after they've reminded us of how superior they are. When NDPers piously insist that only they will stand up for the weak and disenfranchised—incorrectly implying that no one else will—they invite students of history to point out that both Woodsworth and Douglas actively supported eugenics, the practice of sterilizing mentally and physically disabled people and placing them in camps. In fact, Tommy Douglas' sociology master's thesis was entitled *The Problems of the Subnormal Family* and expounded on ways to deal with both "defectives" and people of "below normal moral standards" by sterilizing them, which he thought would "meet the requirements most aptly."

In the early 1990s, when the NDP refused to bring in prosecutors from outside Saskatchewan—as is customary in criminal cases involving public figures—and went after former MLAs and staff of the Grant Devine government, it was a huge boost to NDP morale: the "bad guys" were going to jail or at least being seen every night on the TV news doing the "perp walk" outside the Courthouse.

If one's view of politics is to keep a running scorecard of wrongdoing, these were the best of times for the NDP. Virtuous and beyond moral reproach, the party was shooting par while its double-bogeying immoral and sinister right-wing opponents were constantly in the rough. To top it off, former Devine Cabinet minister Colin Thatcher was in prison at the time for murdering his wife.

Since then, however, if keeping a tally is your thing, the NDP has not done so well—in fact they've fared badly. In the late 1990s, a candidate in an NDP nomination in Saskatoon, a union leader, was fired when it was revealed that he had beaten his wife. In Prince Albert, drunk driving cost ex-NDP MLA and Mayor Don Cody a conviction, his license and the next election. Also in P.A., politically well-connected NDP civil servant Murdoch Carriere was alleged to have sexually assaulted some of his staff and was convicted of common assault.

Later, after years as a suspect, former Romanow advisor Mark Stobbe was charged in the murder of his wife. Shortly after the 2007 election, prominent NDP supporter and AIDS activist, Eric Braun, who had been an NDP appointee to the Saskatoon Health Region—and who the NDP trotted out as a "concerned renter" during the 2007 election campaign at an impromptu renters rally for NDP candidates—was convicted of drug trafficking and child pornography after he was found with $19,000 in cash; a large cache of drugs (including crack cocaine), and videos of boys involved in sexual activity.

And, the former President of the NDP Aboriginal section, Ernie Morin, was charged by the RCMP in connection with a membership fraud in the party's 2009 leadership campaign.

I've always thought that keeping a "good and evil" ledger for the purposes of lording your moral superiority over opponents does not enhance politics. It ultimately diminishes politics by deliberately obscuring the fact that human beings, with all their frailty and regardless of party affiliation, make mistakes and sometimes do wrong. It also discourages good people from seeking office. And it shows that the NDP is no better, no worse, no more or less moral than anyone else—just a lot more self-righteous.

There's a Mouse in Here

If the tendency toward sanctimoniousness and a religious sense of purpose is unique to the NDP, we should remember that all great faiths find strength in the written word—the scriptures of the prophets who have come before.

One of the most enduring remnants of NDP icon Tommy Douglas is his famous "Mouseland" speech, which has been printed in illustrated books, with the audio even available on the NDP website, along with an introduction from Douglas' grandson, actor Kiefer Sutherland.

Mouseland was designed mainly to promote party solidarity and argue that NDPers were not communists. But Douglas also used it to reinforce the importance of class conflict and to remind supporters of the historic vote splitting that has benefited the NDP. He used a parable of cats and mice to explain the success of his NDP. Douglas spoke of mice historically voting for cats —black ones, white ones, spotted ones but always cats. And the cats made laws that were hard on mice.

The trouble, according to Douglas, "wasn't with the colour of the cat. The trouble was that they were cats. And because they were cats, they naturally looked after cats instead of mice. Presently there came along one little mouse who had an idea. Watch out for the little fellow with an idea. And he said to the other mice, 'look fellows, why do we keep on electing a government made up of cats? Why don't we elect a government made up of mice?' 'Oh,' they said, 'he's a Bolshevik. Lock him up!' So they put him in jail. But I want to remind you: that you can lock up a mouse or a man but you can't lock up an idea."

While clever and easily illustrated, Mouseland always perplexed me. When I first read this speech as a high school kid, I wondered why someone would compare his supporters to mice. At our old tumbledown family cottage we always had mice. Even though Walt Disney did wonders with the mousey thing, I hated mice. They were rodents that chewed on stuff, crapped everywhere, multiplied in great numbers and never made anything better.

I always wondered why Douglas chose "Mouseland." Mice are small, innocuous and rarely a threat—unless they happen to chew through the wiring and burn down the house. And you will never find a mouse proudly walking around in daylight like he owns the place. Because he doesn't. He just infests it.

If Douglas' metaphor for Saskatchewan people had been something more industrious and proud like squirrels saving nuts for winter or a busy ant colony or bee hive that would have made more sense. But mice—tiny, timid, afraid of pretty well everything? No thanks.

Being the Natural Governing Party When the Gatekeepers Have Your Back

Because they've governed so long, the NDP has a big advantage over every other party. Their fingerprints are all over provincial institutions and the working machinery of government—from younger employees to seasoned bureaucrats and all the way to deputy ministers with NDP pedigrees. The NDP is everywhere.

One political insider estimates that the SaskParty government of Brad Wall, which replaced a 16-year NDP run, has a 60-20-20 formula to deal with. Sixty percent of civil servants are professionals who work for government, regardless of political party—the politicians come and go but the "business" of government is their job. Twenty percent of the civil service is sympathetic to the new government, either personally annoyed at the NDP or being SaskParty friendly. And, the remaining 20 percent are hard-core New Democrats who wake up every morning wishing they could bring Wall down. With more than 12,000 civil servants, this means at least 2,400 people inside government spend their days hoping and even plotting ways they can hasten Wall's demise.

The NDP side of the civil service is Hydra-headed. There are long-term employees who had a bad experience with the Devine Tories and swore off anyone who wasn't NDP. Others have drunk the union and NDP Kool-Aid for so long that they think any new government will be bad for them. Still others are NDP apparatchiks whose jobs are payback for loyalty and discipline to the party machine. Many of these NDP partisans work deep inside the foundations of government or Crown corporations where they were placed at various points in the NDP's lifecycle.

A good example is Dale Schmeichel, the NDP partisan who's been ensconced in the civil service during every NDP government since the 1970s. As a young campaign worker 35 years ago, he was given a management job in a mining Crown corporation and, since then, has moved between government departments, Crown corporations, and the executive and political branches of government and was even made the CEO of a health district for a period during the Romanow government.

Between government postings, Schmeichel sometimes goes back into the NDP's head office as its provincial secretary and CEO. An intense and engaging guy, Schmeichel is smart, tough and ruthless. He has also managed most of the NDP's recent provincial election campaigns except for 2007 when he mysteriously withdrew. At least Schmeichel is so partisan that when governments change both he and the newcomers know that he will leave, which he did after the 2007 election when his job as a senior vice-president of the Crown Investments Corporation disappeared.

So, where does an unabashedly left-wing, savvy and professional NDP organizer go when government jobs dry up? Beyond the CBC or being a university professor—and Schmeichel isn't qualified for either—there aren't many good paying jobs for socialists outside of government. Within days of leaving government, Schmeichel was hired as executive director of operations for the large and powerful Saskatchewan Government and General Employees Union (SGEU). Following the NDP's choice of Dwain Lingenfelter as leader, Schmeichel left the union and returned to the NDP where, as party campaign manager, he remains the consummate partisan—ready and capable of doing battle.

Any time a government changes, dozens of people are fired by the outgoing government as one of its last acts. These are staffers who work in Cabinet ministers' offices and in Executive Council, the politicized department that supports the Premier and Cabinet. When government goes, so do these jobs. But no new government is naïve enough to believe that this is the extent of it—there are always hard-core partisan holdovers that must be dealt with in Crown corporations and inside government itself.

But in Saskatchewan there are hundreds of NDP partisans deeply embedded inside the "professional civil service." Many began as political assistants to Cabinet ministers or MLAs, or as junior staffers inside Executive Council, eventually migrating into management jobs in the relative anonymity of government departments or agencies.

One example is Jason Nystrom, son of career Saskatchewan NDP MP Lorne Nystrom. In addition to working inside the political branch of government and unsuccessfully seeking an NDP nomination in Regina in 2003, Nystrom the Younger even wrote a flattering entry on the life of the NDP's Dwain Lingenfelter in the Encyclopedia of Saskatchewan. Before being defeated, the NDP hired Nystrom as a professional manager in the Highway Traffic Board, the government regulatory agency legally responsible for the operation of motor vehicles in the province under certain laws like Saskatchewan's *Traffic Safety Act*.

Here's the problem. Can someone who got their job because of their NDP connections, pedigree and loyalty to the party machine switch off deeply held partisan instincts—including, in some cases, contempt for the people who "took" government away from the NDP? Can a hard partisan be loyal and professional to a government headed by people who aren't of his party? Common sense and human nature being what they are, you can be forgiven for being skeptical.

When hiring senior staff, former Premier Roy Romanow said that governments must "try to be objective...have competent people" but admitted there are limitations both in "salary and ideology so that civil servant advisors must be knowledgeable and in general support of the ideology and philosophy that the government of the day—elected by the people to govern—is pursuing."

The Media: Fair, Balanced & Snoozing

When I returned to Saskatchewan to start the radio show in 1998, I'd been away from the media business for nearly 15 years, having spent time in politics and the legal profession. My last direct news media experience had been as an MP where the Parliamentary Press Gallery in Ottawa regularly feasts on raw politicians.

Living in Alberta, my daily news fix came from Edmonton and Calgary, both mature, top-10 national media markets. Back home in Saskatchewan, it was obvious that this was a smaller media market where political giants didn't have to stand very tall to tower over the media. Beyond the CBC, which has always been a professional and experienced news-gathering organization (with distinct NDP sympathies) and a few good print journalists there just wasn't much going on here.

Shortly after starting my talk show, I remember a news conference—the topic long forgotten—where Premier Roy Romanow opened with a prepared statement and the first question came from a shining-eyed coiffed TV reporter who breathlessly fawned, "Mr. Premier, can you provide another example of why your policy will work so well?" Gee, tough questions, I thought.

Historically, Saskatchewan has been an entry-level media market where it's training day every day as journalism grads start their first jobs here and hope to move on—quickly. Place names are mispronounced, history and context are unknown, and in some cases it becomes apparent, while they're inflicted on us here for a time, that some people working in the news business are just too dumb to move on.

For NDP governments the rules are pretty basic—be cordial to the media and take the time to explain to them how things work. Usually, once this is done the media will fall into line and be hand-fed. And, besides, most of the media will not be here for long anyway. If a reporter challenges or questions, repeat the cordial part and the explanation. If this behaviour persists, more firmly explain that you are correct. If you weren't always right you wouldn't be in government.

The University of Regina is one of Canada's few degree granting schools of journalism. Its faculty and reputation extend hard to the political left on most issues. The J-School's department head is Mitch Diamantopoulous, a pleasant enough guy who was a guest on our talk show when he was the self-professed left-wing founder of the "alternative" newspapers Prairie Dog and Planet S. With other faculty members in the alt-journalism field, including one who recently left a 10-year stint as editor of the NDP's Commonwealth magazine, the U of R Journalism program is about as balanced as MSNBC's "tingling" Chris Matthews on President Barack Obama's inauguration day.

Since my first career years ago as a journalist reading radio news and hosting a news-based, non-opinion talk show, I came home to a media business that had dramatically changed. Once locally autonomous TV stations were now merely smaller branch plants of large Toronto-based networks. The newspapers, which at one time had a staffed legislative bureau with separate reporters and columnists, now had one legislative columnist and a rotating cast of reporters who had neither the longevity nor understanding of politics or public policy. Even the halcyon days of Canadian Press and Broadcast News were gone, when journalists like Joe Ralko imposed standards on politicians and other news people.

When I returned to Saskatchewan, the Canadian Press staffer was Jay Branch, who would later quit to become the NDP's director of communications and media under Calvert. I had met Branch years earlier when he had done a hatchet job on me in the early days of the newly elected Romanow government in the early 1990s. I had nearly forgotten about him but then my Irish Alzheimer's started acting up—I forget everything except someone who's wronged me!

After federal politics in the late 1980s, before going to law school, I'd worked for the Devine Tories for eight months advising on communications strategy in several privatization efforts and travelling Saskatchewan doing speeches for the government. After starting law school, I worked on a part-time retainer basis for several more months. The NDP transition team in the early 1990s got a copy of my consulting contract to Branch, which resulted in his story that I'd been "paid to go to law school," which was incorrect. This was repeated by politicians like the NDP's Eric Cline who whined that this was a "horror story" without ever asking me about the files I still have from those days. On the very small list of regrets in life, not suing Branch, Cline and a certain NDP transition member is one of them. But the water passed under that bridge long ago.

Upon arriving back in Saskatchewan, and reading the Legislative Committee transcripts of the NDP's Channel Lake scandal in the late

1990s, I was struck by the absence of anyone in the media holding government accountable even for its explanations—if a government says it did something, does no one check? Does no one in the media press government to explain the rationale for what it did, or did not do? In matters political, there was such a trust, an unquestioning acceptance, even a seeming obedience among the media to the NDP, it struck me as odd.

Lest it be thought that Saskatchewan's media is universally weak or indifferent, there are notable exceptions. I was going to name them, inside our company, and others like the CBC, CTV or the newspapers. But if I did, someone gets missed and then cranky. You know who you are.

The undisputed media dean of the Saskatchewan political scene is Leader Post/Star Phoenix columnist Murray Mandryk, whose joyless and often angry columns are like the dour witches of Macbeth, foretelling the dark chaos that will soon reign over us. An equal opportunity naysayer—NDP and SaskParty alike at the end of his spear—Mandryk's role seems to be to tell readers that there's always more to the story, usually worse, and that politicians, especially when they're in government, really are untrustworthy and even venal.

I feel genuinely sorry for Mandryk. He has the unenviable and ultimately untenable job of being both reporter and commentator, having to neutrally report political news from the Legislature and then try his hand at actually weighing in with opinions in his columns. He succeeds at narrative reporting and back-grounding, but fails at opinion. Beyond seeming to take the generally negative tack that "everybody sucks," Mandryk's opinion columns tend to start with a position critical of one side and then double back to smack around the other side just to show he's being "balanced."

Opinion columns, by their nature, are not balanced. They pick one side over another. They take an opinion, lay the foundation with facts and evidence and then reinforce the opinion. In the long run, a columnist's overall batting average may be balanced by agreeing or disagreeing in roughly equal proportions with both political parties. But it's frankly tough to read a column that states an opinion, starts to cogently argue it but then lurches to a conclusion that often leaves the reader with the impression that Mandryk can't agree with the side with which he aligns, because he doesn't actually like them either.

Sometimes seeming grouchy, Mandryk can dial up meanness, too, in his columns. When critics accuse me of getting too personal at times on my talk show—and we're all human, sometimes I probably do—I'd be hard pressed, even on my nastiest day to trump Mandryk on his view of Premier Brad Wall: "Wall would belly-crawl over shards of broken beer bottles just to reach a live microphone and probably wouldn't let go until he bled out." Ouch.

The Academy: Loyal & Left With a Dog in the Hunt

One of the NDP's greatest achievements is its complete domination and ownership of the university professors who write political history and teach our kids. In academia, it's no secret that there are plenty of left-wing scholars, as there are a few moderates and right- wingers. But in Saskatchewan, most political discourse and history are framed, directed and mediated through socialists.

With the notable exception of a small handful of political scientists and historians who seem to have no discernable political tilt—Professors John Courtney, Bill Waiser, Gordon Barnhart and David Smith, to name a few—most of the academics who write Saskatchewan history are NDP apologists, former deputy ministers, party apparatchiks, staff and even advisors to NDP governments. When it comes to chronicling politics, most of these writers have a dog in the hunt. They're sympathetic at least, loyal at most, to the goals, ambitions, past mythology and future of the NDP.

Many of Saskatchewan's left-wing professors are nice enough people; some are even intelligent and fairly original thinkers. But there's conformity of thought on politics that is puzzling for supposedly free thinking academics. They fervently believe that everyone else thinks like them: (a) the NDP is a force for good and a moral example to all; (b) Tommy Douglas wasn't just the greatest politician in history but, indeed (thanks to the CBC), the greatest Canadian to have ever lived, and (c) no one in their right mind could disagree with them.

A frequent contributor to all things NDP literary is historian Jim Pitsula, of the University of Regina, which has housed many of Saskatchewan's best known left-wing academics, from the rancorous John Conway to Gerry Sperling, Lorne Brown, John Warnock, Joe Roberts, Ken Rasmussen, Joyce Green, Jeffery Webber and the radical left-wing social justice professor and anti-nuclear crusader Jim Harding.

One day when interviewing Pitsula about a book he'd written on Tommy Douglas, I asked him if Douglas' insistence on government owner-ship of business and his hard line against resource development may have held Saskatchewan back and made us the perpetual poor cousin to Alberta. Pitsula seemed both puzzled and confused that I didn't seem to understand that Douglas had actually made Saskatchewan better off. He sounded disappointed, even hurt, like I was some disobedient and willful child who deliberately doesn't listen. He just didn't get me. Or people who think like me.

Inside this unitary political thought, the list of NDP academics is long. And they're prolific. Howard Leeson, a deputy minister and advisor to the NDP in both the Romanow and Blakeney governments, has edited two recent books on Saskatchewan political history chock full of essays by left-wing academics, two NDP Premiers and an all-star cast of socialists.

The first book, in 2001 was entitled *Saskatchewan Politics: Into the 21st Century.* It attributes Romanow's near loss in 1999 to a "harvest election" and this "catastrophe" happened when the white male, "neo-liberal" and ideological Saskatchewan Party got more votes than the NDP. Even the book's chapter on the SaskParty is written by a former NDP media services employee with no practical or academic knowledge of the party but who still comfortably concludes in his central thesis that the SaskParty appeals to "neo-liberals" susceptible to the "libertarian lexicon of 'common sense'."

Also in Leeson's book, an entry written by NDP youth vice-president Sarah McQuarrie and University of Regina political scientist Jocelyne Praud gushed that the NDP had greatly contributed "to the definition of Canada." Really? For those of us who've spent time in national politics, the NDP with its couple of dozen MPs is not near the edge of definition. The NDP is hardly even noticed, if even relevant in defining Canada beyond a 50-year tenacious grasp on Medicare which, nationally, was introduced by Liberal Prime Minister Lester B. Pearson.

Although Leeson gets some help in his books from neutral or non-NDP writers like former Liberal leader Lynda Haverstock, ex-protocol chief Michael Jackson and former Treaty Commissioner Judge David Arnot, the books overwhelmingly represent a Saskatchewan viewed through the lens of socialist scholars and NDP advisors. They range from former NDP Premiers Romanow and Blakeney to NDP ex-Deputy Ministers John Whyte, Duane Adams, Brent Cotter, Greg Marchildon and prominent leftist aca-demics Sperling, Pitsula, Rasmussen, Green, Brett Fairbairn, Dan De Vlieger, David McGrane and left-wing lawyer Merilee Rasmussen. Even former NDP

MP and Canadian Labour Congress media advisor Dennis Gruending and NDP environmentalist and ex-MLA Peter Prebble get in on the act.

In Leeson's second book, the 2009 *Saskatchewan Politics: Crowding the Centre*, the pictures on the cover say it all. Featuring Wall and Calvert, one has a hopeful, heavenward glance; the other stares with lips uncomfortably pursed like he was sucking a lemon. Guess which one was which? Both of Leeson's books seem desperately dedicated to preserving the NDP mystique and mythology, even as the 21st century loomed—arguably one of the lowest points in recent NDP history due to policy failures, public discontent and a 2007 election which the party lost.

These writers continue a long NDP tradition, adding to the library of "any recent Saskatchewan political history has to be written by a socialist." The seminal work on Tommy Douglas, *The Road to Jerusalem* was a labour of love by Tommy McLeod—Douglas' life-long friend, advisor, confidante, trouble-shooter and deputy minister. McLeod's daughter, Beth Bilson, a genial NDP law professor and former U of S Dean of Law, would go on to be appointed by the Romanow government as head of Saskatchewan's notoriously pro-union Labour Relations Board.

The intrigue, life and murder trial of Colin Thatcher, son of Liberal Premier Ross Thatcher, is chronicled in *Love and Hate*, written by left-winger Maggie Siggins, wife of the U of R's Gerry Sperling.

For a policy critique of the nine years of Grant Devine's Conservative government, there are two choices. The first is NDP caucus employee Stobbe's *Devine Rule: A Decade of Hope and Hardship,* a predictable collection of essays by Leeson, Fairbairn, Ken Rasmussen and the usual suspects, edited by Stobbe and U of S left-wing feminist studies academic Lesley Biggs. The other Devine book is *Privatizing a Province: the New Right in Saskatchewan* by Rasmussen and Pitsula, a predictable socialist critique of how limiting government involvement in Saskatchewan's economy, even slightly, constituted the "privatizing of a province."

The book that details the Tory fraud scandal of the early 1990s, *Sask-Scandal* was penned by Gerry Jones, the left-wing CBC reporter married to the head of the Saskatchewan Federation of Labour at the time, Barb Byers, whose father was former NDP MLA and Cabinet minister Neil Byers.

In addition to its decidedly socialist journalism school, the U of R is also home to the Encyclopedia of Saskatchewan, which, thanks to Pitsula, Marchildon, Leeson, Rasmussen, Gruending and other left-wing academics and contributors, shows great loyalty to NDP history and symbolism. Just one example of the Encyclopedia's bias is the tale of two politicians in Northwest Saskatchewan.

Bert Cadieu, a rancher and long-time Conservative MP, was elected with John Diefenbaker and served with great distinction and one interruption from 1958–1979. Long before the Internet and cable news, Cadieu kept the nation awake in 1972 when he lost his Meadow Lake seat as Liberal Pierre Trudeau clung to a razor-thin minority and narrowly deprived the Conservatives' Robert Stanfield of government. Cadieu, with 19 years in political service and public life, rates no mention in the Encyclopedia of Saskatchewan. By contrast, Doug Anguish, a one-term NDP MP who went on to 10 years in provincial politics, is fawningly described in the Encyclopedia as a "leading NDP politician in West-Central Saskatchewan." I knew and defeated Doug Anguish, and knew and admired Bert Cadieu. These two men were not in the same league.

The U of S, Saskatchewan's largest university, isn't blameless either in the NDP love-fest. In its famous "100 Alumni of Influence", Premiers Romanow and Calvert are properly included but there is not a single mention of the only Saskatchewan premier educated at the U of S and on faculty at the university before entering politics. It is petty and classless for the U of S to pointedly ignore Grant Devine. And it is ironic that the two NDP premiers on the list were in the party that excoriated Devine for his pursuit of a new state-of-the-art College of Agriculture building which he delivered for the U of S as one of his last political acts, and of which the university continually boasts.

This stuff matters because history matters. And history is owned by the historians. In Saskatchewan, the only political thought that seems to count and endure—as it is continuously mythologized by its fan club in academia—is the NDP version of Saskatchewan. And the library of books, many written by NDP academics and supporters, takes careful pains to not only under-sell the accomplishments of non-New Democrats but to keep the NDP's image carefully glossed. From its policies to even its underlying values, the NDP is rarely critiqued by its gatekeepers on the same standard that others are held to. And, considering that the NDP's death grip on Saskatchewan politics has spanned three generations, this is pretty important stuff.

Before the CCF/NDP and Douglas, before being Canada's "place to be from," before state-owned government enterprises and nationalization of private business, there was a Saskatchewan that was Canada's most robust and "banner" province, as our first Premier Walter Scott called it in the early 1900s. As Saskatchewan built the immense and towering Legislative Building, which opened in 1912, Scott saw this as the seat of government for a province that would one day be home to 10 million people. That's how big the dreams of this place were. And, in today's "it" province of Saskatchewan, there are thousands of stories of a place breaking out from the eternal state of NDP-induced low expectations and the "Saskatchewan way" that so often ensured we always fell just a bit short.

Years from now when kids ask why and how certain events shaped us, why certain things happened—and equally important, why they didn't— the varnished, NDP-friendly version of history will simply not be accurate. But, hey, if you're a natural governing party, it doesn't hurt that the political historians always have your back.

What's in a Name, Comrade?

The Sturdy Stone building in downtown Saskatoon is a huge government building perched atop a parkade. It is a 1970s eyesore from the "Brutalist" school of architecture—aptly named because this is one brutally ugly building. As a young reporter present at the opening of the building, I thought someone was being cute by calling the big windowless concrete bunker the "sturdy stone" building. Then it was explained that the building was, in fact, named after two long dead Saskatoon CCF MLAs, Jack Sturdy and Arthur Stone, who were elected in 1944. Who knew? But the NDP historians ensure that rather than erect statues of the once great, we name buildings after them.

It is correct, smart and only proper to name buildings after our premiers. These people make an immense personal sacrifice, are forever the figureheads of their governments, and are defined by their times—good, bad or indifferent. And to honour the contribution of our premiers by naming buildings after them is a permanent way to pay tribute to them.

After leaving office, every premier should have at least a building named in his or her honour. These people are our history.

But NDP governments use your money to name buildings and provincial facilities after long dead, gone and forgotten Cabinet ministers or, even worse, obscure MLAs who never even made it to Cabinet. After a while, it starts to smack of the propaganda efforts around the workers' revolutions of the Soviet Union or China where the peoples' heroes are memorialized for all time to be thanked by the grateful masses.

Walking past the SGI tower on Regina's 11th Avenue at Lorne Street, one sees the name "CM Fines Building" embossed in brass on the side of the building. It is named after Clarence Fines, a brilliant CCF organizer and member of Douglas' 1944 Cabinet. But it's incomprehensible why anyone would want to remember this guy today. Fines, who began life as a school teacher, grew very rich while sitting in the Douglas Cabinet, with "investments" including gold mining, commodities trading and even directly investing in projects with a friend who happened to be receiving loans at the time from a Crown corporation controlled by Fines. And Fines accepted gifts—plenty of them—while in Douglas' Cabinet, even cutting Tommy Douglas himself in on at least one business deal.

Rumours and allegations abounded both in the Legislature and around Saskatchewan—stories of Fines and alleged kickbacks, skimming money from people given Crown contracts and worse. One day in 1960, Fines disappeared. Surfacing later in Florida, having left both his wife and Saskatchewan behind, Fines lived out his life with his substantial and beloved investments. If Fines had been anyone but a member of the powerful NDP political establishment, you can only imagine the firestorm.

The worst that is said by NDP historians (in this case, left-wing writer Walter Stewart) is that Douglas should have reined in Fines for "improper and idiotic" acts but the problem was that Fines was "too real a free enterpriser". So, just to get this straight: The NDP literary establishment avoids the words "immoral" or "crook" but finds a way to blame Fines' unethical behaviour on free enterprise!

In certain Saskatchewan towns, the local government offices are named after long dead, old time NDP MLAs like Yorkton's Alex Kuziak, Kindersley's John Wellbelove, North Battleford's Eiling Kramer (whose name is also on a local campground) and Tisdale's John Brockelbank.

The choice of Saskatchewan government building names is often tainted by politics. While some of our early premiers were recognized, not all were; the NDP had been busy naming buildings for ex-MLAs and ministers. It wasn't until our Centennial year that the NDP decided to name government buildings after former premiers William Patterson and Charles Dunning.

Patterson was a distinguished two-term premier who led Saskatchewan through the worst of the Great Depression and then the Second World War. His name graced no building in Saskatchewan until the fall of 2005 when an old and tired rundown three-story building on Regina's Albert Street was named "Patterson Place."

On the same day, Charles Dunning's name was attached to the small but historic provincial revenue building on Smith Street in downtown Regina, nearly 80 years after he left office as Saskatchewan's third premier. Dunning, who came to Saskatchewan as a penniless teenager would lead the largest grain handling company in the world, be elected premier, and following provincial politics, would also go on to a distinguished federal career as Canada's minister of finance and later, in business, as CEO of a large flour company and member of the board of the Canadian Pacific Railway (CPR). He was also chancellor of Queen's University where a building and public policy chair still carry his name today.

As Patterson and Dunning, both memorable premiers in the develop-ment of Saskatchewan, finally got their due, the larger provincial environment department building down the street from "Patterson Place" was named after Woodrow Lloyd, the shortest serving premier in history whose time in office, in the early 1960s, was just one-third of Patterson's. Lloyd, of course, was an NDP premier.

Ironically, on the very same day that the buildings were being named, the newest, largest and fanciest (the 11 story finance department building) was christened "Cooper Place" by the Calvert NDP. Who was Cooper? Marjorie Cooper—never a premier, not even a Cabinet minister. She was a long-serving MLA, an NDP MLA. But it took decades to finally honour both Patterson and Dunning, and at that with small, nondescript buildings. They had the misfortune of being Liberals in the long-ignored era before Tommy Douglas.

Like controlling history through historians, the NDP practice of naming institutions after prominent New Democrats isn't coincidence. It is part of the natural governing party being all-present, at all times.

Are We Having Fun Yet?

Like people in any political party, there are bright and engaging New Democrats and dumb ones; good, decent and classy people along with irredeemable jerks. But there is one type of NDPer who is more difficult to find—one with a sense of humour, a genuine ability to observe life's absurdities and share a good laugh, often at their own expense.

As an entertainer (you'll note that I avoid the lofty "journalist" tag because I'm not one), there's been no end of amusement exposing one of the great Achilles' heels of New Democrats: their congenital inability to poke fun at themselves.

Many in today's political left are nice enough people but they're so damned earnest and self-righteous, swept up by their own sense of importance and mission to improve humanity, that to laugh, kick back and take joy in humour is seen as almost a betrayal of their noble purpose.

This is not to say that all NDPers are humour-challenged. Some like past and present politicians Chris Axworthy, Deb Higgins and Frank Quennell have always been good for a laugh. And they're able to laugh at themselves, which is the ultimate test of humour.

But this NDP humour deficit is surprising, given the modern pedigree of the party and the defining role played by Tommy Douglas. Douglas' claim to fame was as an orator—and a very funny one. Long before TV and mass communication, when town hall meetings and radio ruled, the spoken word mattered. Leaflets and notices were circulated around town, word spread and before long hundreds of people would crowd the hall to hear a political speech.

Douglas rarely disappointed. His oratory was inspiring enough but more than that, it was very funny. As a preacher with a filing cabinet full of anecdotes, jokes and stories for every occasion, Douglas would keep the crowd rollicking and rolling. Never afraid to point out human foibles in himself as well as in his opponents, when Douglas used humour in an attack, it was often like a scalpel rather than a club. In public, Douglas was a funny guy.

Not surprisingly, the two best NDP friends I have—both with long family pedigrees in the party—are drop-dead funny. One does impressions and parodies that make my sides hurt. The other shares many of my views of life and affection for the same type of humour. But for some reason, humour isn't the long suit of many NDPers. Perhaps all that piety and moral sense of mission trumps a good laugh. I dunno. I'm not the left-winger here. But NDPers would do much better to lighten up. A lot.

A long-time friend, a federal Liberal with an infectious sense of humour, tells the story of being approached during the Calvert years by a senior NDP strategist who asked my friend to chair the province's public utilities rate review panel, a much maligned job that was even dubbed by one of its first members as a "rubber stamp" controlled by the Cabinet. Although my buddy was honoured to be asked, he didn't have the time and declined the offer.

Several days later he picked up his phone to hear the impressive words "please hold for the Premier". Moments later Premier Calvert was on the line. It was never clear whether Calvert had not received my friend's turn-down or the Premier was personally trying to make the sale himself but Calvert formally, and with great gravity, offered the position. My pal (who is truly a gracious and good man) joked "Gee, Mr. Premier, what did I ever do to make you mad at me?" Silence. Then, without another word, click, the call was over. Calvert had hung up. My friend put it down to the premier having a bad day. A laugh would have been much easier. And probably therapeutic.

American writer H.L. Mencken observed that Puritanism was the haunting fear that someone, somewhere, may be happy. In Saskatchewan, along with keeping expectations low and assuming the dour worst, many of the political left have a distinct Puritan streak: it's almost not right to have fun.

My Irish dad and Australian mum came to Canada in the early 1960s with me, the toddler, in tow, after having spent time in Asia patching up Her Majesty's soldiers in the Malayan Emergency. Moving to Saskatchewan for a new opportunity and new life, they were completely unprepared for institutions like the Saskatchewan Liquor Board stores. In those days they were staffed by stern old guys in uniform who would make the customer write and sign their order on a chit before disappearing behind a shelf to retrieve the product, which would be handed over with great solemnity.

Within months of arriving to this Prohibition-era throwback, Dad would keep himself occupied by creating names to sign on the chit. His favorite was "Mr. Douglas," with the first name alternating between Tommy, Thomas and T.C.

Even in my coming of age, the NDP made it illegal to privately own a telephone in Saskatchewan. Phones could only be rented from SaskTel, the last phone company in North America to do this. This had everything to do with preserving the government-owned phone company's profits. As young Saskatchewanians, we would cringe every Christmas when national advertising flyers had phones for sale, with the fine print that the offer was void and prohibited in Saskatchewan. Some of us even sneaked into Alberta, bought phones and smuggled them into Saskatchewan—crimes against the people for which we were never prosecuted.

Like the government curtailing choice of telephones 30 years ago to the continuing modern-day restrictions on private liquor sales, getting government to lighten up is more difficult than it should be. Some of the resistance comes from ideological decisions influenced by organized labour fearing that union jobs might be lost if customers are allowed more freedom and choice. Some opposition comes from civil servants simply afraid to give up control. Assuming that public standards and safeguards are met, government can move beyond its constant default of saying "no."

A good example was the Calvert government's decision in 2004— made with the stroke of pen and no consultation—to abolish front license plates on vehicles. This permitted motorists to have only one rear plate and to opt for front promotional plates saluting everything from Saskatchewan's Centennial to favourite sports teams and hobbies. The change was not difficult, long overdue and, like the end of the phone ownership ban, no one even missed it. Ironically, in 2010 when the SaskParty government unveiled an official license plate promoting the Saskatchewan Roughriders, thousands of the plates were ordered within days. I wondered at the time how many of the purchasers standing in line were staunch NDPers finally able to understand that governments can actually lighten up and allow citizens to occasionally have fun.

In 2004, before his license plate move, Premier Calvert had mused aloud about lowering the drinking age from 19 to 18, as is done in Alberta, Manitoba and Quebec. As one who agrees with this, I encouraged Calvert; after all, if you're old enough to have sex, drive cars, smoke cigarettes, own guns and die for your country, a legal drink or two along the way shouldn't hurt.

Unless we were going to have a U.S.- style universal 21-year-old drinking age—which effectively keeps college students, university undergraduates and trades apprentices out of bars—"should it be 18 or 19?" is really an academic question. But before any provincial debate broke out, and as quickly as he had proposed the idea, Calvert abandoned it, no reason given.

Beyond the well-known NDP fun deficit, Saskatchewan's natural governing party has the toughness, the people and the relentless campaign edge to always be within one election campaign of coming back to government. No party I've ever witnessed is as strategic, ruthless and deeply embedded in society as the NDP. They never sleep and winning elections, at any cost, is all that counts.

Another hallmark of the party of Douglas is a seven-decade run of fear, gloom and an attitude of low expectations and mediocrity. It's the main weakness of the NDP in the "new" Saskatchewan.

Chapter 2

ATTITUDE: THE OLD SASKATCHEWAN COLLIDES WITH THE NEW

Paging Mr. Lombardi

The greatest football coach who ever lived was Vince Lombardi, coach of the Green Bay Packers from 1959–1967. Although I was a kid when he died in 1970, I read some of Lombardi's inspirational speeches. They changed my life.

Lombardi's philosophy was clear: "The price of success is hard work, dedication to the job…and the determination that whether we win or lose, we have applied the best of ourselves to the task at hand. The quality of a person's life is in direct proportion to their commitment to excellence—regardless of their chosen field of endeavor."

In life, attitude is everything. What you believe, what you tell yourself and how you plan, prepare and persevere during your day will usually determine the kind of day you'll have. At least that's how I've lived my life.

But coming home to host the radio show, I was struck time and time again by one inescapable fact: the Saskatchewan attitude really sucked. Everywhere I turned it was there—an intricately woven web of inferiority, self-loathing, negativism and pessimism, like a movie zombie, shuffling along sucking out the life and hope of everyone in its way.

Beyond being terribly depressing, the bad Saskatchewan attitude had become a big impediment to our collective psyche and even to our economic climate. Who'd want to live in a place where people were just so down all the time?

Managing Expectations Downward

It is puzzling how Canada's hardest working, most generous and adaptive people came to be such merchants of gloom. But it's understandable. The earliest roots of our bad attitude grew from the Great Depression of the 1930s which stole hope, wiped out peoples' futures and saw Saskatchewan topple from our perch as Canada's third largest province.

From this was spawned an understandable reserve and caution that soon became pessimistic: Why get too excited when everything from this year's crop to your life savings can evaporate in a drought and the world's worst economic crash, both unexpected and beyond your control?

Pessimism also led some people to aim low and hope for luck to pull them through. Even the innocent and hopeful "next year country" optimism of Saskatchewan was little more than an excuse to repeat last year's failings by not learning from the experience of making the same mistake over and over.

This was most apparent, and troublesome, in the Saskatchewan obsession for football where we eventually slipped into accepting mediocrity for the beloved Saskatchewan Roughriders (as long as they didn't lose money and finished 9-9 "it could always be worse"). This set us up to keep the bar low and fall back on "there's always next year." On the football field this began to change when people committed to excellence took over.

Every small town had (and still has) the "King of the Coffee Shop," the guy on Coffee Row who can be counted on to complain about pretty much everything. "It'll never work" is his opening line; if something actually does work "it won't last long"; and, if by chance it succeeds, it's only because someone is stealing everyone's money.

Another feature of small town life that made its way into the psyche of Saskatchewan was the belief that it was wrong to "show that you're doing well"—it would only make your neighbours envious and people might treat you differently. As a result, for years, even in Saskatoon and Regina, people with millions of dollars in the bank preferred the nondescript house in a quiet neighbourhood and the comfort and safety of a Chevy Impala or Ford Taurus.

Having spoken dozens of times at conferences and events on the "Saskatchewan Attitude Adjustment," I tell the story of a businessman in a small Saskatchewan city who, after years of hard work and success, finally bought the car of his dreams (a fancy M-series BMW) but kept it parked in his son' s garage in Saskatoon. He'd drive to his son's, take the car for a spin, even the occasional road trip to Alberta or BC, and then return, switch back to his Taurus and drive home. He told me "if any of my customers knew I had a $90,000 car they'd stop coming to my business—they'd think I was charging them too much money." Only in Saskatchewan could this kind of silliness make sense. Ironically, as I tell this story to laughing audiences, at the end of many speeches usually someone will approach me, look carefully both ways and then tell me their story—whether buying identical cars to fool prying neighbours or going to lengths to conceal the existence of vacation homes, "you can't show off your wealth," they'd say.

When low expectations are allowed to prevail, their effects go deeper, like not striving for excellence, not challenging ourselves or enforcing accountability. And, as alcoholics know from their inspiring Big Book, "we do as we think," which might explain something about Saskatchewan's historic failure to perform.

Another pattern of post-Depression Saskatchewan rural life was for some people to compare themselves to their neighbours—after all, it was easy, and why work so hard when all you needed was to be no worse than your neighbour? An unintended and bad consequence of this is *schadenfreude*, or delight in the misfortune of others. *Schadenfreude's* big problem is that you don't actually have to do anything to improve your life—just wait for others to screw up. And all that hoping for misfortune doesn't make you the most positive person around.

There's also a problem when your neighbour does better than you; your smugness soon turns to envy. And when the measuring stick for success isn't personal bests or excellence but instead keeping an eye on your neighbour, how can anyone feel really good about this? So, it isn't long before a collective poor self-esteem takes over. As a result, even when good things do deservedly happen, we believe that we're somehow unworthy. One of my first observations on coming home to Saskatchewan was a reverse sense of entitlement—we were only deserving of the not-so-good things.

Combine this with the self-perpetuated myth that somehow Saskatch-ewan is "unique" when in fact our people and lives are really little different than anywhere else, and soon uniqueness becomes an excuse for ignoring best practices elsewhere. With all of this, it isn't long before a negative attitude takes root, as it did in Saskatchewan.

At a political level, as NDP governments from the time of Douglas did, there was an advantage to politically keeping expectations low, or at least doing nothing to raise them. Raising expectations might encourage voters to expect more. And this could lead to expecting better performance from governments.

Like comparing ourselves to neighbours, it doesn't take much to achieve expectations when they are kept low. And, conversely, when setbacks, mistakes or policy mishaps happen, the fall isn't as far when the bar is set low. As a result, perennially low expectations also don't do much for account-ability and holding ourselves to higher standards.

Sometimes in life I stumble on little discoveries. If they were bigger and more significant they'd be full blown epiphanies. But they're not, so I call the small revelations "epiphinettes." I know that's not a word but it should be.

One day, waiting for some friends, I overheard two young guys in their twenties, fresh-faced, baby broker types, expounding on "under promising and over delivering." This is the practice (I did it for years as a lawyer) where you avoid bold and flashy promises, keep expectations manageable and then over-serve clients by delivering more than they expected and, hopefully, outcomes and results which also exceed their expectations.

Eavesdropping on the young business guys, I had the epiphinette: this is what the NDP had messed up. Lacking, for the most part in NDP governments, people with actual experience in business or any credible advisors who knew this, the NDP had tried the "under promise/over deliver" approach but had missed a critical part. Under promising does not mean driving down expectations and actually lowering them; it means managing expectations so they don't grow beyond the capacity to deliver on, in other words, they don't get higher than you can control. This also allows you to actually deliver beyond those expectations to create what Keinginham and Vavra called not customer satisfaction, but "customer delight." There is a big difference. The former ensures ongoing mediocrity; the latter strives to be better than average.

The Lorne Calvert government had so diminished public expectations (as had Roy Romanow's earlier) that a type of collective negativism and depression had taken hold in Saskatchewan. Once this happened, even when the economy began to turn around as it did at the end of Calvert's political career, the voters were left with several emotions, all negative. There was an unbelieving incredulity: "It can't really be good here, they said it never would be." There was open skepticism: "If good times really have finally arrived, which I doubt, they'll never last." And even churlishness: "Nothing good ever happens here and I think the government is lying."

The NDP's own bad attitude and mismanagement of expectations had come back to bite the party at the very time it most needed positive expectations and hope. I almost felt sorry for them.

Nothing is as contagious as attitude. From the positive, upbeat and confident "can do" approach of winners to the self-defeating, negative "can't do" gloom of losers, attitude shapes and defines every one of us as individuals and in groups.

The NDP & the Relentless Pursuit of Mediocrity

By the power and influence of their messages, behaviour and attitudes, governments have a profound effect on how citizens eventually view the world. For years, critics of the NDP have fooled around with the party's initials, turning them into slogans like "No Darn Progress" or "Nutty Doomed Party" and other combinations. One of my buddies calls them the "Negative Downer Party." I think he nailed it.

When it comes to attitude, decades of NDP governments took pains to not lift the veil off low expectations and under-achievement. Even in the early 2000s, Premier Calvert's tepid declaration that we will always be "in and out of have-not province status" was hardly a ringing endorsement of either confidence or high standards. Even when Saskatchewan began to show signs of emerging economic growth toward the end of the Calvert years, it was always greeted by the NDP as a kind of apologetic success: sort of good but always wondering aloud about those "left behind" or "not sharing in the boom."

This merely reinforced the historic skepticism and "sky is falling" attitude of many NDP governments about development, prosperity and getting ahead. For the political left, some of this negativism is politically necessary—class struggle and pessimism need to be in place for socialism to take root. Even when governing, the NDP subtext is that failure is just around the corner; things might be good now but they can always get worse.

Some NDP partisans actually want people to fail—they can't escape the desire to wish ill because it helps sell various social policies. Gloom and unrest helps convince other left-wingers that capitalism, business and the market economy are flawed and the "victims" will always need to be saved by government; workers exploited by management will need protection; the poor marginalized by the rich have to be helped by wealth redistribution and everything works better under the time-honoured NDP messages of fear, loathing and envy.

As a result, from the Great Depression onward, many dour prairie socialists and trade union leaders in NDP governments worked tirelessly to perpetuate the Saskatchewan mantra that things can't get done, you'd best not get your hopes up, and someone else is always to blame when things don't work out.

When in opposition (those rare times the NDP loses political power) the party is not just negative but relentless and excoriating in its criticism of anyone else that tries to govern. It is almost as if Saskatchewan belongs to the NDP—they own the province—and someone else has stolen it by defeating them at the polls.

In 1989, the last time the NDP was out of power, a union leader pledged that "we, in concert with the NDP, will work to make this province ungovernable." The resulting strategy of the NDP involved one of the most acrimonious and negative periods in Saskatchewan political history. Twenty years later, in 2009, a brochure from NDP leader Dwain Lingenfelter declared that Saskatchewan had gone from "boom to bust" even as we continued to lead the nation in economic growth and job creation. The modern NDP lifeblood is often bad news and a negative attitude. By 2010, an NDP MLA reading a statement prepared by Lingenfelter's office took small-mindedness and envy to new heights when criticizing Premier Wall for promoting Saskatchewan but also owning a vacation home in the United States.

Thinking Small in the "Wee Province"

When low expectations and settling for mediocrity are your game, the rules require that people think small…wouldn't want someone dreaming big and actually forcing the bar higher for the rest of us. Calvert, in the early days of his premiership (perhaps channeling some long lost ancestor tending cattle in Yorkshire) took to calling Saskatchewan "the wee province." Wee, of course, means tiny.

What was tiny about Saskatchewan in Calvert's mind was never made clear. Twice the size of Germany, we're not geographically small and are not going to be mistaken for Prince Edward Island. Although our population was plummeting at the time, we still had more people living here than in four provinces and eight U.S. states. So what exactly did Calvert mean by "wee"?

It seemed that he'd conjured up some idyllic Saskatchewan that disappeared years earlier—like something from an Everett Baker photo of the 1950s—a largely rural and quaint Saskatchewan full of hard working people in a bucolic, simple place, quietly toiling to get their grain grown, loaded and off to the local Wheat Pool elevator. At the time, and since, I've often mocked this "wee province" stuff on my radio show by putting on a prairie preacher voice and cautioning that we'd best be careful not to have our backsides hanging out of our dungarees.

The "wee province" was a hokey allegory portraying us like something we're not—simple, small folk obediently accepting our fate from larger forces beyond our control.

Not long after his first "wee outbreak," something odd happened at Calvert's 2003 Premier's Dinner when he was talking up the Saskatchewan economy, as every premier does at these dinners. Calvert paused and then unexpectedly jogged off script with a degree of frankness and puzzlement rare in modern politicians. Saying he was frustrated why people would not invest in Saskatchewan, he mused that it was about our attitude toward success. He was partly right. But he could have said so much more.

For years, our perennially crappy outlook on life (a friend calls it "rectal oculosis") extended from farmers whining about the weather to the "glass half empty" crowd to Calvert's predecessors in the NDP talking down success by campaigning on the envy themes of "share the wealth", "make the rich pay" and "people before profits". While not an exclusively NDP-caused problem—many on the political right did an effective job of bitching, whining and virtually driving their kids to the Alberta border—many naysayers inside Calvert's party had only themselves to blame.

From the promise of the *Regina Manifesto* to eradicate capitalism and save the world from "wasteful competition, the inevitable outcome of capitalism," to the mid-'70s potash nationalization, Saskatchewan's NDP went out of its way to ensure that many savvy investors steered clear of Saskatchewan.

If you believe these statements, you might be part of the problem:

- Any new idea—particularly from around here and not from government—won't work. Or if it does, not for long;
- If things are good now they'll never last;
- New businesses only force out old businesses;
- Profit is greed;
- If you're such a hot-shot, what are you doing in Saskatchewan?;
- Lower taxes reward big business and make "rich" people richer;
- People who prosper—nice cars, houses, clothes—got that way because they screwed someone else;
- Successful people and companies got that way by charging too much;
- If you're successful—rich, even— don't show it because it might make other people feel bad;
- Who wants to invest here?

In progressive and modern economies which prosper (like today's "new Saskatchewan") most citizens don't necessarily traipse around worshipping business or reading Ayn Rand. But they get the connection between investment, new business activity and profits which then means good jobs, new people coming here, spin-off businesses being created and more money being spent. It's not complicated. And people understand attitude: don't criticize the successes of others—admire, learn and emulate.

A few years ago, I met a guy in rural Saskatchewan who grew his small business into a large and successful agriculture service company. He laughed at what he discovered when travelling the world. In the U.S., particularly, when people discovered his success they would say "good for you," implying that they shared his joy. Only in Saskatchewan would he get "must be nice," which suggests envy and distance from someone's success.

That night in 2003, as Premier Calvert stood at the podium, pausing uncomfortably and expressing his honest frustration (which I gave him credit for), I wanted to jump up and say "Lorne, don't you know that changing the way you view the world can change you? The way that you and your friends think of Saskatchewan is keeping us small. And, haven't you heard the saying that insanity is doing the same thing over and over and expecting a different result?"

In 2002, when prominent New Democrats on Saskatoon City Council voted to kill a proposal to host the World University Games, one Calvert Cabinet member echoed the left wing faction on City Council and said "we are too small for this". It was sad how far Saskatchewan had fallen, when less than a century earlier Premier Walter Scott had spoken proudly of a big land for big men with big ideas.

For many hard-core NDPers, thinking small is virtually coded in their DNA— anything that might elevate Saskatchewan to world-class status or attract more people, development, money and prosperity is to be skeptically regarded. In fact it would be better not even to mention it.

Within days of talk about a new covered stadium in Regina in 2009, prominent NDP activist, Fraser Needham, played the "think small" card perfectly in a letter to the Leader Post, arguing that it was pointless to spend money even on a feasibility study because Regina is "simply too small and isolated" to attract acts "largely from the United States." Although he didn't explain his conclusion that big acts would be "even less likely to come in winter" to a covered facility, Needham implored the idea be "killed" before it got too far. I thought (at the time and since) what a strange existence one must live when they fear even discussing new things or big ideas.

Premier Calvert had two minor but telling moments that seemed to define his role in perpetuating the Saskatchewan attitude. In late 2004, when he announced that Saskatchewan had become a "have" province and would no longer be receiving equalization, it was an oddly uncomfortable moment. Although Calvert was in a dispute at the time with Ottawa over what he saw as an entitlement to more equalization money, his demeanor and voice had an almost consolation prize look about them.

While the premier spoke proudly of Saskatchewan's achievement, he begrudgingly conceded that we could be slipping back into "have-not" territory at any time and might soon be in need of equalization again. This has not happened. But it struck me as I watched the confusing array of mixed messages that only in Saskatchewan would a premier look like he's mourning moving into the big leagues. It was like a bronze medal performance where the athlete made sure that he did whatever was necessary to avoid the gold medal at all costs.

Calvert's other attitude moment came during Saskatchewan's 2005 Centennial year when the premier proudly talked of being in a northern community where a three-day canoe race was ending. As the receiving party waited on a bridge around a bend, there was a delay. Calvert spoke stirringly of seeing the remaining canoes and crews who had survived the grueling race, finally rounding the corner together, all abreast, the teams holding hands so that "everyone finished in first place...together."

As the premier beamed with pride about a cooperative spirit, a unified effort and the importance of sharing, a young female reporter sitting at our table leaned over, cocked an eyebrow and muttered, "Does this mean everyone finished in last place together and no one won?"

A couple of weeks later at another event Calvert told the same story to a different audience. Around the tables, people began snickering and one young man whispered, sotto voce, "so, in a race, people who are faster and better should never beat people who are slower—and we all lose together. Hmm."

The NDP is often in a tough spot when its own core voters misbehave and the party decides to publicly distance itself and not pull its own people into line. Like in 2010, when both federal leader Jack Layton and provincial leader Dwain Lingenfelter refused to criticize 15 radical professors at the U of R for an offensive anti-war letter insulting Canadian forces veterans, fallen heroes and their families, Calvert would often find himself standing silently and awkwardly on the sidelines as hard-core left-wing radicals in his own party perpetuated the worst NDP stereotypes of talking down Saskatchewan and thinking small.

In 2007, as the Saskatchewan boom began gathering steam—and Premier Calvert desperately wanted to take credit for new development and expansion—he would stand mute rather than defend growth and prosperity when NDP activists and opponents of the boom would go on the attack against increased economic activity.

A group called "SHEEP" (Should Exploitative Economics Persist) began rallying against further expansion of city boundaries and the construction of shopping centers. A broad coalition of Wal-Mart haters, socialists and anti-development activists, this group was, so far as I could tell, a subset of the well-known Saskatchewan organization, CAVE, "Citizens Against Virtually Everything." It was also related (with apologies to Lil' Abner) to SWINE, "Students Wildly Indignant about Nearly Everything" and BANANAS, "Build Absolutely Nothing Anywhere Near Anything and Soon". While we're on the initials kick, while these activists were opposing the consequences of the boom—success and growth—Calvert and his Cabinet were AWOL.

If the NDP government truly wanted to shape the positive attitude of Saskatchewan and take credit and promote economic expansion, the government had a responsibility to lead. And this included facing down the anti-development NDPers. Instead, from Calvert to many of his senior Cabinet ministers there was the sense that they were trying to have it both ways—claim credit for growth but "tut-tut" that wealth and development might be a bad thing.

On the issue of attitude, there is no bigger attitude boost than a winning season for our beloved Roughrider football team. A huge irritant for many New Democrats is the relationship between their party in power and the Riders hitting the pinnacle of success: winning the Grey Cup. In the storied 100-year history of the Riders, they have won the Grey Cup only three times—never when an NDP government is in office.

Saskatchewan Roughriders' Grey Cups	Government	Premier
1966	Liberal	Ross Thatcher
1989	Progressive Conservative	Grant Devine
2007	SaskParty	Brad Wall

Change We Can Really Fear

For generations, a hallmark of NDP politics has been the fear of change—fear of the unknown, fear of a government that is not the NDP, and fear that someone might change long held NDP traditions and views. In both of Premier Calvert's elections, there were frightful anti-change campaigns—in the successful 2003 election, and in 2007 when a "wolf in sheep's clothing" might have changed us into Alberta. More often than not in NDP political campaigns, change resistance and fear succeeds.

In 2002, Calvert himself was forced to look change resistance in the face when his government finally changed farmland ownership restrictions that had hobbled Saskatchewan for years and held us back.

Nearly 30 years earlier during a boom in farming and strong land prices in the 1970s, the Blakeney NDP decided not to encourage more investment but to severely restrict non-Saskatchewan residents from owning land. Playing into the fear of "foreigners" buying up Ma and Pa's farm and turning them into barefoot serfs and peasant farmers, the NDP decreed that Canadians living in other provinces—even our kids living in Alberta—were "foreigners" restricted from owning more than 320 acres of land in Saskatchewan. This also applied to farmers in neighbouring provinces who wanted to expand their operations and bring their money and investment into Saskatchewan.

In contrast to Alberta, where there was no limit on land ownership by Canadians living elsewhere in Canada, it made Saskatchewan look insular and backwards. It also blocked investment from other Canadians wanting to sink money into an increasingly diverse agriculture industry, from ethanol potential to alternative crops, irrigation and intensive livestock.

The opponents of more liberalized farmland ownership laws—many inside the NDP and its proxy groups like the National Farmers Union—felt betrayed: after all, investment and capitalism might break out in farming; land prices could rise; people might own land without living on it, and "outsiders" should not own things. Many of these objections about big, boogey-man landowners were typical left-wing fear tactics designed to frighten the timid and weak-minded.

I supported Calvert on this issue and pointed out that if the same restrictive rules applied to business in Saskatchewan cities, it would kill the successful blend of local, national and internationally-owned businesses that ensures competition, investment and innovation—just like it does in farming. Calvert and the NDP, looking at times uncomfortable, pained, even queasy, finally pushed through the farmland ownership changes.

Within weeks and since, not a whisper of objection was heard. Ironically, that's what often happens with change. The fear and anticipation are far greater than the actual change.

While not a psychologist (I only play one, badly, on the radio), we all know the so-called "stages" of personal change: pre-contemplation, where we don't yet acknowledge a need to change; contemplation, where the problem is identified; preparation and determination, where we make a plan and get ready to change; action, where we make the change; and maintenance, where we maintain the changes that have been made.

But institutional change often comes from other stages, like dismantling the existing change resistance by identifying and overcoming objections, bypassing defense mechanisms and challenging the old ways by explaining the changed future and its benefits. It's also important to re-assure people that existing approaches will be replaced but not worsened. And there's the need to move people into a comfort level that helps them adapt to the new world.

When we consider most changes in our jobs and ways of doing things, the benefit of time shows us that fear of the unknown and speculated risks were usually far greater than what actually happened. But in Saskatchewan NDP politics, often we don't even get past the fearsome spectre of what horrors—always unknown—would be brought by change.

The 5 Stages of Innovation
What People Do When Things Change:

1. Deny that the innovation is needed.
2. Deny that the innovation is effective.
3. Deny that the innovation is important.
4. Deny that the innovation will justify the effort required to adopt it; and finally
5. Accept and adopt the innovation, enjoy its benefits, attribute it to people other than the innovator, and deny the existence of stages 1 to 4.

Bill Bryson, "A Short History of Nearly Everything"

The Saskatchewan Myth—No Thanks

From the comfort and safety of Ottawa, where he jumped into a communications job with the federal Liberals, long-time Saskatchewan political columnist and author Dale Eisler was shopping around a theory in 2006. Fortunately, his timing couldn't have been worse.

In a book called *False Expectations: Politics and the Pursuit of the Saskatchewan Myth*, Eisler reviewed our province's history through the lens that Saskatchewan people are attached to the "universal belief of an unrealized potential and a better life." According to Eisler, this is actually an enduring myth that identifies us and gives our lives "greater meaning and purpose." And because real prosperity is unattainable in Saskatchewan, suggested Eisler, the hope for better things lives on as "a defining myth." Feel free to retch here.

Eisler's book then explored government decisions over the years which he believed had tried and failed to make the myth come true. While his theory was thought-provoking, it was ultimately annoying because it excused many of Saskatchewan's chronic under-performers who have so valiantly tried to keep our province firmly rooted in the 1950s.

The book also gave consolation to certain left-wing academics at the U of R who, while population and hope were in freefall during the Calvert years, were trying to defend declining population as both inevitable and actually good for us. This was the same crowd arguing that our "uniqueness" made it futile to compare ourselves to other more successful Western economies.

Fortunately, within one year of Eisler's book, events began to overtake his theory. Robust economic growth in 2007 turned into a full-on boom in 2008 and Saskatchewan has continued to lead the country both in economic performance and in positive attitude, with population growth unseen since the early 1950s (more people now live in Saskatchewan than any time in history) and economic development in Saskatoon and Regina has rivaled the boom of the early 1900s. Much of the economic growth since 2008 has no modern basis of comparison.

With attitudes like Eisler's and decades of fluctuating population, pessimism and the belief that "this is all there is," Saskatchewan's new confidence will have to extend beyond an "up and down" wait for the next negative cycle. Here's to hoping the Saskatchewan myth is put to sleep for good.

> "Winners in life think constantly in terms of I can, I will, and I am. Losers, on the other hand, concentrate on what they should have or would have done, or what they can't do."
>
> *Denis Waitley, Psychology of Winning*

Take That, Shame Lady

Let me introduce you to the "Shame Lady," an elderly caller who became a legend on our radio show. She phoned the morning after the 2003 provincial election when I was criticizing the NDP for its hatchet job win on the SaskParty's Elwin Hermanson. I was equally knocking idiot Sask-Party strategists for being outsmarted in an election that wouldn't have taken much to win.

I never learned the old woman's name. But she was angry with me—very angry. And, like a lot of people who detest me, she would not call the on-air line but left a voice mail:

"Gormley, you're such a big bully and sour grapes. Now you just keep on knocking the victory. Shame, shame on you because everyone knows you were pulling for that rotten Saskatchewan Party. They're nothing but the resurrected crooks of the PCs. Shame, shame on you!

You're disturbing the community again today by giving all these digs to our wonderful victory. Mr. Calvert is such a dignified and upright man and you can't hack it.

And you're going to have to leave the time alone, too, thanks be to God for that! I'll tell you what. The Great One above was working last night so you creeps—you and the creeps of your friends—couldn't get in.

Shame on you."

Click.

Dial tone.

On the talk show, we often define the way people think about Saskatchewan as being in two great camps—"Saskatchewinners," who are positive, forward-thinking and optimistic; and, "Saskatchewhiners," who are negative, pessimistic and "nothing good will ever happen" people.

To be fair, not all left-wingers are Saskatchewhiners. But many are. Nor are all Saskatchewinners right-wingers—there are some nay-saying, whining right-wingers who are so far backwards that they're still hoping to get out to Vancouver to catch Expo '86.

So, to the Shame Lady and her friends everywhere, the following handy guide is for you.

| The Saskatchewan Attitude Chart ||
Saskatchewhiner	Saskatchewinner
Mouseland	Our Saskatchewan
A "wee" place	A "we" place
"Must be nice"	"Good for you"
Fear, loathing and envy	Rejoice in success
It'll never work	"Let's try it"
Schadenfreude	Support and empathy
"If you're so great what are you doing in Saskatchewan?"	"Good to have you here"
"If you don't like the way we do things then go back to Alberta"	"We welcome you and your good ideas"
"Omigod, we might be turning into Alberta"	"Cool, we may even be better"
How are you? "Not too bad."	"Good, thanks!"
Lobster pot—pull one another back in	Help one another out to success
King of the Coffee shop	We'll sit at the table where people talk about positive stuff

Subtly, something has changed in Saskatchewan's attitude. These days, Saskatchewan people seem more optimistic, forward thinking and positive. In part, this is due to strong economic performance that has buoyed people's hopes and sense of destiny—success will do that to people. It is also a welcome tonic to the traditional Saskatchewan NDP sense of small and cautious insularity.

The attitudinal change sweeping Saskatchewan is not a boastful, false pride built on boosterism: there is a genuinely serious examination going on of our place in Canada as the "it" province. With conventional oil production positioned to overtake Alberta's and undeveloped oil sands that may rival those of our neighbour, Saskatchewan is positioned to become a North American energy powerhouse that has learned some of the valuable lessons experienced by Alberta.

"There's been no spiking the ball in the end zone by Saskatchewan's people. Maybe it's because we know how long we were a have-not, and I think we just want to keep our head down and be modestly, humbly self-assured about this new status."

Premier Brad Wall, 2009

With 25% of the planet's uranium deposits, the source of 33% of world potash supplies and more arable land than all of the other provinces in Canada combined, Saskatchewan's people seem to be bearing down on a serious look at our economic prospects. And they're good.

In large part, it's a human factor that contributes most to the new-found "can do" attitude of optimism, hope and knowledge. Thousands of people from around Canada and the world have chosen Saskatchewan and they didn't get the memo about thinking small, fearing change and engaging in fear, loathing and envy.

Some are families and individuals that were part of the Alberta Diaspora in the 1980s and '90s who left Saskatchewan as an express protest against the NDP brand of socialism. Others, less politically aligned, are international newcomers who have experienced economies and lifestyles more cosmopolitan than ours. Yet other returnees are the children of Saskatchewan left-wing school teachers and Crown employees who have come home from Calgary and Edmonton more informed, experienced and accustomed to change and adaptation. They do not understand fear of the unknown.

The Millennial Generation—those born since 1982 either here or transplanted to Saskatchewan—come from the best-travelled, most plugged in and technologically informed generation. Their experience, even at a young age, with different standards, attitudes, best practices and change, has equipped them to engage in a dialogue that starts at a point well past the "old" Saskatchewan. There is a new vibe, a positive, "can do" attitude that has taken hold.

How the Saskatchewinners Do It

> "It's never too late to become what you may have been."
>
> *George Elliott*

Winners don't look much different than the rest of us. But their mental game, focus and attitude are over-powering. After the Saskatchewan Roughriders' 2007 Grey Cup and the Detroit Red Wings 2008 Stanley Cup, I chatted on my radio show with the winning coaches Kent Austin and Mike Babcock, two guys who bring out the very best in others. And when you meet these winners, they have remarkable insights.

I asked Coach Austin about his "guiding personal beliefs" and as he talked I could feel something magical happening. His words on football are as applicable to politics as they are to our own personal lives.

- **Preparation.** It's the most important. More than anything else;
- **Care.** You have to care at a level that honors the position you're given. If you're not willing to sacrifice and care at the level required to win a championship, then you don't deserve to be here;
- **Investment.** Being here was going to cost the players something. I told them at the beginning that it was going to cost them some of their emotions. There were going to be ups and downs. And they needed to invest at a level greater than they had ever invested before;

- **Accountability.** You need it to each other. I need to be able to look across the room at my teammates and know I'm accountable to them —accountable in how I prepare, how I play, how I practice, how I pay attention in meetings. All those things have to be important to me because I have to be accountable to those teammates;
- **Unselfish.** Any success that you have is directly proportional to the success of the players around you. It should matter to you that you build those teammates to be the best people they can be, because you're going to benefit by proxy as a result.
- **Excellence.** Strive for it in everything we do. You can't compartmentalize being excellent as a player on the field. You need to strive for excellence in all parts of your life—be the best father you can be, the best husband, the best friend, the best teammate. All of those things matter because the little things add up. And they do affect your play on the field.
- **Common vision and goals.** We have to move in lockstep in our philosophy—where we're trying to go and the values that we're trying to establish throughout the organization;
- **Buy-in.** Everyone is not going to buy-in at the same level—some are going to be at the front end and some are going to be at the back end. But what's important is that we're all heading in the right direction and that the guys on the fringe are pulled into the center more and more as the season goes on;
- **Excuses.** We don't believe in making excuses. When people and teams make excuses for injuries and other things, you start to fall back on excuses and you've actually set up a safety net for people to inadvertently fail. Whether they consciously think about it or not, it doesn't matter. With excuses, you've provided a foundation that allows people to fail;
- **The pendulum.** Don't let the pendulum swing too far. We can't let our emotions gravitate too far to euphoria and too far to negativity. We need to focus on getting better as a team and as people, regardless of emotional swings. It's important we set a standard that buffers those swings and helps us focus on becoming the best;
- **Learn.** To win it all you have to be able to learn from the good experiences and the bad. It's not just the trials and the setbacks but you also have to learn how to handle success.

Unlike Austin who's a Memphis guy and Ole Miss alum, Mike Babcock is from here, educated at the U of S and a summer resident of Saskatchewan when he's not in Detroit or coaching Canada's Olympic men's hockey team. Coach Babcock describes overhearing people on flights "bragging how great things are, how vibrant it is, the economy and the opportunities in Saskatchewan." He says there are two striking similarities between the new Saskatchewan attitude and the psychology of winning.

- **Choose the Contagious Positive.** When people are happy for one another, prepared to share in success and do good things, it's contagious—like the energy and enthusiasm that comes from motivated people
- **Avoid the Negative**. Negative thinking perpetuates, too. Winners have to avoid "Duracell drainers—the people who can sit down beside a battery and drain the life right out of it."

When Babcock talks of sports success and the great Saskatchewan attitude, he emphasizes the values of perseverance, commitment, accountability and being tested by adversity. "Knowledge and preparation and experience defeats fear," he says.

Applying this to Saskatchewan politics, no truer words have been spoken.

Chapter 3

THE EMERGENCE OF LORNE CALVERT

Can a Trinity Fit Four People?

Nothing ranks higher in the pantheon of Saskatchewan NDP heroes than its Holy Trinity—the Father, Son and Holy Ghost of Saskatchewan socialism. Of course, the Father is Tommy Douglas. The Baptist preacher helped create the party, re-invented Saskatchewan in his own image and won five elections in a row, which has never been done before or since. Even though he died in 1986, Douglas has achieved eternal life for NDP supporters.

The Son of the Holy Trinity is Allan Blakeney, the Rhodes Scholar recruited in 1950 as a young civil servant who, 10 years later, became an NDP MLA and then 10 years after that won the party leadership and became a three-term premier. Blakeney set up new Crown corporations, nationalized the potash industry and even created a land bank where the government bought up farms and rented them to tenant farmers—the kind of stuff that makes socialists giddy.

And, the Holy Ghost of the Trinity is Roy Romanow, the smooth and handsome lawyer who lost the leadership to Blakeney in 1970 but served faithfully for 15 years as Blakeney's lieutenant and spear carrier before being acclaimed as leader. Romanow's mission was to slay the NDP's most hated and feared dragon, the government of Grant Devine. For all his panache and promise, Romanow served nine rather joyless years as premier, but in fairness his career was defined by cleaning up the fiscal mess left behind by Devine's government. And, like the Holy Spirit of Christianity, Romanow proceeded from the Father, reminded the unredeemed of their sins and gave comfort to NDPers that they were on the righteous path.

So where does this leave Lorne Calvert, who succeeded Romanow? To be blunt—there's only room for three in a Trinity, and Calvert was number four. From the day of his swearing in, Calvert never stood a chance—partly due to his own approach and style, and because of lingering negatives from the Romanow years that would come back to haunt Calvert and the NDP in the first decade of the 2000s.

> "Leadership is a combination of strategy and character. If you must be without one, be without the strategy."
>
> *U.S. General H. Norman Schwarzkopf*

On a personal level, I always liked Lorne Calvert. As a man he seemed a decent enough human being—kind and considerate and never said a bad word to me. There were times, doubtless he said bad words *about* me, but they were entirely deserved. I also respect the office of premier. And, because Calvert was not the NDP's premier but the premier of every one of us, I always respected what he represented.

What I'm about to say will sound harsh, no matter how gently it is put. So let's not duck it—and this isn't personal either. Calvert never struck me as a political leader and, in particular, as having the stuff of a premier. On a personal level he seemed a genuinely friendly, unprepossessing and nice man. At a political level, Calvert appeared to be a caring politician with a distinctively left-wing, social gospel agenda that fitted well within his theology as an ordained United Church minister. Right-wing friends who knew Calvert as a local church minister supported him—no, loved him— in his capacity as leader of their local faith community. He would baptize and bury, marry and counsel and did so with great empathy, wisdom and compassion. But the same people who would do anything for Calvert as their religious minister were puzzled by his political ambitions beyond being a local MLA. They just didn't see him as a leader, strong or capable enough of transcending his religious calling.

It is not that Calvert lacked intelligence (he always seemed intellectually engaged enough in policy) or toughness, but there was something that did not fit. In part, it was the lack of that intangible *gravitas*, the sense that you were in the room with an important person. There was also a governing style that seemed as if the premier was merely part of something bigger than himself—something that was making the decisions and pushing him along. He seemed, at times, to be simply explaining decisions as if they were made somewhere else. Of course they weren't: In Cabinet the premier gets the last word.

It was these times that I went hardest on Calvert, sometimes too much so. But, from helplessly trying to deflect certain scandals to not stopping truly offensive political campaign advertisements, there was the sense that Calvert was more influenced by handlers, advisors and bureaucrats than he should have been. All premiers live in a constant and swirling vortex of advisors pushing advice but the natural leaders put their own imprint on decisions. And they convey the impression that they ultimately control the decisions being made and are responsible for them. Calvert always seemed as if he was being blown by winds beyond his control.

Lorne Calvert came from humble beginnings. He would remind people of this, even as premier, when talking about family members working part-time in big box stores or him tinkering under dilapidated old buses he'd convert to campers. A small man in stature, friendly, folksy and generally unassuming, Calvert was ordained as a United Church Minister after receiving degrees in Economics and Theology.

After several years as a clergyman in rural congregations and then in Moose Jaw, Calvert was elected NDP MLA for Moose Jaw South in 1986. Following the election of the Romanow government in 1991, Calvert was bypassed for a Cabinet appointment but one year later was made a junior minister and then eventually rose to the powerful health and social services portfolios and was named minister responsible for SaskPower and SaskEnergy after being re-elected in 1995.

In a surprise announcement in the summer of 1998, Calvert suddenly resigned from Cabinet and said that he would stay on as an MLA but wouldn't run again in 1999. At the time, Premier Romanow thanked Calvert for his service, noting Calvert's respectful approach to politics and that "by acknowledging other people's dignity he underscored his own."

Although not public knowledge at the time, Calvert's departure from politics coincided with a difficult family matter—his teenage son had fathered a child who Calvert and his family helped raise and support. Close to his grandson, Calvert would later, in both the 2003 and 2007 elections, mention how he decided on the election date while out walking with the young boy.

Although out of public life after 1998, Calvert stayed deeply inside politics. As is common in the NDP political machine, he was hired as a social policy advisor to Premier Romanow which kept a pay cheque coming and ensured that Calvert stayed closely plugged in to the political world. When Romanow announced his resignation in September 2000, seven candidates stepped forward, including Calvert, who was the best organized and financed. When the leadership votes were counted on January 27, 2001 Calvert won on the fourth ballot.

Calvert's first days as Premier were tumultuous. He'd inherited a coalition government from Romanow which relied on three Liberal MLAs to keep the NDP in power. In Romanow's last election, in 1999, the NDP had received fewer votes than the two-year old SaskParty, a new party made up of former Progressive Conservative and Liberal MLAs. Although the SaskParty received 39.6% of the popular vote to the NDP's 38.7%, the SaskParty took 26 seats and the NDP 29, exactly one-half the seats in the 58 seat Legislature. But with the appointment of a Speaker, which usually comes from the government side, the NDP would not have had a majority of votes so it entered into a coalition agreement with the three Liberal MLAs, convincing leader Jim Melenchuk and his two member caucus to agree to support of the NDP in exchange for two Cabinet seats and the post of Speaker.

By the time Calvert arrived in early 2001 the Liberals, an erratic and disorganized cabal at the best of times, were starting to unravel. Arrangements had to be made for the swearing-in of the new government and, without a seat in the Legislature, Calvert needed to call a by-election and get himself elected. It was a hectic time.

Calvert and his Cabinet were sworn in on February 8, 2001, nearly two weeks after his leadership win—apparently delayed by confusion over when outgoing Premier Romanow and his staff were vacating offices. During this time, at a Saskatoon dinner and roast, former NDP Deputy Premier Dwain Lingenfelter, who had left Saskatchewan months earlier for a job in Calgary prior to Romanow's resignation, mocked Calvert's transition to power: "I leave town for six months and they elect a leftie. He can't get into the premier's office because Roy won't let him. I hear Al Blakeney is sitting up there, pretending he's the premier and Lorne's down in the basement. What the hell is going on down there [in Regina]?"

The early days of Calvert would set in motion a perception that would follow him for the rest of his political life. There was little doubt Calvert was tough enough to make difficult decisions and weather political storms —after all, he'd been a politician for nearly 15 years and a senior Cabinet minister. But did Calvert have the combination of likeability and gravitas that would make people do what he wanted them to do? Along with the ability to persuade others, was Calvert the type of person that people wanted to please because they either inherently respected or even feared him?

Leadership Means Standing for Something

American political strategist David Gergen had a front row seat in politics for more than 30 years, working in the West Wing of the White House under both Republican and Democratic Presidents from Nixon, Ford and Reagan to Clinton. In his bestselling *Eyewitness to Power: The Essence of Leadership Nixon to Clinton*, Gergen brilliantly analyzes the internal leadership attributes of character and sense of purpose. And he explains how leaders must tap into the core values of the people.

7 Keys to Leadership
LEADERS NEED:

1. The character to lead
2. A clear, compelling and central purpose;
3. The capacity to persuade;
4. The ability to work within the system;
5. A sure, quick start —hit the ground running;
6. Strong, prudent advisors; and,
7. The ability to inspire others to carry on the mission.

A few years after it was published, I read Gergen's book and something clicked: Lorne Calvert was a nice enough guy, well intentioned, connected inside the NDP and plugged into the machinery of government, but he wasn't driven or defined by any one specific, compelling objective or purpose that he would dedicate to putting his own mark on Saskatchewan.

Leaders can usually be summarized in one short sentence: Roy Romanow was defined by cleaning up Saskatchewan's debt mess; Grant Devine was driven to diversify the economy away from solely farming, and Allan Blakeney was focused on using government as a central planning tool to "manage" the 1970s resource boom with Crown corporations and the welfare state.

> "When you don't know where you're going,
> any road will get you there."
>
> *Cheshire Cat, Alice in Wonderland*

So what precise political purpose defined Lorne Calvert? What did he stand for? Calvert actually stood for a lot of things but depending on the time and place, the themes would change. And they usually weren't very compelling or specific. In fact, a lack of clear and defining purpose actually ended up defining Calvert.

Within days of becoming leader, even before being sworn-in, Calvert met with the two Liberal MLAs in Romanow's Cabinet, Jack Hillson and Jim Melenchuk. They seemed to be having second thoughts on propping up the NDP, which they had done since signing a coalition agreement with Romanow after the 1999 election. Hillson told the media that Liberal supporters "seem to prefer the idea that we be free to support, or not support, the government on a case-by-case basis, rather than joining the NDP." This same thought had obviously eluded Hillson 16 months earlier when he'd joined the NDP Cabinet and the coalition. After meeting with Calvert, Hillson promptly quit the Cabinet.

What Lorne Calvert Stood For	Where	When
"Building a just, civil and prosperous province based upon the spirit of Saskatchewan people" by listening, creating opportunities, improving quality of life and fostering provincial pride.	Swearing In	Feb 2001
"We need to work hard and work together"	"State of the Province"	Jan 2002
"A green and prosperous economy"	Election Campaign Speech	Oct 2003
Examine, stimulate, listen, encourage expand, attract, explore, increase, support, develop, build on, promote and partner on 81 issues while addressing specifics on two issues.	Saskatchewan Action Plan for the Economy: A New Century of Opportunity	Sept 2005
"The vision of the Lorne Calvert NDP was to build Saskatchewan into a 'have' province with a heart."	Official Biography on NDP Website	2008

A week later, Calvert named his first Cabinet and replaced Hillson with Ron Osika, the third Liberal MLA, who had been Speaker of the House under Romanow. So, with Osika and Melenchuk in the NDP Cabinet, Calvert reappointed every Romanow minister except one, dropping Saskatoon's Judy Junor. Later described by the Star Phoenix as "in and out of Cabinet more times than you slam the screen door at the cottage during a hot Saskatchewan summer", Junor was elected in a 1995 by-election after giving up her job as president of the powerful Saskatchewan Union of Nurses, a strongly NDP-allied union.

In Calvert's inaugural Cabinet he appointed the mercurial Saskatoon NDP MLA Pat Lorje who he would fire 16 months later amidst controversy. The only other newcomer to Calvert's Cabinet was Regina's Kim Trew, an MLA since 1986 and overlooked in every single Cabinet appointment since. Trew was not what could charitably be referred to as a sparkling minister.

With a new boss came a shuffle inside the Premier's office. Calvert brought in long time bureaucrat Dan Perrins to be his deputy minister and the province's top civil servant. Perrins would stick by Calvert for his entire run as Premier —the only senior staffer to do so. Calvert's new Chief of Staff, NDP insider and former candidate Kathie Maher-Wolbaum would last only six months. She was replaced by Deb McDonald, a longstanding and reliable senior NDP advisor who would later leave and become the

NDP's Provincial Secretary. McDonald was replaced by one of the NDP's most versatile go-to guys, Gord Nystuen, former party treasurer, government bus company CEO, Deputy Minister and political jack of all trades. He would leave before the 2007 election for a top vice-president position at SaskPower.

As Calvert got down to the business of governing, it took only days (20, actually) for one of the most senior and respected members of Cabinet to promptly quit without explanation. Janice MacKinnon, who had been Canada's first female finance minister in the Romanow years, later admitted that she left politics because of the "direction" being taken by Calvert's government. There was grumbling that MacKinnon ought to have voiced any misgivings earlier and not have accepted a Cabinet job for less than three weeks. But those of us who know and respect MacKinnon suspect she stuck around for enough Cabinet meetings to confirm the worst—the new direction meant a lurch to the political left and a retreat from the careful budget plans and tight spending of the Romanow years.

Down to Work—and Now What?

As Calvert's first legislative session came to an end in June, 2001, a news release was issued, breathlessly announcing that "the government created hundreds of jobs—new water inspectors, new highways workers, and new child care employees." Usually, even left-wing governments don't publicly boast about using millions of taxpayer's dollars to create government jobs. They may do this and quietly brag to their supporters in the civil service unions, but it's not shouted from the windows. The government news release went on to point out that private companies had created even more jobs by "partnering with the government." Nowhere was any mention made of jobs not related to government. Obviously there was a new sheriff and posse in town.

Within a year of taking office it became increasingly clear that the NDP did not seem to know how to overcome the hemorrhaging of over 12,000 jobs—the greatest decline in Canada—and a provincial out-migration of 10,000 people leaving Saskatchewan. Faster than a frozen hockey puck rattling around a small town rink, the excuses flew, and there were a lot of them: drought, low oil and gas prices, and the post-9:11 economic slowdown and even (as Calvert talked with pride about being the 'have not' province closest to the cut-off line) Ottawa was blamed for shortchanging us on equalization money.

At the same time, while many people leaving Saskatchewan headed next door to Alberta, our neighbouring province had the same oil and gas and agricultural markets we did. With far less a diverse resource economy than Saskatchewan, Alberta was more reliant on oil and gas, and their economy continued to have a lot more people wanting in than out.

In early 2002, faced with these challenges, it was Calvert's *carpe diem* moment—he could seize the day and provide leadership—concrete ideas, a workable plan and a strategy to grow the economy, keep people here and create jobs. But all we got were more excuses. The premier also began reciting a new mantra, "We need to work hard and work together." He didn't offer what work we'd have to do and what results we'd hope to achieve together.

At his Premier's Dinner in 2002, Calvert paraphrased Henry Ford's description of obstacles as "the troublesome things we see when we take our eye off the goal." But then he ran down a gloomy list of obstacles and concluded that the solution was "working together," which Calvert explained could include using tax dollars to buy parts of businesses wanting to operate in Saskatchewan or having the government "partner" with business. It was a weird feeling, sitting there and realizing that while modern governments have all manner of ways to drive economic development, here was the premier treading water and waiting for the 1970s to throw him a lifeline where governments got bright ideas and we ended up paying for them.

Months after Janice MacKinnon's resignation, as a deepening fog of uncertainty and inaction swirled around the Calvert government, I wondered if MacKinnon's comment about a different "direction" might have had nothing at all to do with political ideology. Perhaps she meant a complete lack of direction and focus. It's all I thought of every time Calvert implored us to "work hard and work together."

"Canada's first Prime Minister, Sir John A. Macdonald referred to the "art of Cabinet-making" as one of his pastimes. He didn't mean woodworking."

John Gormley in full rant

In Calvert's nearly seven year run, he brought in 16 new Ministers during five Cabinet shuffles. Most of his senior ministers were holdovers from the Romanow years—Pat Atkinson, Clay Serby, Eldon Lautermilch, Harry Van Mulligen, John Nilson, Eric Cline, Maynard Sonntag, Joanne Crofford and Buckley Belanger.

With the loss of several strong Romanow Cabinet members and the emergence of generally weaker new talent in the elections of 1999 and 2003, I couldn't help but think the ascension of certain people in the Calvert era was explained by the old proverb that in the land of the blind the one-eyed man is king.

Some of Calvert's new ministers, like Pat Lorje, Kevin Yates, Kim Trew and Joan Beatty ranged from weak to walking disasters. Others were good ministers. Long time and experienced NDP strategist Frank Quennell, first elected in 2003, took easily to Cabinet and performed well. Andrew Thomson grew into an impressive minister and Deb Higgins was generally effective. Other ministers, like Len Taylor, Graham Addley, Peter Prebble, David Forbes and Mark Wartman were neither shining stars nor political liabilities. The final four Cabinet ministers (Warren McCall, Lon Borgerson, Sandra Morin and Ron Harper) were all virtual unknowns and low on the political depth chart but, having been appointed just months before Calvert's defeat in 2007, they had little time to prove themselves.

With his background in the social gospel and the United Church, Calvert is considerably to the political left of Roy Romanow. While he could make tough decisions on policy or finances, Calvert had difficulty saying "no" to the perpetual demands of the hard-core left and organized labour, two factions in the NDP which often felt ignored and even alienated during Romanow's time.

It was not surprising, therefore, to find in Calvert's first Cabinet the only new faces being left-wingers Trew and Lorje. Later, after the 2003 election, Calvert named to Cabinet environmentalist and rabid anti-nuke Peter Prebble, who had fought uranium mining in the 1970s, opposed a uranium refinery in the early 1980s and was well staked out on the political left of the party.

Union MLAs Wake Up the Job-Killing Monster —"It's Alive!"

Two appointments from organized labour would cause Calvert heart-ache—one resulted in a controversial public issue that could have been avoided; the other was just a bad choice.

The controversy arose after putting Deb Higgins into Cabinet in 2001. Choosing Higgins wasn't a bad move. She is a congenial, unpretentious and hardworking MLA who took over Calvert's Moose Jaw seat when he left politics in the late 1990s. In the union world she was a powerhouse, starting as a Safeway cashier and rising to head the powerful provincial council of the United Food and Commercial Workers Union. Higgins was not to be underestimated.

After the 2003 election, when big unions saved the NDP from defeat by running a successful scare campaign about Crown corporations, Higgins convinced Calvert to enact a law that organized labour had been lusting after for years. It was called the "most available hours" law and had actually been passed in 1994 by Roy Romanow, who never proclaimed it into law, fearing the harm it would cause to Saskatchewan's employers. The law made it illegal for any company with more than 50 employees to hire new staff or even pay overtime if new hours of work arose. Instead, the new hours would have to be offered to all existing part time employees on the basis of a government supervised seniority list in the workplace. Higgins liked the seniority part; it would "stop employers from giving work to whoever they like" and she convinced Calvert to proclaim the law because it would "help people move to full-time work."

The problem with this ideological approach is that it would actually end up doing the opposite—costing jobs, as the seniority lists would reduce or eliminate hours for new, young workers. And, the law would be a huge disincentive for new businesses to come to the only place in North America with a law giving government so much power. Unlike Romanow, Calvert wasn't strong enough to say "no" to big labour and to Higgins. Calvert naively talked about his friends and family members working in big box stores and Higgins did the bidding for organized labour, all the while trying to sell this assault on common sense.

Then it happened. Saskatchewan's business community, normally fickle and not known for standing together for anything, finally stood up—way up. By early 2005, after four months of blistering public heat and protests—fuelled in part by a certain radio host who called it the "job-killing monster" and played the Frankenstein "it's alive" soundtrack every day—the job-killing monster was being chased down with pitchforks and torches. At the same time, Calvert, Higgins and Big Labour's Larry Hubich were high-tailing it with upset citizens at their heels. Finally, a government source confided to me, "we need to find an honourable way out of this—it's killing us." Two days later, Calvert backed off and repealed the law.

Et Tu, Kevin?

The union appointment by Calvert that was bad news from the start was the decision to put Kevin Yates in Cabinet. A Regina NDP MLA, Yates is an oddity in image-conscious politics—short, rumpled and roly-poly and with a slight speech impediment. He's brash, loud and tends to exaggerate. Just a couple of years before being elected in 1999, Yates was a senior SGEU executive and chair of the Public Service Negotiating Committee for the union.

Yates worked for 15 years at the Regina Provincial Correctional Centre (RPCC) and was a union shop steward. In 2006, Calvert decided to put Yates in the Cabinet and named him minister of corrections, which transformed Yates from a jail guard to the guy in charge of the entire corrections system, including overseeing the same senior managers for whom Yates used to work.

Later, in 2008 after a sensational jail break from the RPCC, which happened when accused murderers tunneled for four months while 87 different guards appeared oblivious, an investigation revealed years of bad morale, fear, complacency and even intimidation among jail guards. The investigation also identified a "long history of an adversarial and controversial relationship between the SGEU shop stewards and management that has limited management's ability to manage."

It was also discovered that during Yates' time as minister, there was a decree that union shop stewards at the jail could personally contact the minister and bypass the chain of command.

In the short term, though, Calvert's concern wasn't Yates' buffoonish behaviour or union shop floor politicking style—it was his lack of loyalty. Just seven months after entering Cabinet, Yates began openly questioning Calvert's leadership and talking up NDP ex-Deputy Premier Dwain Lingenfelter who was living in Alberta and sending none too subtle hints that he wanted back in the game.

Accused of leading an attempted coup—a rare thing for the usually well disciplined NDP machine—Yates was dumped from Cabinet by Calvert. But inexplicably, just a few months later, in his final Cabinet shuffle in May 2007, Calvert reinstated Yates, a move described by the Star Phoenix as "the oddest choice by far."

Of the new Cabinet Ministers created by Lorne Calvert, the longest journey from backbench lightweight to senior and respected minister was taken by Andrew Thomson. Thomson was an NDP staffer elected as an MLA in 1995, just four years after graduating from the University of Saskatchewan where he was the students' union president in 1991.

An MLA at age 27, Thomson had some maturing to do. A hard partisan in the Legislature, he once suggested that SaskParty MLAs were Nazis by calling them "brown shirts." Another time, while sitting on a government committee purportedly examining the NDP's Channel Lake scandal, Thomson boasted to a constituency meeting that the committee's final report had actually been written in advance, before the hearings had ended, and had been authored by Premier Romanow's Deputy Chief of Staff—not committee staff—all of which set off a controversy and confirmed suspicions that the committee's true job had been to further cover-up the Channel Lake scandal and whitewash it. For more than six years Thomson had been ignored in every Cabinet shuffle until Calvert named him energy and mines minister in late 2001.

Thomson progressed through several Cabinet portfolios until being named, after the 2003 election, as minister of learning (as the NDP preferred to call education). He would later become minister of finance. In these last two jobs, Thomson grew into an impressive minister— tightly controlled, well messaged and one of Calvert's strongest and more effective ministers.

When moderating an industry conference one day, I was impressed by Thomson's ability to establish a point, explain and defend it and disarmingly concede that other options were open but not always possible. On education property taxes, he bluntly admitted that he agreed with Alberta Premier Ralph Klein's removal of school board taxation powers but could not convince the Cabinet. Later, the SaskParty brought in this measure. Thomson also impressed the crowd with his mantra "I love cutting taxes," even offering the audience an opportunity to weigh in on where he should cut next. I commended Thomson for an enthusiasm that was good policy and good politics.

But, Thomson had two weaknesses. Like the NDP's subsequent leader Lingenfelter, whose muckraking and personal attacks were legendary, Thomson couldn't help himself and sometimes chose gutter fighting when his smarts, charm and personality would have carried him further. Just before his retirement, with the NDP desperate to take a piece of the SaskParty's Brad Wall, Thomson went on the attack in the Legislature, suggesting that Wall had personal knowledge of criminal activities during the Devine government years. Although Thomson apologized the next day, the damage was done—not to Wall but to Thomson's reputation as a guy who could go negative and ugly, making him look like a young Lingenfelter instead of the telegenic, articulate and savvy politician he'd grown into.

Thomson's other vulnerability was a personal matter—ultimately irrelevant to politics—over which he had no control. As a gay man in a committed relationship, which was well known in political and social circles, Thomson would not have survived an NDP leadership convention. Inside the core of the NDP (particularly the old CCFers who pray every night to God and Tommy) the party's path of chosen leaders will not include a gay man, not yet. In this way, the NDP is like any other political party. While many of its members will tolerantly judge people on their abilities and their hearts, many will not countenance a gay leader. Thomson, on leaving politics in 2007, took a job in Toronto with a computer company.

In 2005, Saskatchewan celebrated a magnificent Centennial celebration, with concerts, galas, homecomings and festivals around the province. For citizens, there was a general sense of optimism, pride and growing confidence that with improved economic prospects and a growing population, maybe Saskatchewan was ready to turn the corner; that it finally might be "our turn." But in political circles, the bright horizon was obscured by a dark ennui covering the landscape—Premier Calvert just couldn't get happy or focussed on a specific agenda beyond the trite "green and prosperous economy," the slogan which he'd unveiled earlier during the 2003 election campaign. Never answering the question of which "green" measures would result in prosperity and how this would happen, the uncertainty made it difficult for Calvert to engage and ultimately inspire citizens to follow him.

As 2005 rolled on, Calvert was not experiencing the bump in popularity that good times, celebrations and a big provincial birthday party should have brought the NDP over the opposition Saskatchewan Party and its new leader Brad Wall. Rumours continued to persist, both inside and outside NDP circles, that the premier would finish the birthday year, announce his retirement in 2006 and move on to a nationally prominent job in the United Church of Canada. But it didn't happen.

"Do, or Do Not. There is No Try."

Early in 2005, the government convened a summit to map the future of the Saskatchewan economy. Its findings and recommendations were released at the end of the year in a 38-page document called the *Saskatchewan Action Plan for the Economy: A New Century of Opportunity.*

With great fanfare, Premier Calvert unveiled the plan, which contained 81 recommendations. It began with a detailed summary of impressive statistics outlining a recipe for a booming economy and great potential in energy, mining, forestry, oil and gas, agriculture, innovation, technology, tourism, skills development, and so on. The main theme of the report was that Saskatchewan should "act now to seize new opportunities and ensure a high quality of life."

Each heading in the report contained statements like "build healthier, safer and more supportive learning environments with investments in our educational infrastructure" or "build on our momentum to boost manufacturing and enhance access to capital." But, full of verbs like "build, attract, expand, support, examine, explore, stimulate, develop and encourage," the document contained only two single concrete, detailed objectives and benchmarks: Saskatchewan should expand beyond 175 megawatts of wind-power "as opportunities permit" and we should have 5,000 immigrants by 2008. That was it.

Years earlier, in 2000, the Romanow government had unveiled "Partnership for Prosperity," a document which identified 19 specific targets (later revised downward to 16) which were regularly monitored until Calvert's action plan took over. Saskatchewan went from regular updates on targets to an "action" plan that was short on action.

The word "action" suggests something being moved, altered or accomplished. But this report had far more talking points and hopeful verbs than action. The NDP political staff and bureaucrats who wrote the plan were savvy enough to know that the public had given up on "consultation" in the 1990s, hence the word didn't appear even once. But the report repeated 19 times "working" or "partnering;" reference was made 11 times to "supporting," four times each to "develop" and "promote" and the government promised three times to "build on." On royalties and taxes, the pledge was made to "continuously monitor"—not to raise, lower, study or adopt best practices but to sit and watch taxes.

Think about your life. Success comes when we have specific targets to achieve and a time to do them in—hitting a goal weight, paying down debt, upgrading our education or working on most personal objectives. And it's the same for governments that set out specific objectives and measurements: literacy and training goals, social assistance collection rates, immigration targets, population growth, tax policy and targeted sector development. Ironically, while Calvert's action plan was struggling here, next door in Alberta the "performance measurement" system of government was requiring every ministry to set out each year in advance specific benchmarks along with detailed objectives and targets—actual, attainable outcomes which were then measured against results at the end of the year.

By keeping its action plan deliberately vague, the Saskatchewan NDP tried, as it so often did, to ignore the rule that has always worked everywhere else: "You can't manage what you can't measure."

Worse, the lack of detail almost seemed designed to keep public expectations low—low enough that the government could not be held accountable for under-performing because there were no benchmarks to perform to. When I read this "action" document with no action, this "plan" with no plan—it brought back Yoda's immortal words in Star Wars that trying doesn't count: "Do or do not. There is no try."

Calvert's action plan was full of try.

Equalization: Picking Up the Welfare Cheque in Your Lexus

"Equalization is an essential part of the glue that holds Canada together, East-West, provinces and citizens alike. When the equalization formula is revealed to be generating problems, the glue just could become unstuck."

Thomas Courchene

In 2005, Saskatchewan-born economist Thomas Courchene wrote a paper that found a weakness in Canada's equalization program, the decades-old scheme that has even been included in our Constitution. It transfers money from the richer "have" provinces to the poorer "have nots," which supposedly enables the poorer provinces to provide public services like health care and education to their citizens at a level comparable to the wealthier provinces.

Equalization is mind-numbingly complicated and is about "fiscal capacity" where the feds top up the revenues of poorer provinces so that their per-capita revenues are equal to the average per-capita revenues of the five so called "mid-provinces" of BC, Saskatchewan, Manitoba, Ontario and Quebec. Revenue is calculated from at least 33 different variables—all plugged into 1300 simultaneously moving parts in the equalization formula. Very few people really understand the formula and when they try to explain it, it's not easy to get.

Courchene's point was that Saskatchewan—for years a perennial "have not"—was being forced to pay out more than a dollar for every dollar we earned from oil, natural gas and resources. The federal Liberals refused to change this claw-back formula, despite promising two Atlantic provinces that their oil and gas revenues would be exempted from the equalization formula. In late 2004, Newfoundland's fiery Conservative Premier Danny Williams ordered all Canadian flags removed from provincial buildings over a dispute with Liberal Prime Minister Paul Martin over this issue.

By the 2006 federal election, Saskatchewan's Lorne Calvert had demanded that Saskatchewan be given the same treatment—not the flags part, the exempting of resource revenue from the calculation of our income. Before the election, then-opposition leader Conservative Stephen Harper promised to give Calvert what he wanted: a national 10 province standard for calculating equalization—rather than 5 provinces—and all Saskatchewan's resource revenues would be excluded from the equalization formula.

After winning the election, Harper delivered on the promise. But there was fine print—he put a cap that limited the amount of money coming to Saskatchewan to $226 million dollars in 2007 and zero thereafter. This was clearly a broken promise by Harper. But the PM explained that Saskatchewan had become a strong, "have" province and it would not be appropriate to still be receiving money from provinces with less fiscal capacity than us. Harper also committed more money to Saskatchewan than the $800 million dollars that Calvert had anticipated under an improved equalization formula.

....

"Equalization and transfer programs "…have a perverse impact and make regions more dependent. They give very little incentive to create greater on-source revenue because those revenue sources are taxed back. Well-intentioned but generally speaking they aren't transformational."

Former New Brunswick Premier Frank McKenna

....

Calvert, on the lookout for an issue in the coming 2007 provincial election, thought he had found it in equalization. The NDP would run a provincial campaign against Stephen Harper, claiming that only they would "stand up" for Saskatchewan, as the SaskParty were puppets of Harper's and couldn't be counted on. Repeatedly using the word "betrayed," Calvert accused the Prime Minister of lying, refused to shake his hand at an Ottawa meeting and Saskatchewan filed a lawsuit.

Finance Minister Andrew Thomson was Calvert's lead on equalization and fared no better than his boss. Thomson and his officials were isolated both at the political and bureaucratic levels throughout 2006–2007 by the strategic and tough Harper. Thomson even tried playing the Western alienation card saying, "they're buying Quebec votes with Western oil," which earned him criticism from former NDP Finance Minister Janice MacKinnon. She argued that it was not good policy to change Saskatchewan's historic role of being a "builder" into a "divider" on national issues. MacKinnon also argued convincingly that, on the logic of fiscal capacity, it made no sense for Saskatchewan to receive funds from provinces that were less well off than we are.

Unfortunately for Saskatchewan, the NDP position resulted in our province being frozen out on important files beyond equalization, like the consultations for the 2007 federal budget. Even before he lost the 2007 election, Calvert's equalization pitch failed for at least four reasons:

1. Equalization was difficult to understand;

2. Attacking Stephen Harper as the "bad guy" was a tough sell when Harper was more popular in Saskatchewan than Calvert. Federal voters generally supported the PM and gave Harper 13 of 14 federal seats;

3. In a booming Saskatchewan, a solidly "have" province with the hottest economy in Canada, it was difficult to justify ignoring revenues from our huge oil, gas, potash and uranium revenues so we could collect a welfare cheque paid for by people in other provinces with a lower per-capita income than us; and,

4. Continuing a temper tantrum made us look like whiners, which didn't fit with the new Saskatchewan winning attitude. And, besides, if doing the same thing over and over and expecting a different result is the definition of insanity, why would Calvert keep up a fight that was going nowhere?

In the equalization campaign, the Calvert NDP government spent more than $340,000 dollars on public relations, slick advertisements and a website. In late 2005, in the run-up to the federal election two months later, Calvert stumbled; it wasn't a hard fall but it was amusing.

Doing a riff on Danny Williams' flag removal in Newfoundland, the NDP dubbed its equalization campaign "raise a flag for fairness" and there was an on-line web poll asking people to vote on the question, "Do you think that Saskatchewan deserves a fair Energy Accord?"

I mentioned the poll one morning on my radio show, commenting on how silly it was—what kind of idiot would vote "no" to a fair deal? As I suggested listeners check out the website, something odd began to happen—within minutes I was laughing about how the "no" votes had suddenly shot up to 25% percent, as some listeners had disabled their "vote-once" feature and repeatedly voted "no" to cause some mischief. Within an hour, as a couple of listeners later confessed to me, they'd skewed the poll so that 77% of votes were against a fair deal!

Several hours later, as another listener observed, "Looks like someone decided they didn't like the 'Gormley Effect' and decided to 'correct' the poll." So the NDP re-set the on-line poll and locked it to show that 90% of voters said "yes" regardless of how many votes were actually received. After the government locked the poll, the great conservative blog Small Dead Animals.com got involved and, with thousands of daily visitors to its site, asked its readers to check if the poll was rigged. It was, as the poll never moved despite thousands of "no" votes.

What should have been dealt with by the government as a silly prank went one step further when Calvert was scrummed by the media and sputtered about "b-b-b-b-logs" and how a "security fence" would have to be put around the site which had been "hacked." Calvert's look of utter exasperation told the story. So did his dismissive, "Small Dead Animals doesn't speak for the people of Saskatchewan." He'd be surprised.

In many respects, this one-day tempest for the NDP was a metaphor for the Calvert years. The entire silly notion of running a website and having the public vote on a loaded question was someone else's idea, yet Calvert was cast as the front man having to defend it. Later the NDP ran a companion campaign on equalization asking Saskatchewan people to imagine what we could do with $800 million dollars if Prime Minister Harper would write us a cheque, like we were playing a giant province-wide fantasy game, led by the premier. I'd rather imagine what it would be like to get drafted at my age by the Saskatchewan Roughriders and quarterback the team to next year's Grey Cup win—the odds were about the same of Ottawa ponying up the equalization dough.

The Raise a Flag mishap was another example of Calvert's NDP reacting to forces seemingly beyond its control. Like tectonic plates shifting beneath the earth's surface, the agenda for Calvert was either lurching into yet another scandal or trying gamely to respond to an economy and population loss that had pushed Saskatchewan's morale and psyche to all-time lows.

From advertising campaigns using millions of dollars of our own money to tell us how good things were, or the NDP helping fund events like a speech by climate crusader Al Gore, the Rolling Stones concert or bringing the Junos to Saskatchewan, the Calvert government seemed to be trying almost too hard to manufacture relevance, a sense of place and even fun. In most other places in Canada, contented and optimistic people don't need the government as an entertainment promoter.

In his time as premier, Calvert never seemed to shed the image of a caretaker, the shepherd tending the flock until something happened. He did not seem a visionary leader or even someone with a clear plan to get from point A to point B. A generally likeable and respectful man, Calvert never seemed entirely comfortable and secure in the job of premier, as did Romanow and Blakeney before him and Wall after him.

Had it not been for the infamous NDP election machine, I would today have been left with an entirely favourable assessment of Calvert as a nice guy. However, my opinion of him slipped after several particularly vicious and personal campaign attacks by the NDP in the elections of 2003 and 2007 against their SaskParty opponents. As much as any party leader is always pushed and pulled by advisors in the heat of battle during a campaign, the leader still bears ultimate responsibility for the behaviour of the party. In my view, the NDP's negative tactics diminished Calvert.

Chapter 4

BRINGING A KNIFE TO A GUNFIGHT: THE 2003 ELECTION

The Future is Wide Open. So is the Election

As Saskatchewan's natural governing party, with a knack for getting elected and then tenaciously hanging on to power, the NDP's high holy days come during election campaigns. They have the longest record of winning elections against usually weak and less organized opponents. And, for those who thought Lorne Calvert's ecclesiastical and folksy approach made the gentle vicar above the fray of politics, his first election as premier in 2003 opened a lot of eyes. It was a vicious, nasty and very personal campaign that set a new low, even by Saskatchewan's often ugly campaign standards.

In the parliamentary system, when someone wins the leadership of a governing party between elections they automatically become the premier, even though they have been chosen by party members and not elected by the public. The last NDP leader to do this was Woodrow Lloyd in 1961, who succeeded Tommy Douglas and was beaten three years later in his first election as premier. With recent Saskatchewan campaigns tending toward autumn—the last one being Romanow's minority government in 1999—by the fall of 2003 it was likely that Calvert would face the voters for the first time, nearly three years after becoming premier.

The NDP was usually at its tactical best leading up to election campaigns: early issues are put in play which helps the longstanding campaign rule that winners set the agenda, decide the time and place of the fight, define the issues and then make their opponents react. Another NDP commandment that would come into play in 2003 involved attacking the opposing leader and forcing a response.

In late 2002 the NDP unveiled a three year, multi-million dollar campaign called "The Future is Wide Open," designed to improve Saskatchewan's image both inside and outside the province and to promote business and investment here. Taking the NDP at its word (which future events suggest may have been a mistake), the campaign was to run up until the province's Centennial in 2005. I was a big fan—it spread the word outside Saskatchewan, featured glitzy ads and even scoreboard advertising at CFL Roughrider road games. And I especially liked Jason Plumb's catchy theme song where he sung "I know a place well worth living." Promoting Saskatchewan in other parts of the country was a great idea. Provinces like B.C., Alberta, Ontario and Quebec had done this for years in business promotion and tourism.

But in 2003, six months before the expected fall election, the Wide Open Future campaign dramatically changed, cranking up its frequency and focusing nearly exclusively inside the borders of Saskatchewan. This coincided with the arrival behind the scenes of Ed Tchorzewksi, one-time NDP deputy premier, who began working on the NDP's pre-campaign strategy.

The provincial "feel good" campaign at taxpayers' expense was so manipulated by the NDP campaign machine that the government sheepishly admitted later that the original two million dollar budget for 2003 actually exceeded $5 million. By the time the entire Wide Open Future campaign ended, its cost was $8 million.

They're Off: The Tortoise & the Hare (Watch the Tortoise)

As the 2003 election began, the NDP was unpopular and beset by scandals including a Crown computer and land titles corporation called ISC losing millions, the "Spudco" scandal and the revelation that Cabinet minister Eldon Lautermilch had deliberately misled a businessman about Spudco. These blows to NDP trust and popularity, plummeting population as young people continued to flock to Calgary and weak government economic policy had the NDP enter the campaign on shaky footing.

Several weeks before the election, amidst the BSE or "mad cow" cattle crisis, Premier Calvert unveiled with great fanfare a province-wide petition calling on the U.S. to re-open the border to Canadian beef. But the effort was derailed when a leaked memo to NDP MLAs and political candidates joked about "President Shrub," instead of Bush, and suggested that the petitions—which had been created at taxpayers' expense—be widely distributed "as a campaign canvassing tool" and be used politically for "whatever creative flim-flam you can come up with." The NDP had managed to cynically take a crisis destroying ranches and farm families and turn it into a political stunt.

During this time I had an interesting revelation about Calvert's political savvy. In mid-September, with speculation rampant that he would soon call an election, the premier and I had dinner one night. As we chatted, Calvert mused whether he should call the election later that autumn or wait. When I asked him how he felt about election prospects, he leaned across the table and predicted a tough election but said the NDP would make gains in three SaskParty seats—Saskatchewan Rivers, Weyburn and Lloydminster.

I was stunned—why would he tell me, not exactly one of his confidantes? Was this a test to see if I'd blab? Was I being set up? Or was it just the premier speaking frankly to someone who was a keen political observer? I never mentioned our dinner or conversation to anyone. On election night, when the SaskParty lost Sask Rivers and held on to the other two seats with reduced majorities (in the case of Lloydminster a mere 66 votes), it was a good lesson in not underestimating the premier.

As the election campaign began, the NDP was on the defensive and slowly plodding along, while the popular SaskParty clipped along with a lead in the polls. Within days a scandal hit the NDP hard when its campaign team had circulated a cartoon depicting SaskParty leader Elwin Hermanson in a Nazi uniform loading NDP sympathizers into boxcars. This was in response to a so-called "hit list" that emerged weeks earlier where the SaskParty had identified NDP partisans on government job lists.

While the idea for a cartoon began as a harmless morale booster for party troops, it soon showed the politics of hate that often lurks beneath the surface of the NDP hard partisans. The cartoon surfaced several days after longtime NDP apparatchik Dave Degenstein noted that he'd like to see a cartoon of uniformed SaskParty people tattooing the forearms of NDP supporters, a none too subtle reference to the Nazi atrocities at Auschwitz. At a symbolic level, this cartoon showed that some NDP campaign workers evidently believed it was acceptable to compare their political opponent to a murderous Nazi because he wanted to defeat them. And, presumably in the minds of party hacks, losing their politically-granted jobs would be a fate comparable to human genocide.

Save Us from the Scary Bald Man Who is Going to Fire Mommy and Daddy

When the NDP is lagging in the polls during an election, as it was in 2003, it will usually unleash a strongly negative attack strategy during the second or third week of the campaign. And so it did, targeting SaskParty leader Elwin Hermanson in one of the nastiest and most counter-productive campaigns in living memory.

Hermanson, a genuinely good and decent man and a farmer from West-Central Saskatchewan, had the unfortunate appearance of being middle aged, bald and unassuming. This wasn't so bad—particularly when the other contestant in the beauty pageant was Lorne Calvert, whose folksy, plain look was a cross between Martin Short's character, Ed Grimley, and comedian Don Knotts.

Somewhere, in part based on appearance, the perception began to emerge in focus groups and polling that, while Calvert was seen as a kind and trustworthy preacher, Hermanson was negative, uncomfortable and untrustworthy. And unlike Calvert, who looked non-threatening and even nerdish, Hermanson had this "thing"—an indefinable factor that made women uncomfortable. I can't describe it; I'm not a woman. But all the women I know, including even ardent right-wingers, said Hermanson scored high on their "ick meters."

But Hermanson's biggest problem was an honest answer he gave to a hypothetical question (media savvy politicians never answer hypothetical questions). Asked about selling Crown corporations, he said "no" but when pressed as to whether he would reconsider if offered huge amounts of money, he said he'd obviously have to look at all options. That was all the NDP needed.

The party's BC-based advertising agency, at the direction of NDP campaign manager Dale Schmeichel and with advice from NDP consultant Garry Aldridge, unleashed a brilliant and ruthless fear and smear campaign warning that Hermanson and the SaskParty would sell off all the cherished Crown corporations, throw thousands of hard-working civil servants into the abyss, and threaten "the Saskatchewan way."

The attack campaign worked on several interconnected principles:

1. Elwin Hermanson will sell the Crown corporations;

2. Hermanson will take away your sense of security by raising car insurance rates and power bills, which will result from the selling of the Crowns;

3. With the Crown corporations gone—sold by Hermanson—we'll get a lower minimum wage, more poor people, there'll be no money left for Medicare. And, the kids who haven't already left for Alberta will be fleeing;

4. Hermanson will fire thousands of hardworking employees of Crown corporations (your neighbours) because he's selling the Crowns; and

5. In summary: NDP=good (will protect you), Saskatchewan Party=bad (have a hidden agenda to sell Crowns).

The NDP attack ads, with a single focal message—Hermanson will sell the Crowns—followed the marketing laws of frequency and consistency. Everywhere the message was the same: Don't trust Elwin Hermanson. It didn't matter if this was true or a damnable lie—there was no evidence that Hermanson and SaskParty were planning to sell Crown corporations—but it was all in the perception and messaging. And in politics, perception is reality.

Lorne Calvert, like most New Democrat politicians and strategists, never gloats. As the shock and awe campaign against Hermanson was unfolding and a strong SaskParty lead in the polls was crumbling by the day, a determined and serious Calvert quietly told his advisors that "if you're explaining in politics you're losing." And the SaskParty's Hermanson was doing plenty of explaining as he lost.

Counting Out the NDP & Other Fatal Mistakes

The NDP attack was so thorough and withering that it caught rookie SaskParty strategists off balance. People would never believe this "made-up garbage," a SaskParty insider sniffed to me with days left in the campaign. Bravely maintaining that their polls had them ahead by eight points, the SaskParty whistled past the graveyard as the NDP went unchallenged with their fear and smear campaign.

In the final days, one Saskatoon SaskParty candidate boasted to a friend of mine that the campaign was "in the bag" and the SaskParty would pull through despite the NDP counter-attack. I asked my friend "he didn't really say 'in the bag', did he?" My friend nodded yes. I told my pal that in my political experience, rookies invariably talk like this and in every campaign where I've heard someone say "in the bag" they are usually missing one word—"body." My friend looked puzzled. I said to him "you guys are finished."

The ultimately fatal tactical mistake by the SaskParty was not to "bomb the bridges" of the NDP on attack advertising. It is a well accepted strategy: if your opponent strikes first with negative ads, take the initial hit, keep your head down and allow your adversary to commit themselves to a single issue of attack, in this case, Crown corporations.

Then—after the opponent has fully committed—you launch a two-pronged counter-attack: first, an equally withering salvo of attack ads hitting back at their ads, meeting their issue head-on and calling it a lie or setting the record straight; second, at the same time, you launch a wave of aggressive attack ads designed to "bomb the bridges" behind your opponent by going hard on their fall-back issues. In this case, these were population and job loss, hospital waiting lists, post-secondary education line-ups, the worst highways in Canada and the most expensive government scandal in history, Spudco. The effect is that when your opponent gets blasted off its initial attack issue it cannot get back to its other issues because the bridge has been taken out. SaskParty strategists did not understand this. Some were such rookies that they didn't even know the strategy existed.

In the last five days of the campaign, pollsters were seeing incredible movement. The SaskParty lead had evaporated and was in free fall, as the NDP chugged steadily upward. I sensed this from calls to the radio show and from hearing friends talk. People were starting to say "better the devil I know than the devil I don't"; a way of saying that they'd stay with an unpopular NDP government because it was better than a party that may bring change they fear. The subtext to this, for the people who typically fear anything new or unknown, was "what we have now is as good as it's going to get."

Another story I heard was a chilling illustration of how effective the NDP campaign was. One of my Regina friends was driving some kids to school when a group of eight-year-old girls began talking about Jessica, whose mom and dad worked for a Crown corporation. Jessica was sad, they said, because "if the SaskParty wins the election her Mommy and Daddy won't have jobs anymore."

In addition to chopping down the SaskParty, the beauty of the NDP cleavage tactic on Crown corporations became apparent too late for the Liberals. Because the fear message broke into clear "yes" or "no" camps, it didn't allow voters to go to the Liberals. You couldn't say "yes, I'll save the Crowns from the bad man, so I'll vote Liberal." There was only one way you could vote if you were frightened by the Big Lie.

On election night the Liberals were decimated, losing their three seats and the Liberal popular vote dropped by six percent, while the NDP vote rose by the same six percent to 45%. The SaskParty vote remained virtually unchanged at 39%. In a tactically brilliant but brutal campaign, Lorne Calvert had taken 30 seats to the SaskParty's 28.

Later, U of S political scientist Joe Garcea coined the expression "Ouija Board Effect" to describe voters, many wanting change, who paused with their pencils hovering above the ballot, amidst all the uncertainty over Crown corporations, and then slowly moved the pencil toward the NDP candidate's name, placing an "x".

As the election results rolled in, Elwin Hermanson and his advisors, looking for all the world like guys who'd brought a knife to a gunfight, learned a valuable lesson: the NDP can never be counted out.

Meet the New Boss; Same as the Old Boss

It did not take the NDP long, after the election, to return to a defensive position of public unpopularity.

As the province's finances were revealed to be in worse shape than disclosed during the campaign (something admitted by Finance Minister Harry Van Mulligen to be "outrageous but true"), he further confirmed that the NDP was contemplating tax increases but this was the kind of thing "I don't think you'd want to get into" during an election. The NDP then hiked the PST from 6% to 7% with no advance notice or consultation.

It was also confirmed, shortly after the election, that the government's two million dollar budget for the 2003 "Future is Wide Open" campaign had actually ballooned to over $5 million which had amounted to paid government propaganda not being claimed as an election expense. And, the NDP had "forgotten" to mention that more than $2.5 million of the money had been secretly kicked in by the Calvert Cabinet directing the government's Crown Investments Corporation to ante up. The government also confirmed, after the election, that the fancy TV commercials for the "feel good" campaign were made by a film company being financially propped up by the NDP government.

As Calvert, fresh off his first election as premier, looked ahead to clear sailing with a majority government and the provincial Centennial celebrations just 13 months away, ominous signs continued to appear. And more often than not they were highway signs, showing the way for a growing number of Saskatchewan people beating a path to Alberta.

Chapter 5

SASKATCHEWAN AND THE ELUSIVE MAGIC MILLION: VOTING WITH YOUR FEET

From Canada's Big Dog to Small Fry

"Just as sure as the sun shines there will be within this Province alone some day a population running into the tens of millions."

Walter Scott, first Premier of Saskatchewan, 1905

Population has defined the hopes and dreams of Saskatchewan for generations. From wanting our kids close to home to knowing that population also determines who's voting with their feet, the stats are coldly unforgiving. They don't lie. Population matters —if people want to be here they will be, if they don't they won't. When people are attracted to an area by opportunity, they come. Then those newcomers need goods and services which, in turn, creates wealth, jobs, economic activity, investment and ultimately more tax revenue for government.

The first one-third of the 20th century belonged to Saskatchewan, as hundreds of thousands of people flocked here from all over the world to open up farm land. Thousands more followed to feed, clothe and provide services and business to this remarkable, brave new land. Saskatchewan's first premier, the visionary Walter Scott, foresaw a day when 10 million people would live here.

By 1911, Saskatchewan was the third largest province in Canada—our 492,432 people dwarfed Alberta's 374,295 and British Columbia's 392,480. Only Ontario and Quebec had more people than Saskatchewan. By the summer of 1912, some promoters called Saskatoon the "fastest growing city in the world." Who could blame them with nine architectural firms, 12 car dealers, 13 banks, nine theatres, 14 poolrooms and five employment offices?

Saskatchewan remained Canada's third largest province until just after the end of World War II when we slipped behind our neighbouring Western provinces.

Super Saskatchewan to "Wee Province"		
Year	SK Population	Population Change
1901	91,279	
1906	257,763	+182%
1911	492,432	+91%
1916	647,835	+32%
1921	757,510	+17%
1926	820,738	+8%
1931	921,785	+12%
1936	931,547	+1%
1941	895,992	-4%
1946	832,688	-7%
1951	831,728	-0.1%
1956	880,665	+6%
1961	925,181	+5%
1966	955,344	+3%
1971	926,242	-3%
1976	921,323	-0.5%
1981	968,313	+5%
1986	1,009,610	+4%
1991	988,928	-2%
1996	990,237	+0.1%
2001	1,003,469	+1%
2006	992,295	-1%
2010	1,041,729	+5%

Statistics Canada

Saskatchewan's promising population of the early 1900s was decimated by the ravages of the 1930s Great Depression which robbed our province of farms, hope and people. The mythology of many NDP academics and apologists is that our population just couldn't bounce back after the Depression; that somehow the die had been cast. While every other province buffeted by the Depression rebounded and outgrew its 1930s-era population—particularly Alberta which saw a 400% growth in population—Saskatchewan never did. In fact, there were times during the 1970s we had fewer people than in the 1930s.

In the mid-1930s, Saskatchewan had more than 930,000 people while each of Alberta and BC had fewer than 800,000. By 1974, Alberta's population had over doubled to 1.7 million people and BC had tripled to 2.3 million. Saskatchewan had 907,000 people…25,000 less than in the middle of the Great Depression.

When prosperity returned to Canada after World War II, Saskatchewan was the only place in all of North America that elected a socialist government and continued to do so for decades. While other provinces saw robust growth, the NDP put an indelible mark on Saskatchewan's politics with less development of resources than BC and Alberta, extensive government intervention in the economy and a culture marked by wealth redistribution and socialism. Only Saskatchewan did things dramatically differently than every other province. And we paid for it by people leaving in droves and staying away. The conclusion is inescapable and brings to mind the words of British novelist Aldous Huxley that "facts do not cease to exist because they are ignored."

Generations of socialism and keeping our thinking small would allow Saskatchewan to be content with a population, at the best of times, lucky to nudge the magic one million mark.

Known as the "place to be from," Saskatchewan would send our farm kids—some seasonally but others permanently—to the lumber mills of Northern B.C., the oil rigs of Alberta or the industrial plants in Ontario. From universities and colleges, too, thousands of bright young Saskatchewanians would leave, never to return except for summer vacations and family visits at Christmas.

The largest proportion moved to Alberta for economic opportunity, jobs, lower taxes and being with their friends, which created a cultural Diaspora where kids were more likely to find their friends in Calgary's "Cowboys" nightclub than they were back home in Saskatchewan.

In my own Alberta years it was always a good opening joke, when people asked me about being from Saskatchewan, to explain that Saskatchewan was a Cree word, loosely translated, that meant "moving to Alberta."

> "Between 1971 and 2008, 885,000 people left Saskatchewan for other parts of Canada."
>
> *Prof. Harry Hiller, University of Calgary and Statistics Canada, November 2009*

Population Pounds Premier

Premier Lorne Calvert was dogged by population—it was the bane of his existence. When Calvert took office in 2001 there were 1,003,500 people living in Saskatchewan. By 2006, population dropped steadily and precipitously to 985,000, a 25-year low, later revised by Statistics Canada to 991,000. Public anger and frustration were palpable—people were annoyed that the Calvert NDP couldn't grow Saskatchewan. As Calvert struggled with 1980s-era population numbers, Manitoba (a smaller province than Saskatchewan in the early 1960s) continued to chug along with more than 7,000 international immigrants per year while Saskatchewan could not find one-third of that number. And the elephant in the room was Alberta, where thousands of our children were living. In the early 1970s Alberta wasn't even twice our size; by the 2000s it had grown to more than three times the population of Saskatchewan, and was performing at more than 10 times our numbers in housing starts and immigration statistics.

"From high public sector employment to an investment-killing tax structure, Saskatchewan has put in place a wide range of incentives for innovative, skilled, entrepreneurial, young people to leave. Not surprisingly, they have responded rationally to those incentives: their hearts may back the Saskatchewan Roughriders, but their heads are at work in Alberta."

Barry Cooper, Director, Fraser Institute Calgary
Policy Research Center, 2002

In 2006, the NDP was losing the population battle on every front. Those on the party's political left tried spinning the story (like Canadians often do with Americans) that we are "nicer" than Albertans, somehow more "unique" and therefore deserving of being smaller and less populated.

Albertans are no different than us. Why would they be? Many of them are from Saskatchewan. With resources and natural advantages that should outstrip our neighbouring provinces, there was no excuse for a Saskatchewan population in freefall. And while I argued in 2006 that all of us were entitled to demand specific strategies of how to grow Saskatchewan's population, we weren't getting it from a vague and evasive NDP. The Calvert government preferred to talk about "potential," "opportunities" and "future" rather than details. And it was starting to sound a lot like trying to make the best of a bad situation. We deserved better.

By 2006, Saskatchewan's population had shrunk by 1.2 percent over four years (a city roughly the size of North Battleford disappearing), while government spending rose by more than 11 percent. This meant a narrower tax base with ultimately fewer people paying taxes. The official government line during this population decline was that population would soon be turning around; a hopeful if not logical tack because it couldn't have fallen much lower. But another more revealing NDP talking point came from senior MLA and cabinet minister Eldon Lautermilch who came to the jaw-dropping conclusion that declining population wasn't so bad… it left "more wealth" for the people who decided to stay.

Saskatchewan Premiers and the Good, Bad and Ugly of Population			
Premier	What They Started With	What They Finished With	Net Increase
NDP Allan Blakeney PSYCHOLOGICAL LOW POINT 1974—population fell to 907,546	932,038 (1971)	983,744 (1982)	51,706
PC Grant Devine PSYCHOLOGICAL HIGH POINT 1987—population high of 1,032,799	983,744 (1982)	1,000,942 (1991)	17,198
NDP Roy Romanow PSYCHOLOGICAL HIGH POINT 1996—population high of 1,019,408	1,000,942 (1991)	1,003,469 (2001)	2,527
NDP Lorne Calvert PSYCHOLOGICAL LOW POINT 2006—population low of 991,000	1,003,469 (2001)	1,005,083 (2007)	1,614

After his continuing ennui over population, the saddest irony came for Calvert in the final months of his government when population grew by 9,000 and we re-entered the One Million Club. By the time Calvert was defeated in November 2007, provincial numbers indicated a small net loss in the population he'd inherited from Roy Romanow. But later adjustments from Statistics Canada showed Calvert's departing population number as a net gain of 1,600 people in his nearly seven years in office.

The population surge in the dying months of the Calvert government not only continued but exploded following the election of the SaskParty's

Brad Wall in late 2007. By July 2008, the three month in-migration from other provinces totalled 8,000 people, the highest since 1980. Overall rates of population growth hadn't been as high since 1952.

In October 2009, Saskatchewan hit a new all-time population record of 1,034,974 which climbed to 1,038,000 in the early months of 2010 and then to 1,041,729 by summer. From a growing national profile as Canada's "it" province to informal license plate counts at local malls, clearly the old Saskatchewan where people were from had become the place where people wanted to be.

Hard-core NDP supporters downplayed and pooh-poohed the good population news by saying that Wall had simply surfed on their population wave and had done nothing to deserve the credit. The NDP were at a loss to explain why record numbers of young people -- many who had earlier left Saskatchewan for Alberta during the NDP years -- chose the year 2008 to make their return.

One of Wall's coups on population was a dramatic change in immigration, including an end to the Alberta Diaspora as kids and families returned to Saskatchewan and an increase in foreign immigration.

For years, Saskatchewan's international immigration levels fluctuated from 1,800 - 2,100, while neighbouring Manitoba regularly exceeded 7,000. In Calvert's final year in office, international immigration reached nearly 4,000. Although the NDP regularly hoped for immigration in the 5,000 range, it was not until the Wall government's specific focus on international immigration that more than 6,300 new immigrants arrived in 2008. In 2009, 8,600 international newcomers came, more than the NDP's combined five-year total from 2001 to 2006 and the highest number of immigrants since records began being kept in 1946.

The Politics of Population—Only in Saskatchewan

One of my buddies tossed out a theory in the early 2000s that NDP governments didn't actually mind a population of around 990,000 people—in fact, they wanted it that way because if population could be held at less than one million, there would always be a high enough proportion of people working for government that NDP-friendly civil servants would swing enough seats to ensure the NDP held on to power, particularly in the larger cities.

I'd discounted this theory (who in their right mind would actually discourage growth for the sake of politics?) until an NDP pal, over a beer one night, earnestly tried explaining why Saskatchewan really didn't need one million people; his preferred number was 975,000 and he trotted out theories explaining "quality of life infrastructure" and how our population didn't need expanding. He was engaging in a slightly smarter-sounding version of the Lautermilch strategy of "more for the rest of us." And he was serious.

So, I ran the numbers. Usually in Saskatchewan, the total number of people paid by various governments is around 145,000—provincial, federal and municipal civil servants, Crown corporation staff, teachers, university staff, and health care employees (we'll call them "government people"). As the 2000s began, government people made up over 30% of the 480,000 people working in Saskatchewan.

Historically, the number of government people is fairly constant — today it's in the range of 149,000. But, thanks to the all-time population high, there are now about 545,000 people working in Saskatchewan so the government people ratio is down to 27%. I'm not saying that government people automatically vote for the NDP but the influence and power of large public sector unions, which are in the back pocket of the NDP, clearly put government people in a category more disposed to support the NDP.

There is a good argument that more people working outside of direct government influence will result in a greater likelihood of political balance away from the NDP as the natural governing party.

Like the old slogan that you can't manage what you can't measure, the Calvert government, besieged as it was by population woes, never set benchmarks or goals for population. Surely something as concrete and indicative of success or failure as population deserved specific discussion.

In the 2003 election, SaskParty leader Elwin Hermanson promised that if he won the election he would commit to growing Saskatchewan's population by one percent a year, or 10,000 new people. Within a decade, he said, Saskatchewan would target a population bump of 100,000 more people. The NDP reaction was puzzling. Considering that most things worth doing in life—from losing weight to watching your kids' marks to growing your RRSP—have greater expectations than a puny 1%, the NDP claimed that this was "statistically impossible" and "wishful thinking". The NDP openly mocked the idea as unrealistic, naive and evidence that Hermanson didn't get the complexities of governing. The theme was clear: "don't aim too high —we can't do it."

At the same time Saskatchewan was debating the one-percent question, the City of Calgary's population was growing by an average of 2.6% every single year. And, while Hermanson laid out more than 35 specific policy initiatives that would result in the 1% solution, it is worth noting that since his election in late 2007, Brad Wall has easily surpassed a one percent population growth in Saskatchewan each year.

By 2010, ironically, for the first time people began talking about a new Saskatchewan population goal of 1.1 million. If this benchmark is achieved it will be a historic and century-bending standard, finally leaving behind years of yo-yoing around the elusive one million.

Chapter 6

UPS AND DOWNS OF THE SASKATCHEWAN ECONOMY

In all but its final year, the Calvert NDP years were financially bumpy. Calvert's first budget in 2001 increased spending and hired many new civil servants. But it wasn't long before the government was in trouble. It frequently dipped into its Fiscal Stabilization Fund, often called the rainy day fund or savings account, in order to balance the budget.

According to budget documents, there was $775 million in the fund in the spring of 2001. By early 2003, the fund had shrunk to $139 million. The government cited several reasons (and some excuses) for dipping into its rainy day fund: the post-9:11 economic slowdown, drought, low oil and gas prices, forest fires, BSE or "mad cow disease" and even not getting enough equalization money from Ottawa.

But there was a problem with the NDP's Fiscal Stabilization Fund. It didn't really exist. Unlike the later Growth and Financial Security Fund of the Wall government—a rainy day fund or savings account with actual cash reserves—the NDP's Fiscal Stabilization Fund was only a bookkeeping entry. Money allocated to the fund, usually from gambling and video lottery terminal revenue would be used to pay down accumulated debt. So when the fund was drawn on, like a line of credit, the province's overall level of debt would rise by the same amount taken from the fund. As a result, the early Calvert years also resulted in an increase in Saskatchewan's debt.

The NDP also regularly took the profits of Crown corporations and had them paid into the government's general revenue fund as "dividends," even though the Crowns borrowed money at the time. But later, when the Wall government did this for the first time in its third budget—following an unprecedented collapse in forecast potash royalties—both the NDP and media and would react in horror.

The Calvert Spending Years

Governments are judged by how they spend our money. In the Romanow years, nine budgets saw government spending go from $5.01 billion to $5.95 billion, an increase of $940 million. In nearly a decade Romanow increased spending by 18.7% while the national inflation rate rose by approximately 16.3%.

Calvert's first budget in 2001 would push spending to over $6 billion and by his final budget in 2007, spending had climbed to over $8 billion. In seven years, the Calvert NDP increased spending by $2.33 billion dollars, a 37% increase. This compares to the national inflation rate at the same time of approximately 15.5%.

And spending can also be judged by whether it's "one-off" on capital items like highways, bridges, buildings and infrastructure or whether it goes to create new government programs, jobs and continuing expenditures that result in a permanent growth in the size of government.

Calvert Government Spending	
Years	Spending
2000–01	$5.95 billion
2001–02	$6.37 billion
2002–03	$6.4 billion
2003–04	$6.69 billion
2004–05	$7.07 billion
2005–06	$7.70 billion
2006–07	$8.22 billion
2007–08	$8.7 billion

Saskatchewan Ministry of Finance, "Schedule of Expenditures," Budget Documents, 1999–2010

If People Are Leaving Why Do We Need More Civil Servants?

It didn't take long (the first budget, actually) to see a major difference with the new, more left-wing Calvert government. The number of jobs in the Saskatchewan civil service jumped by more than 500. I have nothing against government employees; many of them work tirelessly in moving the wheels of government and are not given nearly enough appreciation or credit. Others, in contrast, are lazy, wear sweat pants to work and bitch all the time. I have no idea of the numbers in each category.

After the first big jump in civil service hiring, there was a slight shrinkage, but never to the levels where Calvert started. Later there would be a couple of huge spikes, like 1,100 new civil servants hired during the Centennial year and a 2007 pre-election surge of 700 new government employees. It was peculiar that by the spring of 2006 when Calvert had grown the civil service to 11,677, our population had plummeted to 991,260. Five years earlier, when we got by with 10,242 civil servants, the population was 1,001,643. It was never made clear why a province growing smaller by the day needed more government employees.

Overall, Calvert expanded the civil service by over 2,400 employees in seven years, more than a 20% rate of growth. And that's just frontline government, not Crown corporations and government agencies which also saw growth in the Calvert era.

Civil Servants and the Calvert Years	
Years	Government Employees
2000–01	10,242
2001–02	10,813
2002–03	10,539
2003–04	10,631
2004–05	10,526
2005–06	11,677
2006–07	11,939
2007–08	12,639

Saskatchewan Ministry of Finance, "FTE (Full Time Equivalent) Staff Complement," Budget Documents, 1999-2010

The Tax Turnaround

The NDP was dragged kicking and screaming into an issue that had defined Saskatchewan for a generation. We had among Canada's highest taxes and it was driving people away. To be fair to an underachieving left-wing government bent on keeping expectations low, the NDP deserves big credit for finally doing the right thing on taxes.

In a conversion unlike any since St. Paul on the road to Damascus, NDP Finance Minister Eric Cline had a 180-degree change of mind after his 1999 budget and the NDP's near-death experience a few months later when it nearly lost the election. Saskatchewan had Canada's second highest personal income taxes in the late '90s. The opposition SaskParty tapped into public discontent, calling for tax cuts and preparing a detailed, staged tax strategy that was reviewed and costed by a national economic forecasting company.

Cline, an affable guy never afraid of a good debate, simply denied the obvious. It wasn't a problem he said. When pushed harder, Cline (who could get as partisan and nasty as the crankiest NDPer) waved the fear flag of the left: lower income taxes would be reckless and irresponsible and would hurt the poor, endanger social programs, help already-rich fat cats and (cue lightning bolt and thunder clap) mean less money for Medicare.

But the public didn't buy it. Just two months after refusing to lower taxes in his 1999 budget, Cline set up the Personal Income Tax Review Committee made up of three chartered accountants without an NDP political insider among them, and chaired by Jack Vicq, an accounting professor emeritus and one-time senior finance department official during the Tory government of Grant Devine.

Three months later, in the fall of 1999 during the election, the Sask-Party got more votes than the NDP, forcing the government into a coalition with the Liberals and sending a strong message to the NDP to move quickly on tax reform. In the 2000 budget, Cline accepted the Vicq Committee's recommendations and, by the end of 2002, Saskatchewan had the second lowest personal income taxes in the country. Cline's total flip saw him ditch the "lower taxes won't work" pitch for the mantra that lower income taxes would make Saskatchewan attractive and the government would not lose tax revenue because lower taxes would actually grow the overall economy and with more income being taxed, even at a lower rate, the government's take would still net out positively.

As both the SaskParty and the Personal Income Tax Review Committee had predicted, Cline was vindicated by the numbers. By the time Saskatchewan moved to three simplified tax rates of 15% (for income higher than $100,000), 13% (for income of $35,000-$100,000) and 11% (for income of $35,000 or less), Alberta brought in a single rate of tax of 10% for all incomes, but at least Saskatchewan had scrapped a complex, higher system of five tax levels that had discouraged many people from paying their income taxes here.

Later, in 2008, after the election of the SaskParty, Brad Wall would knock down the final hurdle of income tax reform—something long sought by low-income people and anti-poverty activists. Wall raised the basic personal tax exemption (the amount of money someone can earn before paying any income tax) in the largest personal income tax cut in history. The exempt amount and matching spousal amount were raised by $4,000 to $12,945 along with a nearly doubled child tax credit. As a result, a family of four could earn up to $41,300 before paying any provincial income tax—the highest level of any province.

Although personal income taxes are an incentive to live and stay here, corporate taxes are an important piece in the puzzle of why Saskatchewan has had so much difficulty growing the private sector under NDP governments that typically impose the highest taxes on business. By 2005, Saskatchewan's basic tax on corporations was 17%—Canada's highest — while on each side of us Manitoba had 15.5% and Alberta 11.5%. With B.C. at 13.5%, and money ultimately mobile, it didn't take a genius to figure out where you'd want your business paying tax.

As Saskatchewan's Centennial year kicked off in 2005, population continued to fall like a rock as young people still flocked to Alberta, which was breaking every Canadian growth record. With the same oil, natural gas and opportunity as us, Alberta was on fire as Saskatchewan stood on the sidelines watching and waiting, wondering why it wasn't happening here.

Corporate taxes in Saskatchewan have always been tied up in capital "P" politics. For generations, the NDP's left wing has taken comfort in a small private sector and a complaining one. The left talks about businesses "paying their fair share." And those who won't (selfish, bad capitalists) are better off in Alberta anyway, says the left.

Years earlier the NDP had also instituted a "capital tax," which was both unpopular and a business disincentive, for obvious reasons as noted in 2002 by the Fraser Institute's Barry Cooper.

"Possibly the worst tax that human beings have invented is the capital tax—essentially a tax on investment... before the government permits you to invest and bring jobs and other benefits to Saskatchewan, you have to pay a tax on your investment. It is hard to think of a better reason to invest in Alberta."

Barry Cooper, Director, Fraser Institute Calgary Policy Research Centre, 2002

Ironically, the NDP's historic anti-business bias actually helped the tax reform movement. Because Saskatchewan had such a small private sector (remember that government-owned Crown corporations pay no corporate income tax) every percentage point of corporate income taxes paid to government by businesses equalled only about $18 million.

At the time, I argued on my radio show that a courageous and dramatic cut in the corporate tax rate wouldn't amount to a huge revenue hit on government and would be "a wake-up call for businesses in Canada and the U.S. to take notice of Saskatchewan and our immense potential for business, investment and opportunity."

In early 2005, five years after his personal tax review, the NDP again called out Jack Vicq, this time to examine our high business taxes. Vicq described these taxes as "among the highest in Canada and in some cases, Saskatchewan doesn't even make the short list for investment opportunities because we are known as a high-tax province."

Nearly eight months to the day, Vicq and his committee of two other CAs issued a list of sweeping recommendations that would, in his words, "move our 1980s tax regime to a 2010 tax regime." And he wasn't kidding.

Vicq's four major recommendations included:

- Lowering the 17% corporate income tax rate to 12% and eventually to 10%;
- Phasing out the decades-old NDP tax on corporate capital which actually taxed companies for expanding a plant or building other infrastructure;
- Increasing the small business limit from $300,000 to $500,000—that's where income is taxed at the small business tax rate of 5%; and,
- Harmonizing the federal GST with the provincial PST.

Less than a year after appointing Vicq, the NDP brought in its 2006 budget and Finance Minister Andrew Thomson accepted nearly every recommendation, except for harmonized sales taxes. At that time the biggest package of tax cuts in history, the NDP—historically as business unfriendly as a government could be—introduced the measures to "stimulate the economy and bring in a competitive business environment." On budget day, if you listened really carefully, that faint sound you heard was Woodsworth, Coldwell and Tommy Douglas spinning in their graves.

For years Saskatchewan people paid a 5% tax on goods at the cash register. Known as the "E&H" tax, it stood for education and health because the money supposedly went for schools and hospitals. But it didn't; so-called dedicated taxes are discouraged in Canada. Instead it went into the general revenues of government. In the 1980s, when this was finally acknowledged and the tax was broadened to start covering some services, it was renamed PST, or provincial sales tax. And a uniquely Saskatchewan game began.

In many parts of the world, sales taxes are handled delicately because they're highly visible and politically volatile. Politicians tread softly around sales taxes, even holding public votes on whether to raise a sales tax. In some places, like Arizona's 5.6% sales tax or Missouri's 4.225%, legislators even fractionalize the tax down to "point 1 or 2," cautiously taking money from consumers in tiny bits and incrementally. But not in Saskatchewan. Here, with little justification and even fewer apologies, politicians have no qualms about stepping in and swiping your money at will.

In the Grant Devine 1980s, the 5% PST was shamelessly upped to 7% in an attempt to find money in a serious drought and revenue crunch. During the Roy Romanow era, when government was trying to plug the deficit hole, the 7% tax was hiked to 9% with no debate. By 1999, the NDP gradually dropped the PST to 6%. But just after Calvert's 2003 election win, with not a whisper of consultation —and with the economy taking off next door in zero-sales tax Alberta —the government sneakily jacked the 6% PST back up to 7%. At the same time, the civil service unions which had worked so hard in 2003 to re-elect Calvert were rewarded in 2004 by having their wages capped at 0-1-1% increases for the next three years. The decision to up the PST in 2004 was criticized as an entirely needless revenue grab, confirmed less than three years later when the Calvertistas lowered the PST back to 5% where it remains today.

Governments often claim, when arbitrarily hiking the PST, that "it's only one point." But consider that when 5% becomes 6%, it's actually a 20% increase in the tax—done with no consultation or permission from the consumers who have to pay. The time should be over for politicians who think they can smack on an extra full tax point without asking you. They should treat your money like your money.

Saskatchewan's Embarrassment: The Worst Highways in Canada

I grew up in a small town, worked as a farmhand in high school and still know that Argentinean canola has a longer growing season than the Polish stuff. But try as I might to show my rural side, I'm fooling no one but myself. Farm people are smart enough to see right through me: I'm a city guy, let's face it, and barely know what end of the cow makes the moo. And, like most city people, my definition of highway driving is from here to the lake or to Edmonton and Calgary on the well-travelled Trans-Canada or Yellowhead highways. When the talk show started in the late '90s, many farm and rural callers complained about atrocious highways, but I never really knew how bad things were until one day in the summer of 2000.

More on a whim than anything else, and wanting to go cross country to a golf course I was itching to try, I set off on a highway around Lake Diefenbaker. Venturing down the road was like something from a post-apocalyptic movie. The road was completely abandoned, rutted and with gravel patches and rocks poking up through broken pavement. And this was supposedly a highway. I kept expecting Mad Max to show up at any moment in a dune buggy. Chunks of asphalt flew up as I weaved around car-sized bunkers and potholes on the road.

Finally crawling into a small town, I visited with some people who told their stories. This was their life: front grills, headlights and sometimes windshields were smashed by flying pavement. The price of occasional absentmindedness and hitting a hole in the road was an axle, transmission or oil pan. And tourists stayed away in droves. I was appalled. More like something you'd expect from a third world country or Borat's Kazakhstan…this was our Saskatchewan. It was a bloody disgrace—who would allow people to live this way?

With Canada's largest road network—more than 26,000 kilometers of highways—we've had too many roads for years, at least since towns every six miles disappeared and farms got larger. Some of our highways have been converted into gravel roads, others into thin membrane surface (TMS) highways, where a thin coating of asphalt is laid over a poorly prepared road bed, only to get rutted and worn by the next big truck coming along on a hot day. By the early 2000s, NDP governments had created more TMS roads than primary highways and, for the first time in Saskatchewan history, some of these TMS highways were actually declared unsafe for motorists, so badly deteriorated were they.

During the 1990s, a perfect storm brewed as road maintenance budgets were slashed in the name of government financial restraint and more grain was being hauled longer distances in much bigger trucks that wore down already fragile highways. From the mid-1990s to the early 2000s, the NDP spent less than $200 million every year on actual road repair and construction. At the same time, in gas taxes and vehicle fees—so called "motorist derived revenues"—the government took in over $400 million every year. The biggest gap was in 1997 when the Romanow government spent $300 million less on highways than it brought in. By 2000, the NDP spent less than 50% of its road revenues actually on road maintenance and construction—in every case, the leftover money was absorbed in the general revenues of government and spent on other things.

In Lorne Calvert's first budget in 2001, actual road-related spending went to an all-time high of $289 million, but it was still less than 65% of the overall driver revenues of $465 million. Our highways continued to decline until eventually Saskatchewan developed a national reputation as the home of Canada's worst roads. At the same time, neighbouring governments were spending higher proportions of motorist derived revenue on their highways.

In 2003, the Canadian Taxpayers' Federation (CTF) declared the worst highway in Canada to be Saskatchewan's Highway 47 from Yorkton to the U.S. border, saying that "it stretches the limits on the definition of the word *highway* with its rapid transitions from mangled, pot-holed pavement to deep gravel." Local townsfolk called it "atrocious," pointing out the danger posed "especially to large motorhomes and trailers." At the time, a CTF spokesman remarked that "by far, Saskatchewan was pitifully over-represented with nearly a dozen of the about 100 nominations nationwide."

By 2005, Saskatchewan's laughing-stock roads continued to draw the worst kind of national attention when the venerable Canadian Automobile Association named Highway 51, west of Biggar, as one of Canada's worst. CAA described it as "a network of potholes and patchwork repairs, a very outdated design of road, very dangerous in the winter. "

Locally during the early 2000s, many other communities—outraged at government inaction on highway repair—staged high-profile protests, from a naked calendar to raise funds for Highway 32 near Leader, to a local poster campaign along the decrepit Highway 368 near St. Brieux.

One of the ironies of the NDP's highway debacle was that, on a per capita basis, Saskatchewan actually paid more in vehicle fees, road taxes and gas taxes but got far worse roads. On a per person basis, our motorist-derived revenues ranged from $450-$500 dollars a person while Albertans and Manitobans paid just over $300 dollars per capita. But their governments were prepared to invest a much higher proportion of the revenues back into road repair than Saskatchewan's NDP was.

In the final year of the Calvert government, the NDP hit a new high, both in dollars for roads and proportion of motorist revenues committed to repair and upgrading. In 2007, the government spent $341 million—71% of its motorist revenues.

Following the election of the Brad Wall government in 2007, an election promise was made and kept to invest aggressively to change Saskatchewan's woeful highways reputation by spending over $1.5 billion on road maintenance and rebuilding in the first three years of the new government's term. Given two decades of neglect and the large infrastructure deficit, Saskatchewan's overall highway situation still lags behind Alberta's and many roads remain on the priority list. But generally, from the lack of calls to our radio show to virtually non-existent public debate over highway woes, this is one part of the Saskatchewan narrative that appears to have dramatically changed. Gone are the complaints about dangerous and potholed roads, angry motorists and despondent people living in rural areas with roads looking like a moonscape.

While the Lion Sits at the Water Hole I'm Being Lectured on Economics by a Social Worker

From its roots in the 1930s—and the urging of the *Regina Manifesto* to have government insert itself in essential businesses—the NDP has always seen Saskatchewan's economy as needing more government involvement than any other province. At least 10 commercial Crown corporations are involved in everything from phone, internet and television service to home electricity and natural gas to computer systems, property registration, liquor stores, a bus company, car and property insurance, casinos and grain cars. And this doesn't include the several dozen other Crowns involved in providing goods and services to municipal and provincial government departments.

By the early 2000s, Saskatchewan was in last place in Canada for business investment—every other province was ahead of us in providing the environment for private businesses to bring jobs, investment and wealth. One think tank, the Fraser Institute's Calgary Policy Research Centre, concluded in a 2002 report that "the structure of the Saskatchewan economy is significantly tilted towards government business enterprises (Crown corporations) and thus government intervention. This model of business development has not served the province well either in terms of income growth, labour market development, or business investment." The study showed how spending by Crown corporations was nearly 12 percent of the entire provincial economy, "an astounding 36% more than the second-ranked province, New Brunswick."

I don't have anything against Crown corporations. We can keep every Crown we have (except liquor stores which are a gift to the SGEU and a throwback to Prohibition), but Crowns should be a smaller proportion of a larger and diverse economy. Modern economies aren't a zero sum game of either having Crowns or not. But such a dominant role for Crown corporations in Saskatchewan's economy for so many years has resulted in us having one of North America's smallest private sectors and a culture that lost jobs and our kids to other places.

Whether stand-alone Crown corporations or through significant government "equity" or ownership in business, the NDP has a long and controversial record of investing in businesses since the 1940s.

At times, Crown corporations could double as handy political tools when NDP governments needed to assure themselves, and voters, that something was being done in the economy, even when it didn't necessarily make sense. A good example was the grand announcement in late 2002 that the NDP's Crown Investments Corporation would take a 40% share in a large, $55 million dollar ethanol plant to be built near Belle Plaine. In front of 250 people beneath a large tent (at a swishy event that NDP insider Garry Aldridge's Points West Consulting was paid to organize), a formal sod turning was even held for the construction of the first of three 80-million liter ethanol plants. Premier Calvert breathlessly announced that "Saskatchewan will soon be the number one producer of ethanol in Canada." Beyond sod being turned, nothing was ever built on the site. But it made for great photo-ops.

Many Crowns, because they are government owned, have also tried to play by different rules in the business world. NDP governments have long preferred to appoint as senior executives in Crowns their own political operatives, many with absolutely no private corporate experience outside of government.

The NDP also tends to appoint former deputy ministers and senior government managers to the highest chief executive positions of Crowns. While many of these people are capable public servants, their professional skills—honed by years in government—are often the exact opposite of skills of a successful business executive. Senior government managers tend to be into risk avoidance and aversion, ass-covering and adherence to the status quo. Genuine business executives, on the other hand, work in a more dynamic and fast-moving environment of managed risk assessment, adaptation to change and anticipating movement in the business model and the marketplace in which the corporation is doing business.

Crowns tend to behave like lions at the African waterhole where the other animals come to drink: they either eat them for lunch or force them to stay away and go to another waterhole for fear of being eaten.

In 2005, Deputy Premier Clay Serby explained to me that the province's economy has "four engines": private business, government, cooperatives and joint partnerships between government and business. Considering that government features prominently in two of the four sectors, Serby rankled at my question about how many other places in the developed world have the government in one-half of the economy. It should be pointed out that Serby, when not in politics, is a social worker by training and part-time farmer.

More recently, NDP leader Dwain Lingenfelter said there were "three pillars—business, being one pillar, labour being one and government being the third pillar of a modern strong economy." Considering that unions represent 75% of government jobs but only a small fraction of private business, this seems to imply that government and its unions should control over one-half of our economy. Lingenfelter, when not in politics, is a border guard by training and part-time farmer who spent eight years as a junior executive in an oil company lobbying governments.

Perception, Reality & a "Have" Province

Except for using taxpayers' money to hire more civil servants, as Calvert did, or instructing government-owned Crown corporations to hire more staff, governments don't actually create many jobs. They should create the right environment by focusing on infrastructure, tax policy, labour laws, immigration and initiatives to encourage private investment which ends up creating enduring jobs. This also results in a broader tax base and the need for government to spend public money on quality of life benchmarks like education and health care. And with these come good public sector jobs.

In the Calvert years of the early 2000s, Saskatchewan had two problems: one, being next door to the supermodel of the hot economy, free enterprise Alberta; the other, the perception dogging Saskatchewan's NDP that they are anti-business. And, as every politician knows, perception is reality. If the NDP is seen as anti-business, they are anti-business.

There is a long history of the *Regina Manifesto* pledging to eradicate capitalism—and the NDP has carried this pledge out via punitively high corporate taxation; government confiscation of potash mines in the 1970s; restriction of farmland ownership; establishment of a land bank; creating more Crown corporations to develop resources and even the debacle over the most available hours of work that resulted in withering opposition. All are variables adding up to an equation that the NDP is bad for investment and business, and that means fewer jobs and people.

In the early 2000s, the price of oil moved past $75, natural gas surged and a booming resource sector propelled Saskatchewan into official "have" province status. By 2007 we were into a *bona fide* hot economy and genuine boom. The NDP had, by this time, lowered taxes and removed the absurd land ownership laws, all of which helped reverse some of the historic challenges and helped new money come. But the NDP legacy took some getting over.

"Saskatchewan has everything the developing world needs. The only downside is that we never had a capital market that caused development in those resources.

We are the birthplace of socialism in North America. We had tremendous government oversight of all facets of life, including resource exploration and development. Government hooks in business spook away a regular capital market.

Much like Hugo Chavez expropriating assets in Venezuela today, it tells the rest of the world "stay out" because there's too much risk. We did that to ourselves.

We ruined our economic activity because we thought socialism was the neat thing. We came out of it, but we're still living the hangover."

Tom MacNeill, Saskatchewan mining executive,
The Gold Report, 2010

The Nuclear Dilemma

Nothing causes more division, confusion and anxiety within the NDP than uranium. One-quarter of the world's mined uranium comes from Canada, most from Northern Saskatchewan. The highest grade deposits of this silvery white metallic element come from here. Uranium eventually creates the atomic reaction necessary for nuclear power, after a long and complex series of steps that involves processing, refining and enriching the uranium to become fuel for a nuclear reactor.

From the anti-war movement fearing nuclear weapons to environmentalists, the United Church and anti-development socialists, there is a broad coalition inside the NDP that wants uranium left in the ground. But Saskatchewan has been mining uranium since the early 1950s.

> "The development of atomic energy brings nearer the ability to completely eliminate poverty, misery and want, more than any other discovery in the long history of scientific research."
>
> *CCF/NDP Founder M.J. Coldwell, 1950*

Supporting the uranium industry in 1952, the Douglas CCF government established a town called Uranium City on the shores of Lake Athabasca in the far North, near the border with the Northwest Territories. The town serviced the uranium mines in the nearby Beaverlodge uranium area until the mines closed in 1983. In the 1970s, the Blakeney NDP government approved the expansion of uranium mining in the areas now being mined by Areva and the world's largest uranium company, Cameco, which is headquartered in Saskatoon.

....

"The province of Saskatchewan never was in a position to become the major uranium producer in the world, did not ever anticipate that it would be in that position, and is unlikely to be in that position...Let me make a couple of things clear...We believe that the cornerstone of economic activity in this province is agriculture. Secondly, with respect to resources, it has never been the contention of this government that uranium was the cornerstone of resource activity. In fact, it has always been the contention of this government that both potash and heavy oil were very much more activities which were going to attract capital investment and economic activity than uranium."

NDP Premier Allan Blakeney, December, 1981

....

The NDP is wracked by second guessing, guilt, dissension and a good bit of confusion over doing anything more with uranium than mining it. And, the Calvert government, like its NDP predecessors, ended up stalling on any stage past uranium mining. Rather than explaining the tumultuous ups, downs and intrigue within the NDP of the party's long journey on nuclear, an assortment of "best of" quotations will do the trick. Please note: there aren't as many flip flops on the beach in Maui as there are within the NDP on the nuke issue.

"Given what comes out of the tail pipe, it [nuclear energy] has got to be the dirtiest of all."

NDP Premier Lorne Calvert, January, 2003

"We're ready to refine and process uranium when the time is right."

Calvert, September, 2005

"If there can be a reactor of a much smaller scale that might be more fitted to our population . . . at that point in time we would consider or look at those ideas.

Calvert, November, 2005

"A nuclear reactor would change Saskatchewan's economic prospects. If Tommy Douglas were here it would be exactly what he'd be doing. Tommy Douglas would want a nuclear reactor. Saskatchewan has to become as user-friendly to the nuclear industry as it can possibly be."

Dwain Lingenfelter, November, 2005

"Nuclear power back on agenda"—Premier Lorne Calvert ventured as far as saying that the province might one day consider nuclear power."

Leader Post, June, 2006

"Nuclear power is and will continue to be a huge part of the global solution to our energy problems."

Lingenfelter, May, 2008

"We support the consideration of further value-added development of Saskatchewan's uranium industry including nuclear power generation."

Every NDP MLA, except Deb Higgins, votes in favour of this Resolution of the Legislature, April, 2009

"Be it resolved that an NDP government will not pursue research into the nuclear option and will not investigate building a reactor or storing nuclear waste under any circumstances"

NDP Convention Resolution passed June, 2009

"Now is not the time to consider nuclear power. We don't think there's an economic or business case for nuclear power. It's not something we'd jump into, certainly not at this point."

NDP Leader Dwain Lingenfelter, September, 2009

Through Saskatchewan's uranium and nuclear debate of 2009, the NDP emerged resolutely anti-nuke. Guided by its hard-core anti-nuke left-wing of old-timers like ex-MLA Peter Prebble, perpetual candidate Nettie Wiebe and activist Don Kossick along with the new generation of leadership candidates Yens Pedersen and Ryan Meili, the party is presently at a high-water mark of anti-nuclear.

For Lingenfelter's role in all of this, Leader Post Editor Kevin Blevins put it well on his blog: "I think this is about two things: 1) Taking an opposite position of the current SaskParty government at any cost; 2) Playing to the left-wing of the NDP, something Lingenfelter apparently feels he needs to do after a fractured leadership campaign that split the party in two. He wants to win back the lefties, so they will work hard for the party in the next provincial election campaign…Taking such a stance shows a lack of leadership on Lingenfelter's part."

Chapter **7**

DEATH BY SCANDAL: WEIGHING DOWN THE CALVERT GOVERNMENT

Virtually from his first day as premier, Lorne Calvert was dogged by scandals—those shameful and often preventable acts that bring public disgrace to governments. Unlike controversies or unpopular decisions, scandals often involve dishonesty, evasions, cover-ups and unethical or even illegal behaviour.

Scandals attack trust—the glue of the relationship between voter and politician. When too much trust is eroded, it's sayonara for governments, even the natural governing ones like the NDP that historically get away with a lot.

By the time Premier Calvert called his final election in the fall of 2007, his government had been weighed down by scandals. Some were inherited from the Romanow years and continued to chew away at the Calvert government's credibility; others were created by Calvert's Cabinet and staff; and one damning scandal had been hidden years earlier, buried by the NDP who thought they'd seen the last of it. They were wrong, and it cost them dearly.

A mistake in government or even deliberate wrongdoing is not generally a scandal by itself. But it tends to start the scandal. Scandals take on their own life when there is an improper response to the wrongful act, like lying, trying to cover it up or blaming someone else. Throw in a few more evasions, which are usually discovered later, and then the scandal continues to find fuel. In many scandals, the tipping point is often arrogance—an attitude of entitlement and the belief that the people responsible for the wrongdoing can get away with it.

For the NDP there was often a pattern that if something bad happened the government would evade, deflect or cover up because it seemed to think either that the voters were too dim to catch on or if the truth eventually did get out, the story could be massaged so that the end justified the means. Many longer-term governments, complacent and confident in their abilities, and often without effective media or opposition scrutiny, fall into this attitude and begin to think that a different set of rules applies to them.

It's not unique to Saskatchewan's NDP; many political parties get tripped up by scandals. But the NDP is uniquely vulnerable because of its rampant self-righteousness. Many in the NDP believe they're morally superior to other political types and are simply better people, which sets them up for scandal because when something bad or dishonest happens—which is inevitable so long as fallible humans are involved—the first instinct is to protect the party by denying, deflecting and then covering up.

Rather than simply admitting wrongdoing and coming clean—which would put the NDP on the same moral plane as everyone else—some in the party just can't do it. Consequently, trust is violated twice; once by the wrongful act and again when the cover-up is discovered.

Anatomy of a Scandal

Scandals succeed when they are highly publicized with a strongly reinforced negative message that engages, convinces and outrages the public. When a scandal is in full bloom it has a connect-the-dots feeling: the wrongdoing, the deflection, the minimization, not telling the whole story, continued denial, the revelation of new and previously concealed facts, proof that someone was covering up and lying, and the scandal swirls out of control. When the Nixonian "smoking gun" theme emerges—in how many hands does responsibility lie—the scandal hits a new crescendo; who knew what, when, and how far up the chain of command does the knowledge go? And is there another cover-up going on at the top?

Like ex-politician and convicted murderer Colin Thatcher's ultimately unsuccessful "deny, deny, deny" approach, old school NDP governments typically got away with denying that anything happened, or if it did, deflecting the story long enough for the cone of silence to descend. If critics persisted, then a counter-offensive was launched attacking the people asking the questions.

Historically, the NDP has been good at waiting out the storm by clamming up and saying nothing and relying on the media to lose interest. There were also enough NDP proxies around who would publicly change the channel or at least the subject. There was also an often implied threat that if questions kept being asked, when the storm blew over, certain people in the NDP had long memories. From the Clarence Fines shenanigans in the Douglas era to the excesses of certain Crown corporations over the years, this was standard operating procedure.

But times have changed. With new media, the prevalence of blogs and social networking and an aggressive culture of openness that has even infiltrated civil servants, the likelihood of something remaining concealed is not good.

Public Questions Asked When a Bad Thing Happens

- 5 W's of what happened —what, who, when, where and why?

- How did it happen?

- Did anyone else know? Who?

- If there is a "who," 5 W's again: what did they know, when, where, and why and how did they know?

- What did they do as soon as they found out?

- What are you going to do about this bad thing, the person responsible and anyone else involved?

When bad things happen now, the sound strategy is to get out in front and come clean—quickly. This isn't as simple as it sounds. It's done by immediately gathering all of the facts, anticipating every possible question and ensuring that nothing is unknown at the outset. All of the facts may not necessarily be publicly disclosed at once or ever. But that's a decision to make only when possessed of all the facts. But the facts relevant to the wrongdoing must be quickly, thoroughly and fully disclosed, presented carefully, in detail and a narrative created.

For scandal management, the span of control must be tight enough that no facts will later emerge that are inconsistent with the "official version." Some context or shading may occur but no "you hid this from us" revelations. The known and disclosed facts—however uncomfortable and distasteful—must be acknowledged and accepted early. And they must be controlled with no attempts to evade, deny or blame anyone else.

Although responsibility must be accepted, it needn't be so broad that it includes unforeseeable consequences or factors beyond the control or knowledge of the person taking the blame. Every media question must be anticipated and answered, preferably before it is asked.

As part of the anticipation, there must also be a clear answer to the questions, before they're asked: "What have you done to resolve this?" and "What steps have been taken to ensure that it doesn't happen again?" If needed, a proper apology is also made before it is asked for.

> "Remember the "100 Day Rule"—it can cure you or kill you. But it will do something."
>
> *Gormley the talk show host*

The passage of time is critical in a scandal. In my experience, the public memory for most issues is about 100 days. Think about it—can you accurately recall what you heard or read in passing three months ago? As humans, we're hard-wired to forget. Forgetting (or at least going weak on the details) helps ease our pain and embarrassment when bad things happen. And, forgetting good things keeps our sense of awe alive for the next time we encounter something wonderful.

Good politicians know the 100 day rule: if they screw up (in the old days they kept denying; now they "come clean"), they keep their heads down and know that within 100 days you'll either forget or at least put it in the category of "I think I heard something about that".

Politicians' opponents, of course, try to keep an embarrassing story alive by reviving it every three months or so. Similarly, when politicians make good news announcements, knowing we're prone to forget, they keep recycling the announcement about every 100 days until it eventually sticks.

Keep this in mind in reviewing some of the NDP's most notable scandals.

Scandal 1.0—Channel Lake: The Gift That Kept on Giving

The first great scandal in Lorne Calvert's political life wasn't of his own making or even his government's, but it would be the gold standard against which his government would be judged every time that something went wrong. The scandal was called "Channel Lake" and had been declared closed by the Romanow government several years before Calvert got the keys to the premier's office. But Channel Lake would linger over the NDP as a classic example of how not to deal with scandal. For both the party and its critics, the question would always be "What would Calvert's government do to make the latest scandal not look like Channel Lake?"

The scandal began with a company owned by SaskPower and operating in Alberta. It was called Channel Lake Petroleum and got into the risky natural gas trading and arbitrage business in 1995. Playing the gas futures market while simultaneously selling natural gas to one company while buying from another, Channel Lake would make money off the spread between the buying and selling prices. It would also accept the risk if anyone in the deal defaulted.

In less than a year, Channel Lake did 104 deals totaling $80 million but bought $2 million more natural gas than it sold. And, when two companies it was dealing with went bankrupt, Channel Lake faced "substantial further losses" estimated at $5.6 million.

Because of the trading losses, in 1997 SaskPower quietly sold Channel Lake. But, as Crowns Minister Dwain Lingenfelter later tried to explain "time pressures" had resulted in the sale being done in "an informal and ad hoc manner." It turns out that SaskPower never actually read the sales agreement or understood the sale price, which ended up being $5 million less than SaskPower thought it was getting for the company. Later, after unsuccessfully trying to cancel the sale, the NDP-appointed SaskPower Board of Directors agreed to take the lower price.

This escapade reeked of everything wrong with government employees and political appointees being in business—particularly NDP ones with little practical business experience. Stung by volatile gas prices, poor corporate oversight and weak credit policies, they couldn't even unload a bad investment properly. Like other government misadventures, projects involving civil servants pretending to be businesspeople without expertise, experience or competence generally did not end well.

"The heavyweights at SaskPower never seem to learn. They either never understood or never accepted that they are servants of the people of Saskatchewan, not a law unto themselves."

Star Phoenix, January 1997

These events happened under the watch of SaskPower President and CEO Jack Messer, a former NDP MLA, Cabinet minister, party president and Romanow's 1991 election campaign chair. Messer was the same guy who, according to the Leader Post, within days of the NDP's 1991 win "paraded around the cancelled severance agreement signed by former SaskPower president George Hill, a Conservative stalwart…shortly before Messer became SaskPower president himself, and immediately leased a new Lexus for himself and then his vice-president and former NDP provincial secretary Carole Bryant."

Nearly a year after the Channel Lake sale debacle, Messer was given an ultimatum by Lingenfelter's Crown Investments Corporation (CIC); Resign with a severance package or be fired for cause and get no money. Later, Messer would testify "I did not believe there was cause. It was deemed to be the Channel Lake circumstances, which I think are simply a sham in regard to a political process that's trying to make something out of very little." Rather than wait around and be fired, the NDP insider walked away and was paid severance of $300,000.

Just like bad luck, sometimes incompetence happens. And Channel Lake demonstrated plenty of that. But, rather than getting in front early, admitting errors and containing the facts, the NDP tried downplaying the Channel Lake story for a year, as it swirled from trading losses to the aborted sale and finally a legislative hearing. Only then, in the spring of 1998, did the *mea culpas* come. Lingenfelter reported to the Assembly that the "government is extremely disappointed by these events. We deserve our share of criticism for letting this happen. We ordered a detailed review. We have made that review public. We are acting to ensure events like this don't happen again." Even Romanow, who'd remained above the fray, would later admit "there were some pretty serious mistakes made."

The NDP compounded the scandal when the Legislature's Crown Corporations Committee hearings began into Channel Lake. Usually dominated by the governing party and composed of backbench MLAs, the committee this time was unusual. NDP heavyweight Ed Tchorzewski, a former deputy premier and finance minister, sat on the committee alongside Ned Shillington, a prominent ex-Cabinet minister going back to the Blakeney era who had just days earlier been a member of the same CIC Board that had given Messer the "quit or be fired" ultimatum. The committee also had a paid "special advisor," Saskatoon lawyer and NDP strategist Ted Priel.

The hearings were tightly stage-managed and attempts to broaden their scope or expand the witness list were quickly voted down by the NDP majority. The only embarrassment for the NDP during the hearings was when MLA Pat Lorje, who was chairing the Committee, mumbled under her breath into an open microphone that one witness' lawyer was an "unfathomable prick."

"If there had been a genuine interest in clearing the air, in seeing the truth come out, I'm sure that the governing members who hold the majority on that committee would have been happy to hear from the opposition members and to entertain much more rigorous recommendations. But that did not happen. And in fact the opposition had to release a whole series of recommendations of their own in order to address the failings of the committee process."
Wayne Elhard, SaskParty MLA, 2007

In August, 1998, the committee's final report was leaked to the media before the opposition members had a chance to sign-off or even review the final recommendations. Later it would be revealed that the report was not actually written by committee staff but by Romanow's deputy chief of staff, before the committee had even finished its hearings.

The Romanow government then declared the Channel Lake scandal over and the NDP political machine moved on—after all, Lingenfelter and Romanow had acknowledged mistakes, several audits and reports were done, a Channel Lake employee had been fired, SaskPower's CEO was pushed out and the Crown Corporations Committee report (to no one's surprise) had cleared the government of any wrongdoing.

While Channel Lake was done as a scandal, it was neither gone nor forgotten by the Saskatchewan public. Rather, it had become a cautionary tale for future NDP governments all wrapped up in perceptions—handpicked partisans in a politically-influenced Crown corporation; incompetence and a lack of supervision when a government tried getting into a risky business in which it had no expertise; delay and deflection before finally admitting fault; no apology; no explanation of how future repeats will be avoided; and, then a highhanded and arrogant stage managing of the process to avoid tough questions and arrive at a pre-ordained result.

Just two years after Channel Lake, during the leadership convention that elected Calvert, every time Cabinet ministers' names were recited (Cline, MacKinnon, Lautermilch, Atkinson) or the exploits of retired party heroes were shared (Lingenfelter, Tchorzewski, Shillington), it was a subtle reminder for observers of a scandal against which future NDP governments would be judged. It will never be known if Calvert had thought about the strategic lessons to be learned from Channel Lake. But he would find out soon enough, repeatedly and painfully over the next few years.

Spudco: Is That the Sound of a Falling Potato or a Government Crashing?

The largest financial scandal in Saskatchewan history was the NDP's loss of $34.7 million dollars trying to invest in the potato business. The scandal is one single word: Spudco. Like Channel Lake, Premier Lorne Calvert inherited Spudco from the Romanow government and it had many of the same actors in Cabinet, same pattern of incompetence, government trying to be in business and the "Big Four D's" of denial, deflection, deception and delay.

But unlike Channel Lake, Calvert ended up owning much of the damage from Spudco because of the way he handled the scandal. People were angered, not necessarily over politics or even money but about being betrayed. And it had a lot to do with common sense, values, trust and respect.

Spudco was a brainchild of the NDP. From its cutesy name—the Saskatchewan **P**otato **U**tility **D**evelopment **Co**mpany (Spudco, get it?)— the company was a subsidiary of the Crown Corporation, SaskWater. It was created when the Romanow Cabinet in 1996 approved a strategy to "kick start" the potato industry around Lake Diefenbaker by encouraging people to grow more potatoes to attract a $120 million dollar French fry plant to the area.

To do this, Spudco would use a $4 million dollar line of credit to operate a three-year potato production plan and would develop potato storage facilities with a maximum of $1 million dollars per facility. Potatoes had been grown for decades around Lake Diefenbaker. But this time the government decided to get in on the act.

In principle the deal was simple: local farmers and investors would grow the potatoes and set up a company called Lake Diefenbaker Potato Corporation (LDPC) which had a crop sharing agreement with the government's Spudco, which would store and sell the potatoes. Just one month before the NDP Cabinet approved the strategy to invest in potatoes, Lamb Weston, the French fry company being wooed, informed SaskWater that 1.7 million pounds of Saskatchewan potatoes it tested had turned black when fried. The company rejected the second shipment. Yet the NDP Cabinet went ahead and the government was in the potato business. But it wouldn't be for long.

After the potato collapse several years later, farmers told me that no one in the potato growing area around Lake Diefenbaker would soon forget the sight of career civil servants who wouldn't know a real business if it bit them on the butt, strutting around as if they were venture capitalists or snake oil and tonic salesmen in the Old West, stumping from town to town spreading the gospel of hope through Spudco.

One farmer admitted ignoring his instincts when a civil servant, whose riskiest life decision was cashing a pay cheque, urged people to sign up, telling them to "go big" and even mangling a Jack Welch-ism by saying "on this potato deal, you're either on the bus or under the bus." It had an ominous tone.

After only two potato crops, in 1998 the government's potato play began to sputter when Spudco terminated the crop share agreement with the farmers. One month later, the Cabinet and the Crown Investments

Corporation—the big holding company of all the Crowns—approved
Spudco building up to four new storage facilities with debt not to exceed
$14.5 million. A month after that, Lamb Weston chose Southern Alberta
for its plant and potato prices plummeted. Later that summer, Crowns
Minister Dwain Lingenfelter was told that Spudco had invested far more
money and assumed more risk than initially planned. By year's end,
Romanow, Lingenfelter and the Cabinet approved a bailout of the farmers
and investors of the LDPC.

At the same time, by late 1998 it had taken Spudco just nine months
to destroy a small, family-owned greenhouse business, after earlier agreeing to a five-year supply contract for seed potatoes and then reneging on
it. Why government employees in Spudco would be in the business of
buying seed potatoes, when farmers generally know potatoes best, was
never revealed.

By 1999, the farmer-owned LDPC declared bankruptcy. Spudco was
caught selling several hundred thousand pounds of genetically-modified
potatoes to unsuspecting buyers as regular potatoes. And SaskWater, after
being refused a $17.8 million government bailout for its offspring Spudco,
secretly took nearly $4 million from trust accounts held for Ducks Unlim-
ited and other groups, the money being used to prop up Spudco.

In 2000, with several small towns around Lake Diefenbaker in economic
ruin and the life savings of many farmers gone (some in bankruptcy), LDPC
sued Spudco, which then folded. The next year, Calvert's embarrassed and
sheepish Crowns Minister Maynard Sonntag would admit that Spudco had
lost $28 million.

"The scale of this affair—the mismanagement,
lies, years of cover-ups and failure of governing
politicians to take full responsibility—cries out
for answers and accountability."

Star Phoenix, October, 2004

Personally, Calvert had only two ties to the Spudco debacle and both were tenuous. He was in the Romanow Cabinet that approved Spudco. But, as a health and social services minister, he was never publicly associated with it. Second, as a member of the NDP's left wing, Calvert agreed with the principles of Spudco, using taxpayers' money to enter and compete in the private sector. But neither of these vague ties to Spudco meant anything for Calvert.

However, after two years of the case percolating through the Courts and the stories spreading of potato growers wiped out, by early 2003 white-hot, spewing outrage over Spudco had splattered all over Calvert. But how did this happen? It wasn't his government that embarked on the idiotic, politically rushed and ill-conceived plan to "invest" in French fries and potatoes. That was Romanow, Lingenfelter and the mid-1990s Cabinet.

During 2001 and 2002, Calvert had steadfastly refused to make any comment on Spudco, citing the ongoing LDPC lawsuit. But as he did so often when confronted with continuing heat from the opposition and media, Calvert did a complete reversal in late 2002 and directed his deputy minister, Dan Perrins, to carry out a thorough review of the events which led to Spudco. In early 2003, Perrins' review was made public and Calvert's hellish time began.

Years earlier, in 1997, then-SaskWater Minister Eldon Lautermilch signed a letter assuring a contractor that the government had a "minority interest" in potato storage sheds being built with an Alberta company. Lautermilch actually knew that Spudco was paying the entire tab—an important deception because farmers and others were repeatedly told by the NDP that "private sector partners" were involved in financing potato storage when none really were; the entire financial exposure was the NDP's by using taxpayers' money.

Calvert's deputy minister, in 2003, used words like "troubling," "less than forthcoming" and "inappropriate" to describe Lautermilch's behaviour in signing the misleading letter. For the first time it was also publicly confirmed—to the obvious delight of the farmers in the midst of their lawsuit—that the NDP's so-called "public-private partnership" over potato storage had never existed.

No one knows if Calvert, as a member of the Romanow Cabinet at the time, knew in 1997 of the deliberate Lautermilch deception and subsequent cover-up. But as premier seven years later, there were several options open to Calvert. Had he known earlier of the 1997 incident, he could have ensured when becoming premier in 2001 that Lautermilch was shuffled out of Cabinet and away from politics. That way, when the issue inevitably arose publicly in the lawsuit, he could say that Lautermilch had already left public life.

If Calvert only learned of the Lautermilch lie for the first time in Perrins' report, he could have atoned for the NDP's sins of the past by making a clear statement to distance himself from the Romanow government, apologize for the past transgression and then summarily dismiss Lautermilch as unfit for Cabinet and reaping the consequences of a deliberate deception.

But Calvert did none of this. He meekly apologized on behalf of his government and the earlier Romanow NDP—but without any criticism of the earlier government for a cover-up—and admitted that the public had been "misled" during the Spudco saga. He promised new accountability measures.

Then Calvert made the critical mistake that took 1997 and spliced it into 2003. He not only refused to fire Lautermilch but then said that he would not allow Lautermilch to resign because he was "one of the strongest and most able voices" in the Cabinet. Knowing what Lautermilch was capable of, based on the 1997 letter, what did this say for the "less strong and able" members of Cabinet? By leaving him in Cabinet and suggesting Lautermilch had been punished by being assigned new Cabinet duties showed the public where Calvert's priorities were. And they were not on fixing the sins of the past. Spudco had just become a Calvert scandal.

For his part, Lautermilch said "sorry" and stayed in Cabinet. Later in 2003, after the NDP election win—in a race where the rookies running the SaskParty strategy never once uttered the word "Spudco" during the entire campaign—Lautermilch was quietly dropped from Cabinet. However, he was later rehabilitated in 2005 when Calvert brought him back into Cabinet, which re-ignited the controversy over his role in the Spudco deception and cover-up.

"In spite of the collective bruising Spudco gave Saskatchewan and its reputation as a place to do business, one would hope that this final cheque will be the last that has to be written before the terrible tuber caper fades into the history books."

Star Phoenix, October, 2004

SaskParty strategists eventually got around to raising Spudco at the doors during the NDP's losing 2007 election because of Lautermilch's revival in 2005 and the settlement by the government of the farmers' LDPC lawsuit in 2004, which pushed the original $28 million Spudco taxpayer loss to $34.7 million.

As the court case settled in 2004, the Calvert government was stung yet again when it was revealed that the government's lawyers, in defending the Spudco lawsuit, had counter-sued some of the LDPC farmers and others, including an accounting firm, for $10 million for allegedly over-estimating the potential of the potato venture in the first place. A Queen's Bench Justice threw out most of the government's counter-suit and stopped short of finding the government's case against the accounting firm "frivolous and vexatious" only because of the complexity of the argument.

The Pat Slap Flap

When Cabinet ministers mess up, a premier's job is to get to the bottom of the story, determine the pertinent facts and then do something decisive: defend them and tough it out, get an apology, shuffle them, or fire them. In the spring of 2002, Environment minister Pat Lorje was accused of harassing an employee and Calvert tried several approaches.

A staff member of Lorje's had forgotten to post some personal mail (birthday cards). As Lorje lectured Pearl Yuzicappi in front of other staff, she reached over and her hand made contact with Yuzicappi's face. The staffer said she'd been slapped and felt belittled and humiliated. Lorje denied this, admitting touching Yuzicappi's face but "in a joking and affectionate manner... soft and gentle tapping fashion, transient in nature while I told her to 'smarten up'."

Until Calvert put Lorje in his first Cabinet in 2001, the Saskatoon NDP MLA had been passed over in every Cabinet shuffle since being elected in 1991—for good reason: her public behaviour was often unprofessional, erratic and annoying. A psychologist by training, Lorje had been caught near an open microphone insulting a witness' lawyer during a legislative hearing. On my radio show, she'd mocked critics of bad Saskatchewan highways by saying that her back alley had more traffic than some rural roads. When the media and opposition showed up in her back alley, Lorje burst into tears, blubbering that as a single woman this was an invasion of her privacy. They'd actually found her home address in the public phone book.

Lorje was unsuited for Cabinet and Calvert never should have appointed her. Complaints surfaced about her flashing the finger to opposition parties in the Legislature, and giving a patronizing speech to university students, leaving them with the impression that they should put up with eating Spam and Kraft Dinner on a low budget. Another news report had her comparing the economic pain of being a student to childbirth.

In the interests of disclosure, Pat Lorje detests me. She's called me a "scum bucket"—to my face. She even sued me once, unsuccessfully. You get the idea. To be charitable, Lorje was a hard constituency worker and was re-elected three times in the wealthiest constituency in Saskatchewan, a place not usually fertile ground for socialists—a credit to her chutzpah and campaign savvy.

In 2002, when Lorje's staffer came forward and complained about her treatment at the hand of the minister, Calvert temporarily suspended Lorje from Cabinet and hired a Manitoba human resources consultant to investigate. Three weeks later, the consultant reported that Yuzicappi had "received contact to her face" by Lorje which was physical and inappropriate but not violent or sexual and was intended as friendly and affectionate. For her part, Yuzicappi was justified in complaining because she had been embarrassed and humiliated. When reading the consultant's report, it was also obvious that no one had asked a police officer, lawyer or judge to decide where a glance or touch ended and a slap began.

Relying on the consultant, Calvert reinstated Lorje and Yuzicappi was transferred to another minister's office. Citing privacy, Calvert declined comment on the details of his decision. On the advice of the consultant, he also mentioned needing a code of conduct for ministers' offices, which must have gone down well with the majority of ministers who were mature, intelligent and professional enough to know that a boss doesn't discipline staff in the presence of others and touch their faces.

As Calvert reinstated Lorje—relying not on his own common sense but on the opinion of a hired consultant—I mused aloud that if a male minister had "affectionately" touched the face of a female staffer while telling her to "smarten up" there would have been demands for the minister's head on a platter. But was the staff member more dispensable because of her encounter with a woman? An NDP woman.

But Lorje did not last long back in Cabinet. Calvert fired her just two days later after Lorje tried explaining her version of the harassment case to reporters. Citing a breach of confidentiality, Calvert said, "Ms. Lorje went beyond where we should go in public in describing a workplace complaint."

So, the Lorje saga ended as oddly as it began. The Premier made an unsuitable Cabinet appointment in the first place. When the inevitable problems arose, Calvert caused uncertainty and delay by suspending Lorje and farming out the fact-finding mission. Then, his decision to reinstate Lorje appeared to be a non-elected consultant making up Calvert's mind for him. And finally, giving Lorje her job back suggested that the premier had full confidence in her—which lasted all of two days. This scandal ultimately cost Calvert points on judgment.

For her part, Lorje did not run again in the 2003 election and was subsequently elected to Saskatoon City Council in 2006. It was a return to municipal politics for Lorje, who had been a long time councilor prior to her provincial political career.

Computers & Bureaucrats: ISC

ISC, the Information Services Corporation, is a Crown corporation. By 2002, badly over budget and hemorrhaging more than $1 million a month, the newest child in the NDP family of Crown corporations was playing with matches and the Lorne Calvert government seemed powerless to stop the house from going up in flames. Like so many missteps that began with the Romanow era, the Calvert administration's slow response to the ISC computer scandal cost it credibility, along with millions of dollars. Fortunately, this one had a better ending than other scandals.

ISC was born on New Year's Day, 2000. Its purpose was to create a computerized land titles system for Saskatchewan. The idea had been hatched three years earlier when the Romanow Cabinet faced the choice of either doing nothing with the 100-year-old manual land titles registry or computerizing it, as every other province in Canada was doing. A Cabinet decision item in 1996 approved a five year roll-out for LAND (Land Titles Automated Network Development) to be completed by the end of 2002 at an estimated cost of $20 million.

The need to change the old land titles system was clear. Although it made an annual profit for the government of $10 million, land titles transactions were bogging down under the weight of more than 500,000 new documents issued from eight land titles offices each year. It was unwieldy and expensive to manually track 850,000 land titles, four million cancelled titles and six million instruments registered on the titles. The move to digital automation was a major change. When faced with change, the NDP decided it was time to move backwards to its comfort zone by starting up a new government-owned company to develop software and do what every other province was already moving ahead with.

Led by a career bureaucrat, Fraser Nicholson, the new Crown corporation ISC was kicked off in 2000 with the boast that Saskatchewan would "soon have the most advanced land information system in Canada." It was also announced that the design and implementation of the new system would be done by EDS, the company founded by American business tycoon and political renegade Ross Perot.

With delays in registrations, errors and high costs, the LAND system in June, 2001 created what one real estate lawyer described as the "summer from Hell." Another early user, a land surveyor, called the project a "fiasco." The Calvert government, just six months old, was being publicly pilloried for a computerized land titles system that didn't work. While this was happening at home, ISC's Chairman, Frank Hart, announced in Dallas in late 2001 that an agreement had been reached with EDS to market Saskatchewan's automated land titles system globally—ISC's "made in Saskatchewan" software would be sold around the world.

As Nicholson and his sales team of jet-setting and ambitious civil servants globe trotted, back at home ISC was becoming a sorry tale of misplaced faith in bureaucrats and computers. High-flying government software sales reps visited exotic locales—sometimes by themselves, other times accompanied by members of Cabinet and senior NDP advisors. But there was only one problem—there were no sales of land titles software. None. Nada. Zilch. Information technology experts snickered about Saskatchewan's "vapour ware" sales force. But the growing money pit was no laughing matter.

By this time, ISC was closing in on $60 million of spending—three times its original $20 million budget. A new budget for the LAND project was set: $60 million. So, the project was "on budget" again.

In June of 2002, Fraser Nicholson resigned from ISC and the NDP confirmed that he had accepted a job with a "private-sector company based in Atlantic Canada." The company "based" in the Maritimes was actually the Atlantic office of the government's American partner, EDS.

A few months later, EDS entered confidential discussions with the NDP about spinning-off some of the Saskatchewan government's overall computer operations to the giant American company. The discussions were conducted with Frank Hart, who—in addition to being the chair of ISC—was also the powerful chairman of the NDP's Crown Investments Corporation (CIC), the holding company of all Saskatchewan's commercial Crown corporations.

A trusted NDP advisor and former deputy minister, Hart is married to Diana Milenkovic, an NDP partisan who worked as Romanow's senior political advisor in the 1990s until being given a job in SaskTel as senior vice president. Hart would leave the Saskatchewan government less than two years later. His new employer—EDS. Since then, he's returned to Saskatchewan and works with an investment company.

When Nicholson left ISC, the NDP brought in, on a one-year contract, a well respected Regina businessman, Mark MacLeod, to serve as interim president until a new CEO was found. Young, bright and looking for opportunities after selling a successful software company he'd founded, MacLeod was a perfect caretaker for ISC. As 2002 ended, there was plenty that needed caretaking as the government company's downward money spiral continued.

The original $20 million price tag which had ballooned to $60 million was then over $100 million and counting. The assurances of NDP Cabinet ministers that there would be no additional costs or fee hikes rang hollow as ISC scrambled to find money because its revenue projections were wrong. A basic $100,000 house sale, with a $75,000 mortgage, was about to see ISC's registration fee triple from $200 to $600. For many rural people, where a house sits on several lots or easements, the ISC system—which set fees based on each registration number rather than on a single transaction— threatened registration fees in the thousands of dollars.

Adding insult was the government's announcement in late 2002 that ISC was due to pay a "dividend" to the NDP government of nearly $12 million, this at the same time that ISC was borrowing money faster than a jonesing crack addict.

And then things began to turn around. By March 2003, MacLeod took over as permanent president and CEO, the dividend was cancelled, fees were lowered and the focus was on managing change and expectations, providing better customer service and product value.

"With a 'roll-up-the-sleeves' work ethic and 'if-you're-not-part-of-the-solution-you're-part-of-the-problem' mentality, MacLeod quickly went about making his mark upon the company, which first and foremost, established the customer as king."

Keith Moen, Sask Business, February, 2004

MacLeod was a breath of fresh air in a panicked and confused government environment. Within months, MacLeod had scrapped the plan to peddle software around the world, reduced costs by millions of dollars, empowered employees to take ownership of their work, started paying down debt and focused on turn-around times of under three days.

Within a year, MacLeod brought in Scott Hodson, a returning Saskatchewan ex-pat who left an executive position with Kraft Foods and named him "Chief Customer Officer." Effectively ISC's second in command and managing the company's Saskatoon office, Hodson—like MacLeod—took a strongly customer-focussed approach and the pair travelled Saskatchewan winning over sceptics like me with a refreshing, honest and realistic approach.

To the credit of ISC's new minister, Eric Cline, who gave the duo wide latitude and kept political interference to a minimum, ISC had a customer approval rating of 90% and a profit of $8.5 million by 2006. The following year, with a record profit of over $23 million, MacLeod left ISC, saying that his "turnaround" was finished. Hodson departed shortly after and the two joined forces in running a manufacturing business in Saskatoon.

The Calvert government, which inherited an ill-conceived and poorly run Crown corporation, paid the price by accepting a bureaucratic and inefficient approach and then failing to control the agenda by effective and decisive management. The government got a break, and ultimately so did we taxpayers, when two guys with actual business experience, the former computer whiz kid and the solid, capable marketing executive, teamed up to run ISC professionally. And they got results.

The Klassen Malicious Prosecutions—Wanted: Courage & Decency

Like being struck by lightning or attacked in a random act of violence, truly horrible things sometimes happen to innocent people in the wrong place at the wrong time. And so it was for a Saskatoon family wrongly dragged through the law courts and falsely accused of terrible crimes. The "Klassen Malicious Prosecution" case would extract a huge toll on the credibility of the Calvert government in 2004. And, like so many controversies that embroiled the NDP, this one started years earlier but its mishandling blew up in the face of the Calvert government.

In 1987, three dysfunctional small children—twins Michelle and Kathy and their brother Michael—were seized from their deaf, mute, alcoholic and sexually abusive parents and put into the care of foster parents Dale and Anita Klassen. By all accounts, Dale and Anita were good people doing God's work.

Several years later, after Michael began sexually molesting his own sisters, he was moved to another foster home because he was out of control. Hoping to have his sisters removed from the Klassens and reunited with him, Michael made up a story about the Klassens, telling his new foster family and a succession of gullible social workers and police officers that he and his sisters had been sexually abused while at the Klassens'. The story grew to include wildly bizarre and unsupported claims of satanic ritual abuse, the torture, murder and dismemberment of babies, the sacrifice of animals, and the kids saying they were forced to eat eyeballs and feces and drink blood and urine.

In 1991, with no physical evidence and only the shaky testimony of three messed up foster children, the Saskatoon City Police laid sexual abuse charges against the Klassens and 10 members of their extended family. Some of the accused hardly even knew the children; the shame of the charges drove others to suicide attempts, mental illness and drug addiction; and, the elderly Peter Klassen, was so bullied that he even agreed to plead guilty if the police would stop harassing his family.

One family member told our radio audience years later that much of her counseling and therapy stemmed from the day she was arrested. The cop in charge, Brian Dueck, brought her into the prisoner elevator at police headquarters, stared at her and ominously growled "Now I'm going to send you to Hell."

On the same day, two of the Klassen couples were arrested in front of their crying children, handcuffed, bundled into police cars and then jailed for six days in holding cells—deliberately kept there by vindictive cops who prevented them from appearing for bail hearings. Compounding their agony as they sat in cells, the Klassens were told by sneering police officers that their children had been seized by social workers and put into foster care because no one was able to look after them—every single adult in the lives of the traumatized kids was under arrest and locked up.

By 1993, Crown Prosecutor Matt Miazga decided not to proceed on most of the charges he had brought against the Klassens, saying this was to spare the three child victims the "further trauma" of testifying in court. Trauma had nothing to do with it: Michael, Michelle and Kathy had been lying all along. As the years went by, these dysfunctional youngsters would even sign affidavits admitting they'd made up the entire story.

Throughout the investigation, charging and prosecution of the Klassen families there was a stunning web of deceit, official cover-ups, tunnel vision and professional pride that had run rampant over 12 innocent people. In 1994, the falsely accused Klassen family members—and relatives in the Kvello family—filed a $10 million malicious prosecution lawsuit. For the next 10 years, government lawyers stubbornly fought the case and refused to settle out of court with the Klassens, even though they'd been completely exonerated and at the same time the province was settling lawsuits brought in the similar but unrelated Martensville debacle where trumped up ritual abuse cases had dragged innocent people through the criminal courts.

The NDP had ample opportunity to instruct the justice department to settle the case out of court, apologize to the Klassens and pay them damages. One such occasion was in 2000 when the CBC's Fifth Estate aired its story of the Klassens called "Scandal of the Century." Most of the documentary's damning findings would later be confirmed in court, yet the Saskatchewan government remained dug in.

The malicious prosecution case finally went to trial in 2003 and Queen's Bench Court Justice George Baynton, after hearing the evidence, ruled that the Klassen and Kvello family members had been victims of a "travesty of justice". He found that they had been intentionally and maliciously prosecuted. Although some of Justice Baynton's legal reasoning would later be overturned by the Supreme Court of Canada, in a controversial decision that raised the bar to protect Miazga and prosecutors like him, most of Justice Baynton's findings of fact were unchallenged. And they are damning.

It was "beyond belief," Baynton wrote in an exhaustive 98-page decision, that no one took a step back and asked if any of the wild claims made sense or could reasonably be true. There were findings of bullying tactics used by a cop with tunnel vision. The behaviour of a therapist constituted withholding and stifling of evidence which may have risked her "being charged with the criminal offence of obstructing justice." And to top it off, the prosecutor was not going to let the truth get in the way.

In the days after Justice Baynton's decision, the phone lines on my radio show went crazy. Within weeks we did 13 different talk shows covering the Klassen case as listeners reacted with shock and outrage to the despicable treatment that a dozen innocent people had suffered at the hands of the state—a therapist, a cop and a prosecutor out of control. As listeners actually broke down emotionally hearing members of the Klassen family tell of a decade of suffering, many—including me—called on the government to fire the prosecutor Miazga.

In fairness, the Calvert government did not create this miscarriage of justice which arose years earlier during Saskatchewan hysteria over satanic ritual abuse cases. Although these dubious child abuse cases had already been debunked years earlier in the U.S., it showed Saskatchewan's justice department at its worst—a potent combination of negligence, incompetence and being so ill-informed and arrogant that mistakes could not be admitted, even as they ruined the lives of innocent people.

Instead of anticipating and channeling public concern, the Calvert government of 2004 somehow managed to make the malicious prosecution scandal its own. The Baynton decision and the public outpouring of support for the Klassens left the government with a thorny legal dilemma. But rather than Calvert and his Attorney General Frank Quennell leading with a perception of public decency and compassion for wrongly victimized innocent people, the NDP looked indecisive, inflexibly attached to bureaucrats and clumsily relying on legal advice from the same lawyers who had not only failed to stop the persecution of the Klassens but had then run them through the courts for a decade trying to prevent their vindication. And to top it off, these same lawyers lost the court case.

The legal issue was this: leaving aside Miazga's behaviour, what is the appropriate legal standard that separates a risky and incorrect prosecution from one that is "malicious"? For the sake of the administration of justice, this is important to clarify: no one wins if we allow open season on prosecutors (except criminals).

Days after Baynton's decision the government responded, not with Quennell or a detached deputy minister compassionately separating a narrow legal issue from the compelling personal tragedy of the Klassen families. The government put up the same justice department lawyer who had spent years in court fighting the Klassens, Don McKillop, an able litigation lawyer but abysmal media spokesman. McKillop rambled, at times flippantly explaining the government's intent to appeal because "we don't concede that the therapist and prosecutor did anything wrong" but, at the same time, he would not dispute the innocence of the Klassens. To the thousands of decent Saskatchewan people who never went to law school, McKillop's comments were technical, confusing and showed not a scintilla of humanity toward the innocent victims of a miscarriage of justice.

For his part, when Quennell did speak, he sounded like a lawyered-up CEO, evading the obvious, lapsing into legalese, refusing to apologize and saying only that he was "sorry for what happened" and "sorry for what the Klassen and Kvello families have been through." At the same time, the justice department's communications officer, Debi McEwen, a well known NDP politico and campaign worker, issued a statement on Quennell's behalf justifying an appeal because if the case stands "it has the potential to discourage other professionals such as doctors, nurses, social workers and others from reporting possible signs of child abuse to the police."

This prompted ex-prosecutor and law professor Sanjeev Anand to tell my radio audience that this claim was "ludicrous" because professionals already had clear duties to report child abuse, regardless of this case. And, in any event, the Klassen case was about whether a prosecutor, therapist and cop had crossed the line.

As the government refused to apologize directly to the Klassens, on my radio show we started the "Official Frank Quennell Apology Watch" and did a daily count. By Day #17, Quennell doubled down on the government's public relations disaster by expressing not only his personal affection for the discredited Crown prosecutor but also his professional confidence in the work of Miazga. Rather than staying silent, his personal endorsement of Miazga handcuffed Quennell, his government and the NDP directly to the scandal, which had been widely discussed and criticized.

A few days later, still refusing an apology, Quennell agreed to pay the Klassen family victims $1.5 million for their innocence, pain and suffering. Later, the payment would be upped to nearly $2.5 million.

Finally, on Day #41 of the Apology Watch, Quennell did an abrupt about face and personally apologized to members of the Klassen and Kvello families. In a private meeting, Quennell looked concerned, lowered his eyes and sincerely said "I apologize for the prosecution of your family." While this would not go down in the annals of the great apologies of our time, at least Quennell had taken a first step toward reconciling the pain and torment for the dozen innocent people dragged through the criminal justice system.

After six weeks of public outrage and a media circus, the question about Quennell's apology became "Why was it right after weeks of pressure and not right immediately after the case?"

Inside Sask Justice, certain lawyers believed then, and still do, that during an appeal saying "sorry" will admit liability or responsibility. In this case, a proper apology had no bearing on the government's legal position.

But for the Klassen and Kvello families, an appropriate apology would have been the way that those who represent the government express their sympathy and remorse for what agents of government did in perverting justice.

"The Klassens and Kvellos were pursued in public, debased and ruined in public by public employees financed by public dollars. Criminal justice, trial procedure, prosecutions and indeed the golden thread of justice—the presumption of innocence—are not discrete and private concepts. They are public. And the publicly responsible agency entrusted with the administration of justice owes us, the public, an apology too, for wrongdoing and for breaching our public trust."

John Gormley in full rant, January 2004

Although this was a legal case (an abysmally handled one), it had significant political impact: refusing early on to take a humane and compassionate stand spoke to a lamentable lack of leadership. And in government, leadership ends at the premier's office. Most damning was that throughout weeks of bitter and angry public debate, the government looked insensitive, rigid, deflecting and arrogant.

Eventually the Klassens would fade from public sight and five years later the Supreme Court would rewrite the law and exonerate the prosecutor Miazga in a case described by one legal analyst as "placing crown prosecutors above the law." But the harm caused to the Calvert government's credibility was incalculable.

"Sorry" Seems to be the Hardest Word: The Apology in Politics

Erich Segal's sappy book and movie Love Story introduced us to "love means never having to say you're sorry." Actually, it doesn't. Love *often* means saying sorry, especially when you've hurt someone you love. But in politics, apologies are trickier.

When Justice Minister Frank Quennell couldn't bring himself to apologize in the Klassen malicious prosecution scandal, it was obviously on legal advice: someone in the justice department thought that saying "sorry" might weaken the government's case on appeal or cost them more money. Of course it did neither.

There's an old adage in politics—cynical it may be, but for many practitioners it works well: "never concede, never explain and never apologize." Old-school politicos like former Prime Minister Jean Chretien seemed to live by these words. In Chretien's world, an apology only admitted weakness or, worse, incompetence and your opponents could play back your mistakes forever.

"It is a good rule in life never to apologize. The right sort of people do not want apologies, and the wrong sort take a mean advantage of them."

P.G. Wodehouse

I've always preferred politicians human and humble enough to say "sorry" when they've goofed. But there's a limit—which brings us to the Lorne Calvert government, teeter-tottering to the other extreme where there was just too much apologizing going on. When a government seems always to be apologizing there will come a time that people wonder about basic competence. Or, are all those apologies just a way of asking permission to keep failing?

By early 2005, after the NDP had settled lawsuits against their government for the $35 million loss in the Spudco debacle, SaskWater Minister Peter Prebble had apologized yet again—this time because government lawyers had made frivolous and vexatious claims in the court case. As the minister droned on, I wondered how many times in Calvert's first four years the word "sorry" had been uttered. The results were surprising:

- April 2002: SaskWater Minister Buckley Belanger apologizes to North Battleford citizens for the tainted water that made them ill;
- June 2002: Crown Corporations Minister Maynard Sonntag apologizes for SGI changing its story on using private investigators to check out accident claimants;
- Also in June 2002: Justice Minister Chris Axworthy apologizes to maliciously prosecuted Saskatoon cop John Popowich in the Martensville phony ritual abuse case and pays him $1.3 million;
- February 2003: Premier Lorne Calvert apologizes (with several excuses) for the provincial government misleading the public over Spudco;
- February and March 2003: Industry Minister Eldon Lautermilch apologizes as the guy who actually misled people over Spudco;
- April 2003: Leader Post headline: ISC: Heated Debate over Land Titles Sparks Dual Apologies;
- April 2003: Justice Minister Eric Cline apologizes for "misunderstandings" about the case of Lawrence Wegner, an aboriginal man found frozen in Saskatoon;
- July 2003: NDP Caucus employee Ted Bowen apologizes for referring to US President George Bush as "Shrub;"
- October 2003: Premier Lorne Calvert apologizes to Elwin Hermanson and the Jewish community over an NDP political cartoon depicting the SaskParty Leader as a Nazi;
- December 2003: Finance Minister Harry Van Mulligen apologizes for comments about avoiding financial discussions during provincial election;
- January and February 2004: Justice Minister Frank Quennell refuses to apologize to the wrongly accused Klassen and Kvello families; Premier Calvert has "sympathy" but no apology. Finally, six weeks later both Quennell and Calvert apologize—repeatedly.
- April 2004: Health Minister John Nilson apologizes to a Sask Party MLA he ridicules over a physical disability during legislative debate;

- June 2004: Health Minister John Nilson apologizes to Hutterite family of ill little girl, Kathryn Wipf over her poor treatment by Sask Health;
- October 2004: Corrections Minister Peter Prebble says he would apologize to the daughter of a slain care home owner in North Battleford but he "can't at the moment;"
- October 2004: Corrections and SaskWater Minister Peter Prebble apologizes to people suing Spudco as the government pays out a multi-million dollar settlement of a lawsuit.

If done—sincerely and promptly upon discovering that we've done something wrong to hurt someone—apologies can show remorse, empathy and lessons learned. Of course, every proper apology includes confession, atonement and revelation.

Five Ways to Say Sorry Like You Mean It

1. DETAILS: Specifically describe what you did—no excuses, deflections or minimizing. Come clean, it shows that you have insight into your wrongdoing;

2. ADMIT IT: Acknowledge and admit that you did the act; you caused the hurt, take responsibility and accept the blame;

3. GET PERSONAL: Tell everything about your wrongdoing in a way that shows you understand—where you went wrong and how you intend to never repeat the same the same mistake;

4. SINCERITY: Say sorry—many times if need be—in a way that expresses humanity, humility and sincerity, not defensiveness. And the apology must be absolute without qualifiers;

5. MAKE GOOD: Ask forgiveness and offer reparations. Surrender your power. Granting forgiveness or accepting the "make good" are up to the person you've hurt;

The Hillson Misadventure

One of the NDP's most effective and ruthless skills is not merely to defeat political opponents but to teach them a lesson. One of the best ways is to take away their livelihood, which makes them think carefully the next time before they cross the NDP machine. A former MLA who went from being a critic of the NDP to a close friend and then an avowed enemy found out the hard way the cost of angering the natural governing party.

Jack Hillson, a Liberal MLA elected in a 1996 by-election, was re-elected in 1999 and suddenly became one of the most important people in Saskatchewan when he propped up the Roy Romanow NDP in a coalition with two other Liberals. By the time Lorne Calvert became Premier in 2001, Hillson had grown disenchanted with the NDP and quit the coalition which angered a number of prominent NewDems. Hillson was then defeated by the NDP in the 2003 election.

Before politics, Hillson had been the lawyer in charge of the North Battleford Legal Aid office for 10 years. When he ran for office he used a unique provision of Saskatchewan's *Labour Standards Act*, which requires an employer to give an unpaid leave of absence to any employee elected to public office for as long as the political career lasts. And when the leave is over, the law requires the employer to "allow the employee to continue his employment without loss of any privilege connected with seniority." In other words, ex-politicians get their jobs back at the same seniority, rate of pay and benefits as if they'd never left.

A few days after his November 2003 defeat, Hillson approached Jane Lancaster, the NDP political appointee in charge of Legal Aid—the same person who'd given him the leave seven years earlier—and was told that he had no job to come back to. Lancaster said his job was already filled, his seven years away from legal practice left him inexperienced and if he came back a junior aboriginal woman lawyer would have to be bumped, which would have looked bad for Legal Aid's image.

The very reason this law was passed by earlier NDP governments was to prevent exactly what Lancaster was trying to do to Hillson—deny an employee from returning to work with his former employer after serving time in office. On the "skills gone weak" claim, Hillson offered to re-train himself at his own cost and on his own time. But Lancaster wasn't having it. Within weeks, as if to drive the point home, Hillson was told that the entire Board of Directors of the Saskatchewan Legal Aid Commission voted unanimously to terminate him.

At 59 years old, unemployed and with deep roots in North Battleford, Hillson did two things. First, he landed on his feet by taking a job with a three-hour round trip commute at a Saskatoon law firm at one-half his Legal Aid salary. Then, he fought back and filed a lawsuit against Legal Aid.

Whatever the Legal Aid Commission's motivation was —and it claimed no political agenda against Hillson—and whatever legal advice it was getting, none of this mattered: firing Hillson looked like kicking a guy when he was down. And coming from me, that's saying something: I'm not fond of Jack Hillson —I did not respect his professional abilities as a lawyer when he unsuccessfully sued me while representing NDP ex-MLA Pat Lorje; I also didn't like his decisions as a politician. But his treatment at the hands of Legal Aid looked unfair, arbitrary and vindictive. And his courage at taking on a large government-funded agency was admirable.

Within a year of Hillson's firing, a labour standards officer ruled that the Legal Aid Commission had violated the law. With this, the opposition SaskParty put more fuel on the fire by asking why criminal charges were not being laid against Legal Aid, which can be done under the *Labour Standards Act*. This resulted in the odd situation of the justice minister, responsible for both the Legal Aid Commission and the Department that carries out criminal prosecutions, lecturing the opposition on the importance of administrative and prosecutorial independence.

From the beginning of the Hillson debacle through the months of the lawsuit, the government obviously gave a long arms-length reach to the independence of its Board of Directors of the Legal Aid Commission. As a result, rather than the government suggesting to Legal Aid subtly, early and discreetly that Hillson be given his job back, Calvert and his ministers twisted uncomfortably in the wind and being pilloried in the Legislature and around the water cooler.

Two years after Hillson's lawsuit was filed, the obvious and expected happened—he won and Legal Aid lost. In 2006, claiming vindication, Hillson was awarded more than $200,000 and Legal Aid was ordered to give him his job back. The Queen's Bench Court decision used strong language and criticized Legal Aid for trying to make a "sham" of the *Labour Standards Act*; the questioning of Hillson's legal skills was "condescending;" and the concern over bumping of staff "showed certain intransigence."

Justice Guy Chicoine also found that Legal Aid's North Battleford office had vacancies that emerged shortly after Hillson was fired; including the resignation of the female aboriginal lawyer —despite this, Legal Aid had refused to reinstate Hillson.

Jack Hillson never did return to Legal Aid and still practices law in Saskatoon. The damage done to the Calvert government was significant: even though the incomprehensible decision to fire Hillson came from a government-appointed board, it associated the "nice" Premier Calvert with a decision that appeared petty and mean; thousands of taxpayers' dollars were needlessly wasted and the government's response was to stand on the sidelines, weakly and helplessly pleading "it's Legal Aid, not us."

Baby Paige

In April, 2006, we were talking on my radio show about health care waiting lists. During a commercial break, my producer mentioned that a woman I knew was on the phone wanting to talk off the air. Usually, given the hectic pace of a four-hour talk show, where guests and topics are often changing on the fly, I don't have time to take calls during breaks so I don't. But something told me to take this one. The caller, a well-known Saskatch-ewanian on the national stage, didn't want her name used and explained the dilemma of a young couple she knew. As she quickly summarized the story, she started to sob and said "this is so goddamned stupid." There are two things I'd never heard this woman do: swear or cry.

She told me the shocking ordeal of Michelle and Mike Hansen of Humboldt, whose 18- month-old toddler, Paige, had spent three weeks with swollen limbs, lost her ability to walk and began screaming constantly from pain. With no diagnosis from a Saskatoon hospital, the family was bounced back and forth until her condition worsened. They returned to Saskatoon only to learn that the MRI was not working and there was a three-week wait for a bone scan. With Baby Paige in the car, screaming in agony, the young couple reached the end of their rope and raced off to an Edmonton hospital for help. As I interviewed Paige's mom and aunt on the radio, they described how the arrival in Edmonton brought immediate relief. But it also brought a fast, terrifying diagnosis: leukemia.

Hours after the radio interview, the plight of Baby Paige was raised in the Saskatchewan Legislature and an exasperated Premier Calvert blurted out "it's one thing to criticize the system and it is appropriate, when there is [sic] flaws that we discover those flaws and do the repair but you know, if you are going to be credible, you need to stand up and provide some alternative."

The next day on the radio show I played the Calvert clip, paused and said, "You know what my alternative is, Lorne Calvert? Get the hell out of my way. Act like you are in charge and fix things. And if you can't, get the hell out of the way—there are those who can." For the next four hours the phone lines jammed as outraged callers unloaded on an insensitive and bureaucratic health system, a powerless premier and how a little vulnerable toddler like Baby Paige could be put through such pain. Some callers blew up, one saying he was so angry he was glad he hadn't seen the premier because "if I'd been around, I'd have probably gone to jail." I cautioned the caller to calm down.

As the talk show went on, listeners demanded someone be held accountable for the communications mix-ups and confusion and the fact that still no one could offer a satisfactory explanation to the Hansens. At one point, I said colloquially that the premier should have the health minister's "head on a platter"—I now clarify years later that this was the time-honoured reference to John the Baptist, not anything Al Qaeda terrorists were up to at the time.

Quickly, the CEO of the Saskatoon Health Region came to our studios to apologize and admit they had no valid explanation why the family was told they had to wait three weeks to get Paige a bone scan. And no one told the family they didn't need an out-of-province referral for Paige. As the show went on, we discovered that people with a valid Saskatchewan health card can go to an emergency room, a physician or a walk-in clinic anywhere in Canada and get treatment they require. The only exceptions are MRIs, cataract surgeries and bone density scans. The government also announced an investigation into the Baby Paige case.

The story should have ended there, as our thoughts and prayers went out to Baby Paige, who returned to Saskatoon and was getting first-class treatment at the Cancer Centre. But one of the NDP's most partisan tough guys decided to kick things up a notch—and it wasn't a very bright idea.

Deputy Premier Clay Serby went on the attack against what the NDP saw as the cause of the Baby Paige debacle—me. Whether it was payback for making his premier look weak and flustered or whether it was an attempt to de-legitimize our talk show as a forum for concerned citizens, we'll never know.

After a second day of the Baby Paige debate being raised in the Legislature, Serby blustered "I've never seen a piece of work that has created so much anxiety for people as what I've seen the last two days being reported by Mr. Gormley. I'm of concern [sic] that yesterday's broadcast and this morning's has solicited a response from Saskatchewan people that is hugely troublesome, that you have an individual who phones in and says that had his presence been closer to this place, he may in fact be in jail today, where then Mr. Gormley says that what he would like to see is the health minister's head on a platter."

Then Serby suggested that broadcast industry regulators should review my show because "this kind of action, civil disobedience that is perpetuated by a radio host is in my view over the line."

> "The Deputy Premier accuses John Gormley of creating anxiety and fear. Look where that's coming from—the NDP wrote the book on fear tactics. The only difference is most of the NDP fear tactics are totally made up. The fear that baby Paige's parents felt was real."
>
> *June Draude, SaskParty MLA, April, 2006*

When Serby decided to make my show the story, he had to have known at least two things: first, remember the old entertainer's adage "I don't care what they say, as long as they spell my name right." Making me the issue actually helped promote our talk show—and its always shamelessly self-promoting host—to a much wider audience across the province. Second (and every trial lawyer knows this) if you're going to make a threat, you'd best carry it out.

Serby never filed a complaint to either the Canadian Radio Television and Telecommunications Commission (CRTC) or the Canadian Broadcast Standards Council. Had he, we could have had a public opportunity to examine precisely what part of the show's "civil disobedience" he found so objectionable.

But what grated at me—and, unlike Serby, I didn't make a big deal of it publicly at the time—was his lack of personal courtesy, class and good manners. When Serby attacked me and the talk show, I phoned his office and offered to discuss his concerns. He never returned my call. Later, I spoke directly with Anna Willey, a senior NDP strategist in Calvert's office, who told me "Mr. Serby will not be talking with you."

Months later at a private function at my golf club, I chuckled to myself when Serby (who was there as someone's guest) seemed to keep disappearing from my line of sight as I'd look his way across the room. This guy was the deputy premier—so fearless and powerful when dishing it out in the halls of the Legislature against people unable to defend themselves. But when he encountered someone like me—tougher than him, more stubborn and spoiling to put him in his place—he made himself scarce. If this is what passed for senior Cabinet talent, the time had clearly come for Saskatchewan to raise our standards.

As I'm often asked what became of Baby Paige, the story had a happy ending. Now six years old, Paige is a healthy, active and busy little girl in grade one who recently told me that she likes playing outside with her friends. She loves Ukrainian dancing, even winning her first dance medal. Her cancer is in remission.

The Not-So-Safe "Safe Houses"

In public life, some people are great politicians in the old-fashioned "lookin' after the folks back home" kind of way. But it doesn't necessarily make them good policy thinkers capable of navigating issues, overseeing complex bureaucracies and mediating conflicting political values. The NDP's Northern Saskatchewan lieutenant Buckley Belanger was a good example of this.

I first met Belanger when I was an MP in my 20s and he was a bouncy young guy who looked barely out of high school, sitting in a makeshift office of a radio station he was managing in the Northern village of Ile-a-la Crosse. Funded by federal grants, the broadcast project was Belanger's pride and joy—along with his framed picture of Liberal Prime Minister Pierre Trudeau that he cherished.

A skinny, high energy kid, the affable Belanger's happy-go-lucky manner belied shrewd political instincts for the players, issues and ever shifting allegiances in the political minefield of the North. At that time, bureaucrats in the defunct Department of Northern Saskatchewan were still spreading around largesse, much of it being snapped up and channeled by local kingpins in a government-funded lobby group called the Association of Métis and Non-Status Indians of Saskatchewan. More like something from the Sopranos or the influence-based politics of a third-world country, Northern Saskatchewan had its challenges in those days.

Within a couple of years, the well-connected Belanger was elected Mayor of Ile-a-la Crosse. By the mid-1990s, he became a Liberal MLA by defeating 20-year incumbent NDPer Fred Thompson in the northern seat of Athabasca. Wherever he would go in political life—good, bad or indifferent—Belanger always had my respect for what he did next. Convinced to cross the floor and join the NDP in 1998, Belanger quit the Liberals, resigned his seat and then ran as the NDP candidate, being elected with 94% of the popular vote. As a straight up local riding politician, few are savvier than Belanger.

For much of the Calvert government, Belanger's Cabinet duties included the innocuous environment and resource management portfolio. Before the growing political sexiness of the climate change file, environment was not a high profile job. Although the plain-spoken Belanger was the government's point man during a contaminated water outbreak in North Battleford, most of his focus was on fishing, hunting and conservation—all well suited for a northern MLA. Later, however, Belanger's uncomfortable and suspicious silence in the shocking Murdoch Carriere scandal, which went on for years in the environment department's Forest Fire Fighting Centre, would leave questions about Belanger unanswered that should have been accounted for.

In Calvert's final year, the Premier's decision to make Belanger the minister responsible for social services would coincide with a couple of long-simmering controversies boiling over. Like the Carriere scandal, Belanger seemed incapable of turning down the heat.

In 2003, as part of a child protection strategy, the NDP agreed to fund a so-called "safe house" in Regina for 12 to 15 -year-old girls who had been exploited in the sex trade. A First Nations group called Oyate—which included FSIN and local band council involvement—was under contract and paid to operate the facility, although it had no experience in the residential care of children. One million dollars later, it was revealed that the Oyate Safe House was not so safe after all—far from it, with bad management, nepotism, poor training, slack accounting and a high staff turnover of 60 employees cycling through six positions in three years and at least seven different people being listed as Oyate's executive director.

More disturbing were reports that some of the teens were still involved in drugs and prostitution while living at the house and some staff members were actually driving kids around at night.

In 2006, the provincial auditor slammed the suspicious financial dealings—including the board of directors paying itself $10,000 in "honorariums"—and criticized the provincial government for not properly supervising Oyate's activities. As the responsible minister, Belanger often deferred comment to his senior staff who promised to "work with the Oyate board of directors to tighten its procedures, confident that when those recommendations are implemented we will have an effective and much-needed service." With children at risk, the law being broken and financial accountability non-existent, the time was past for bureaucratic diversion and hope, particularly when Belanger's own senior departmental staff had been aware of problems for over a year. But Belanger stood on the side-lines, leaving it up to his bureaucrats.

Then, two months later, Saskatchewan's Children's Advocate Marvin Bernstein unveiled a sharply-worded report, concluding that Oyate was poorly run and did not provide a safe place for sexually exploited children. And Bernstein openly criticized Belanger's Community Resources (social services) Department for even deliberately closing files fully aware that children "continued to be a victim of sexual exploitation."

Bernstein is a nationally-respected child law expert from Toronto who has spent a career litigating difficult cases in the family courts. Beneath his calm and professional exterior lurks an uncompromisingly tough approach on the protection of children. Bernstein bluntly takes a "child first" stance where the safety and protection of children should override everything—culture, language and even the age-old Saskatchewan social services philosophy of keeping families together at all costs.

"Safety, protection and well-being of children
are compromised in order to preserve the
family unit at all cost."

Marvin Bernstein, Saskatchewan
Children's Advocate 2006 Report

Not exactly a card-carrying member of the vast right-wing conspiracy, Bernstein has little time for political correctness, even taking on the elephant in the room: how the interests and care of aboriginal children are often put behind other agendas like cultural sensitivity and First Nations debates over autonomy. According to Bernstein, "we want aboriginal people to be significant players in carving out solutions for their children but there seems to be a lowering at times of the standard of care—too much flexibility, too much accommodation, too much laxity."

With Bernstein suggesting concrete changes within two months or a shutting down of Oyate, Belanger's response was to hold a news conference, flanked by First Nations politicians and his deputy minister. All spoke hopefully in the future tense and spun what can only charitably be called gobbledygook: we will fix the problems, the process, the partnership with First Nations—all after the accomplishment of consultation strategies to be developed through the efforts and direction provided by Bernstein's report.

None of this happened and Oyate was later closed.

Belanger's constant deference to his department was not good enough, particularly when staff knew about and ignored direct threats to children's safety. Social services and its senior mandarins would have better understood a direct approach from their minister, setting out specific benchmarks, strict time limits and consequences for falling short. The approach of infinite patience, repeated second chances and continuing consultation might have been a constructive strategy for land claims or jurisdictional disputes between First Nations and the province, but when the lives of vulnerable children are literally at risk, the public can see through the bureaucratic smokescreen.

Because money ultimately makes the world go round, it is a sad but immutable rule of life that when all else fails—encouraging, cajoling, threatening, begging and pleading—follow the money. And then take it away and deprive the people and agencies neglecting children of any more money and jobs. Blunt though this may be, it is the long overdue answer of the provincial government to the question, "What is to be done when people receiving public money refuse to be accountable?"

....

"Buckley Belanger is concluding a disastrous performance at the Department of Community Resources, a performance that included his incompetent handling of the Oyate Safe House and questions surrounding the safety of children at the Four Directions residential facility."

Star Phoenix, June, 2007

....

In April 2007, the Oyate scandal would repeat itself. Belanger announced the "temporary suspension of operations" of a 24-bed First Nations-owned facility called Four Directions near Yorkton. Saying only that he was concerned about "core standards of care" in the facility that housed 12 to 15 year olds, Belanger commended the staff, the Board, the local chiefs—everyone, including himself, who, he reminded us, was responsible for children in care.

Then came what Belanger did not say. He did not mention a report he'd been given two months earlier, identifying a lack of recreation programs at Four Directions, an inadequate building and staff who were using force to restrain the children. He was also warned by the children's advocate who had received complaints.

The facility was closed by Belanger in 2007. But most damning, Belanger did not say that his department had one year earlier (concerned about the safety of children at Four Directions) removed from the facility the children who were under the direct care of his department while leaving behind First Nations children, who were the responsibility of local Indian bands.

The final indignity came later when it was revealed that mere days before he closed Four Directions, Belanger had appeared before the Legislature's Human Services Committee and said nothing, not even about the report in his possession outlining serious problems, as the committee voted an extra $1 million to the youth facility—funding that would have been denied had the true state of affairs been known.

The "not-so-safe safe houses" and Belanger's minimization, denial and confusing statements—trying both to appease First Nations leaders and still protect children without assigning blame—showed either (a) a minister completely under the influence of his bureaucrats and incapable of decision making or (b) a local Northern politico more concerned with not losing the aboriginal vote. Or, simply, Belanger was out of his depth in Cabinet.

One of the NDP's historic perception strengths, without necessarily any evidence, is that it's the "party looking out for the vulnerable." By the summer of 2007, this perception was dashed along with even the most basic sense that the NDP was any longer competent to handle the protection of children.

Two Painful Words: Murdoch Carriere

If "Spudco" was the single word that became code for financial mismanagement and the most expensive scandal in Saskatchewan history, there were two words—Murdoch Carriere—that turned into the NDP's neutron bomb of scandals, destroying the party's core values of human rights, workplace protection and fighting sexual harassment. It also showed how bureaucratic incompetence and bumbling, along with looking out for an NDP old boy could undermine an entire government.

From the day Carriere's name first surfaced in 2002 until five years later when a tired Calvert government was hanging on the ropes trying to defend the indefensible, the NDP crumbled under the public outrage from this scandal.

Murdoch Carriere had worked for the government for 32 years and was about as untouchable as any civil servant could be. Politically well connected (he bragged of his influence inside the NDP), he was a high profile aboriginal in government and was much praised in the environment department for coordinating Northern forest fire fighting operations and minority hiring initiatives. Carriere was related to NDP MLA and ex- minister Keith Goulet and was a long-time friend of Environment Minister Buckley Belanger, in whose department Carriere worked.

In the Prince Albert fire protection office, Carriere was one of those bosses that made women cringe. He'd hug, touch and "massage" women at work, remind them they'd better know who their boss was and should be thankful for their jobs. He also made inappropriate visits to female staff at their homes and unwanted comments about their appearance. One day, he even called a woman "pet" when introducing her to a visiting Premier Lorne Calvert.

Finally, by 2002, six women came forward complaining of Carriere's behaviour. And they had a lot to complain about. But everything was kept on the down-low inside the civil service. Carriere was quietly sent home in October, 2002 with full pay, where he'd stay for nearly four months. A consultant was hired to investigate the claims against Carriere and concluded in December 2002 that harassment had taken place, along with abuse of authority and inappropriate sexual behaviour.

> "The consultant's report alone would be ample reason to justify firing Carriere or giving him an option to resign. But this wasn't done. In the timid, unprofessional ass-covering approach so typical of government, they made the decision to "discipline" him instead. Sheesh."
>
> *Another Gormley rant, April, 2003*

With the consultant's damning report in hand—in a stunt that could only be pulled in the artificial world of government—Carriere's immediate boss, Environment Deputy Minister Terry Scott, decided not to fire Carriere but to "discipline" him by changing his job description, telling him to take counseling and then placing Carriere on a three-month unpaid suspension before he would "assume new responsibilities as a senior advisor" in the environment department with no cut in pay.

Scott wrote a memo to staff making this announcement in February, 2003 in which the deputy minister thanked "Murdoch for his valuable contributions." On the same day, the six women got an ominous private note from Scott, warning them not to circulate the consultant's report or to discuss the investigation with anyone: "I want to specifically caution you to treat this decision and any information related to this matter with strict and absolute confidentiality," Scott wrote.

As Carriere's victims read Scott's memos, their incredulity turned to anger. Thanks to Carriere, they'd been ogled at work, their bodies and appearances scrutinized and commented on in front of others, they'd been touched and hugged and had to rebuff unwanted physical advances. One of his victims told me on the radio about her messed up self-esteem, blaming herself for everything that had happened, including the guilt and shame she felt. She also spoke of a fear that would not go away, that nagging feeling of being unsafe, of being paralyzed by the fear of losing her job and sometimes, late on a sleepless night, the fear that she was losing her mind.

After summoning the bravery to come forward and complain, there was no apology, no offer to make things better—only the warning to shut up, knowing that the same man who caused such hurt and fear was being commended by the highest ranking bureaucrat in the Department for "his extensive knowledge [that will] advance our department efforts in areas of high priority."

Within days, someone leaked the consultant's report to the media. Some of the women also filed complaints with the province's Human Rights Commission and the RCMP.

On April 1, 2003 the Carriere scandal exploded on the front page of the Star Phoenix, after more than half a year of being kept hushed up inside the environment department. As the media and Legislature were in an uproar, the Opposition SaskParty called on the NDP to honour its own civil service zero-tolerance harassment policy and fire Carriere.

"Rather than enforce the rules, it conveys the impression that Carriere's touted political connections are covering up for him, to the detriment of women who dare to complain the government needs to explain the department's handling of this mess and the silence from the minister on a situation that's been simmering for a long time."

Star Phoenix, April, 2003

Both Premier Calvert and Public Service Minister Joanne Crofford said they first learned about the case through the media, which made sense—one employee in an office in Prince Albert was not likely to raise flags throughout government. But less credible was the deafening silence from Environment Minister Buckley Belanger. Had Belanger never been briefed by his deputy about a potentially explosive controversy within his own department involving a senior employee who happened to be Belanger's friend? Not an artful or articulate speaker at the best of times, Belanger went mute as the entire controversy was handled by the Premier and the more proficient Crofford and Justice Minister Eric Cline.

On my radio show and on coffee row across Saskatchewan people were talking of nothing else but Carriere. The next day, Crofford rose in a hushed Legislature to say that she had personally intervened and fired Carriere because the so-called discipline was not sufficient. Foretelling what was to come, she observed that the public firing could lead to a lawsuit. At this, Justice Minister Cline backed Crofford, promising to "defend vigorously" in court the government's justified termination of Carriere.

While the immediate political controversy was defused by Carriere's firing, SaskParty MLAs questioned why Carriere was still using his government car and cell phone for six months after he was suspended from his job. And there was more:

"Was Terry Scott, Deputy Minister of Environment, ordered not to fire Murdoch Carriere by someone in the NDP government or did Mr. Scott make the decision to appoint Murdoch Carriere as senior adviser to the government on his own? The Saskatchewan Party has been informed that Terry Scott has not been at work since the Murdoch Carriere scandal broke. What is the current employment status of Terry Scott? Is he currently at work in his position as deputy minister? Or has he been sent home with pay?"

Arlene Jule, SaskParty MLA, Saskatchewan Legislature, April 11, 2003

Days later, the NDP announced that Scott was leaving the civil service with full severance pay—not fired, according to Calvert, but departing by "mutual" agreement because the government's public overturning of Scott's discipline decision made it "impossible" for him to continue as a deputy minister. Neither Scott nor the NDP answered the question of what advice Scott received or who he talked to in advance of his so-called discipline of Carriere.

Within a month, Carriere would sue the government over his dismissal, launching a sequence of events that would re-ignite the controversy several years later when the NDP would mis-handle the case all over again.

By the end of 2003, the Carriere case behind them, the NDP was re-elected. Days after the election, Carriere was criminally charged and in early 2004 nine various women would share $135,000 from the province in settlement for harassment claims arising from Carriere's behaviour.

In early 2006, Carriere went to trial. He was convicted of two counts of common assault and acquitted on two charges of sexual assault. At his trial, two of his victims testified they had been groped and kissed numerous times by Carriere in the workplace. When he took the stand, Carriere defended hugging and kissing as "part of my upbringing" and testified that he must stand close to people when speaking to them because of a "hearing problem and I tend to want to get very close to them." The Judge,

in sentencing Carriere to six months probation, said he did not understand how Carriere's conduct could have gone on for as long as it did
without being detected by other supervisors.

One year later, in February 2007, a bombshell would drop and revive
the entire Carriere controversy. And the NDP would not fare well.

The Calvert government tersely announced that it had settled Carriere's employment lawsuit out of Court. In exchange for Carriere dropping
his lawsuit, the government agreed to pay him $275,000 and top-up his
pension contributions to a full 35 years of service. Dodging more questions than he answered, Environment Minister John Nilson uncomfortably
conceded that the money was payment for Carriere's long service with the
government and was "a way to have this whole thing over".

But it was far from over —at least for the political fall-out for the NDP.

Over 90 percent of lawsuits are settled out of court before reaching
trial. The opposing parties compromise for many reasons—litigation
fatigue, to save further costs, knowing one's position is vulnerable or eliminating the risk of uncertainty that comes when a case is before a judge. In
most litigation, settlements are not so much about winning or losing. It's
about making the lawsuit go away on terms the parties can live with.

But Carriere's case was not "most litigation." It was a significant public
policy line in the sand about anti-harassment policies and the treatment
of women. And the settlement didn't look much like the "vigorous" defense
earlier promised by Justice Minister Cline.

Unlike trials in open court, settlements are private. And the NDP
refused to make available the settlement agreement or any other documents related to the case, including a much-referenced legal opinion that
apparently concluded the government would lose the Carriere lawsuit
and pay dearly. A principle known as solicitor-client privilege protects all
communication between a lawyer and client, including a legal opinion
from a government lawyer in the justice department for his "client,"
the government. But this principle permits a client to waive privilege if
he chooses. The Calvert government could have made public the legal
opinion but it refused to. And, to this day it has never been released.

Later, a five-page settlement agreement with Carriere, obtained through
a Freedom of Information request made by the Leader Post, confirmed some

embarrassing facts. Despite NDP ministers repeatedly insisting that Carriere had been fired in 2003, the NDP gave this up in the settlement, agreeing in 2007 that they had not fired Carriere after all and he was merely "on leave from February, 2003."

In government, Carriere had earned about $85,000 a year. If he really was an employee all along and had been suspended for the entire four years he should have been entitled to a salary for the full period, which amounts to about $340,000. Yet, in the settlement agreement Carriere agreed to take $120,000 for severance or "payment in lieu of notice" and the remainder of the money was for "pain and suffering and damage to his reputation." Income tax is payable on severance because it is treated like income, while damages received for pain and suffering are not taxable. So, of Carriere's lump sum payment of $275,000, only $120,000 was taxable—the remaining $155,000 was a tax-free windfall.

And it didn't end there. The government agreed in the settlement document that Carriere could resign in February, 2007 "or such later date as required to ensure that he is credited with 35 years of pensionable service," so in addition to getting the large settlement payment he would start receiving a pension of $4,418 a month plus an additional $814-a-month bridge until he turned 65.

Carriere's lawyer was Geoff Dufour, a capable and at times flamboyant Saskatoon litigator —a former radio talk show host and lawyer (there are two of us around) who is now a Queens Bench Justice. Dufour strongly advanced the argument that Carriere had never been fired because he couldn't be. Saskatchewan's *Public Service Act* states that the permanent head of a department—the deputy minister—can dismiss or demote any employee in that department when the permanent head "considers it to be in the interest of the public service to do so." Dufour's argument was that when Terry Scott re-assigned and suspended Carriere he had already disciplined him and had therefore determined that firing him was "not in the interest of the public service." So later, the argument goes, when Calvert and Crofford claimed to fire Carriere it was a violation of the *Public Service Act* because it was no longer open to the government to fire Carriere. So, he was never really ever fired.

Dufour's argument was a novel one made by a capable lawyer but by no means was it conclusive. It might have persuaded a judge; it might have failed if the government had called Calvert's deputy minister, who was the *de facto* head of the public service and had actually instructed Terry Scott to fire Carriere. A judge might also have found persuasive the argument that a deputy minister is open to reconsider an earlier decision, particularly when it was unreasonable and prejudicial to the interests of the public service and made in an error of judgment.

Carriere's lawyer laid out his case in a 20-page brief of law sent to the government lawyers before the settlement was reached. And, like any good legal case, this one cited case law and had compelling facts and inferences that could be drawn to the advantage of either side. The brief, which at times became a bit overwrought, claimed that Calvert and Crofford had violated the law "inspired by a media frenzy" and the brief stretched a bit to compare their "arbitrary acts" to fraud and corruption. The brief even shared selected quotations from Thomas More's character in the 1966 movie *A Man for All Seasons*. Like I say, a bit overwrought.

Dufour put considerable weight on the fact that Carriere had been acquitted of sexual assault a year earlier in a criminal trial. To a good employment lawyer this meant little—there was no dispute that Carriere's admitted hugging, kissing, close talking and abundant evidence of inappropriate workplace conduct had more than poisoned the work environment. But apparently the department of justice thought it would not only lose the case but end up paying Carriere for the full four years' salary plus be found liable for other damages.

In public policy the Carriere case was so objectionable—so distasteful—that even if a government lawyer or outside counsel had convinced themselves that loss was an absolute certainty, it would have been better for public confidence in government and the administration of justice that a "vigorous defense" had been conducted and leave the courts to rule that an unduly restrictive interpretation of the *Public Service Act* could be used to exonerate Carriere and the boss who should have fired him outright.

At the end of the Carriere debacle, the public took away some basic messages: Carriere got away with harassing staff; the government paid $275,000 to a man who did what Carriere did while nine victims shared

$135,000. And what happens the next time a senior, politically well-connected civil servant decides to hug and kiss women and comment on their bodies? Will he be fired? For real?

For the NDP this showed, yet again, undue deference to civil servants —where were the people who should have stopped Carriere years earlier? Who allowed the deputy minister to shamelessly re-assign Carriere instead of firing him? And, who was asked to give legal advice to the government on the litigation strategy and law behind Carriere's lawyer's position that he'd never really been fired when, in fact, Carriere had been fired. And which bureaucrat ultimately convinced the Cabinet that $275,000 would "make this go away"?

Beyond this, the Carriere case struck at the NDP's core—the self-righteous view that only this left-wing party cares for women, minorities and workplace inequality. If this is how social democrats protect vulnerable employees in government from exploitation, the NDP claims no moral high ground at all. Quite the contrary.

All Rise: His Honour is Entering the Boom-Boom Room

In the spring of 2007, a sex scandal involving a Judge would hit the NDP government hard. And, like several other scandals inherited from the Romanow government—by now it should be clear that Romanow's NDP was often more lucky than competent—Calvert ended up wearing yet another embarrassment. And this one Calvert couldn't shake as the months ticked down to the 2007 election.

Sixteen years earlier, one of the NDP's first appointments to the provincial court was Terry Bekolay, Prince Albert lawyer, NDP insider and former party president. Calling Bekolay "highly qualified," Romanow's justice minister gushed that lawyers of all political stripes were "enthusiastic" about the new judge. Enthusiastic wasn't exactly the word that sprung to mind in 2007 when Bekolay's dirty little secret got out.

It was no secret that Judge Bekolay was gay, which was no big deal— lots of people are gay and it has no bearing on their careers. But the dirt involved Bekolay's bad judgment in friends and lovers.

Judge Bekolay befriended an ex-con, a master manipulator and disbarred lawyer named Michael Bomek who had been doing jail time for sex offences. Bomek is a psychopath, according to my old friend, Dennis Cann, who had prosecuted Bomek for sexually molesting 20 former clients.

Cann describes Bomek as "interested only in self-gratification. He uses people. He has no moral sense."

After being released from prison, Bomek turned to support from Prince Albert's Gay and Lesbian Health Services group where Judge Bekolay volunteered as the "P.A. contact." Bekolay took Bomek to meetings, including at the judge's home. Usually, judges are barred from even sitting on charity boards because it may give the impression that they have "taken a position" on a community issue. A judge acting as the contact for a group providing support, advocacy and information to a serious criminal just out of jail is nothing short of bizarre. Later, several provincial court judges expressed the private view that Bekolay's involvement in this group was "crazy".

Judge Bekolay would also later explain that he wanted to help the ex-con Bomek "turn things around" and Bomek would call him for coffee once or twice a month.

In the fall of 2005, Bomek hadn't been out of prison long before being arrested for selling drugs from a hotdog stand he ran in Prince Albert. When the police searched Bomek's home, they found child pornography and detailed diaries from 2003 and 2004 chronicling Bomek's exploits. As they read the diaries, astonished officers saw mention of Judge Bekolay having sex with young men at Bomek's house in a bedroom festooned with pictures of naked young men. Called the "Boom-Boom Room," this bedroom was a busy place for Bomek and young aboriginal men he'd befriended from remote Northern Saskatchewan towns.

A couple of months after police read Bomek's diaries; Judge Bekolay was quietly placed on the "unassigned" list, meaning he was still a full-fledged judge but not given any cases. He would never sit on another case. But his status was carefully kept from the public and even from other judges who knew nothing about the cloud hanging over their colleague.

Later, under oath, Bekolay would testify that Bomek gave him pictures of naked, attractive young men. One of them was a young Northern aboriginal man named "JD" who was occasionally in legal trouble. When asked about JD, Bekolay testified that he "had been intimate" with the young man.

Judge Bekolay also testified that he "may have" been at Bomek's house with JD and Bomek at the same time. Bomek's diary put it more bluntly: "JD came over and we got naked…I gave him a blow job…and then he wanted to f**k so I called the judge and then he came over and f**ked JD while I watched and kissed him."

While a judge's sexual partners are usually his own business, turn this image around—picture, for a moment, Bekolay not gay but straight, not a former NDP politico but someone more mainstream. Then imagine a male conservative judge in his late 50s having casual sex with marginalized young aboriginal women in the home of a notorious sex offender and then collecting naked pictures of these girls with the help of the same ex-con. This would have been National Enquirer worthy. TMZ would have been on the front step—or at least the Toronto Star.

Bomek was clearly trying to use his social relationship with Bekolay to influence the judge. There was no evidence Bekolay was ever influenced, but Bomek was charged and convicted of attempting to obstruct justice.

During the police investigation, officers asked pointed questions about Bekolay's relationships with various people to determine if he may have been involved in criminal wrongdoing. The provincial justice department referred the investigation to Alberta Justice which recommended no criminal charges against Bekolay but suggested a misconduct complaint be filed with the Saskatchewan Judicial Council, the self-regulating body that investigates judges' misbehaviour.

When Sask Justice filed the complaint against Bekolay in mid-June, 2006, they used the misleading term "conflict of interest" to describe his activities rather than "conduct unbecoming" or something more descriptive. Four months later the Judicial Council suspended Bekolay with full pay and benefits, the first Saskatchewan judge suspended in 11 years.

Elsewhere, when a judge is accused of making inappropriate comments from the bench or crusading for an issue in his private life or even being accused of a criminal offence, a summary of the details is provided. But in Bekolay's case, the Judicial Council kept a cone of silence over the case, not even revealing the nature of the so-called "conflict."

By May 2007 the Judicial Council announced that it was bringing the complaint against Bekolay to a hearing committee which would have resulted in publicity. Only then did the case get attention in the media and the Saskatchewan Legislature. But still the public knew nothing about the details of the case. It was also revealed that for nearly 18 months, at a salary of $195,000 a year, Judge Bekolay had been paid a lot of money to do nothing—over $275,000 worth of nothing.

As the firestorm continued, on May 18, 2007 the 60-year-old Bekolay abruptly resigned, citing "a professionally-documented medical issue" that he never identified. With his quitting, Bekolay's case was closed. The former NDP party president called the decision to appoint a hearing committee "precipitous" and he argued that his case had been "inappropriately elevated to a level of public profile and discussion" and should have been treated privately as a personal medical condition.

Choosing to have a social relationship with a notorious criminal and have sex at Bomek's home brought this judge's credibility past the point of repair and into the realm of conduct unbecoming of a judge. In addition, Bekolay's abominably bad judgment reflected poorly on a guy paid to have good judgment in upholding our laws and dispensing justice. Without integrity and good reputations our judges have nothing.
A high standard of personal conduct is expected of judges both on and off the bench. They must avoid conduct that is unbecoming.

Bekolay's bad choices and poor judgment reflected, too, on the people who thought him good enough to sit on the bench in the first place. But those people had moved on—a different NDP government in a different time. The only NDPers around to take the fall were the Calvert government, which shuffled uncomfortably and powerlessly on the sidelines as the Bekolay circus played out.

The reverberations were heard well beyond the Boom-Boom Room.

The NDP Caucus Fraud Cover-Up

The NDP's last great scandal of the Calvert years was actually its first, having happened 15 years earlier following the election of the Romanow government. A crime had occurred in 1992 which was concealed for years by NDP insiders in a carefully-engineered cover-up. And it would erupt during the dying days of the Calvert government in 2007, as one of the last gasps of a government running out of air.

Like so many serious scandals, it wasn't the original act so much as its cover-up that cost two prominent New Democrats their jobs and caused the Calvert government a world of political hurt.

Known as the NDP Caucus Fraud Cover-up scandal, the original story was straightforward. In 1992, the NDP caucus office hired a new director of administration named Ann Lord—or at least that was one of her aliases. She'd also been known as Ann Davey and was a convicted thief and embezzler wanted by police in Canada and the U.S. Not surprisingly, she didn't mention any of this to the NDP and they didn't check out her background.

Within a few months, the con artist altered cheques, stole $5,900 of taxpayers' money and skipped town. Lord left behind a detailed confession letter—addressed to NDP Chief of Staff Jim Fodey and the Caucus Chair, MLA Glenn Hagel—in which she admitted the theft, explained how she did it, asked for forgiveness and implored the NDP not to tell anyone. And they didn't.

Neither Fodey nor Hagel reported the theft to the police. In fact, efforts were made to actively conceal the theft from inquiring police officers. Fodey later lied to the Leader Post when asked about the case, saying that Lord had not left under "mysterious circumstances" and an audit "turned up no evidence of wrongdoing." When another employee found the Lord confession letter in a file, Fodey swore the staffer to secrecy.

....

"In 1992 a veil of secrecy and deception was cast over the Ann Lord theft mainly by Mr. Fodey but assisted in part by Mr. Hagel. Mr. Fodey misled the Regina Police Service as to the correct state of financial affairs related to the departure of Ann Lord. He asked an NDP caucus employee to keep secret the existence of the Ann Lord Confession Letter. He misled the press regarding the true facts surrounding the Ann Lord departure. Mr. Hagel played no active role in Mr. Fodey's actions, although at the NDP General Caucus meeting in 1992 he reported that "Ann Lord resigned," a factually inaccurate description . Further, he took no steps to correct the inaccuracies given by Jim Fodey to the press."

Gerald Gerrand, Conflict of Interest Commissioner, 2008

....

Fifteen years later, in 2007, a copy of Fodey's personal file on Ann Lord would surface along with police reports from the early 1990s. What they revealed was an old fashioned political scandal: someone inside the NDP Caucus had covered up the fraud and likely obstructed a police investigation.

The leaked documents, in a brown envelope, were left in the mailbox of a SaskParty staffer in 2006 and held for a year, obviously to maximize impact when they were revealed during an election year. Although the documents revealed the NDP fraud years earlier and the subsequent cover-up, they didn't suggest a theory for why the cover-up took place. They didn't have to. The timing spoke for itself.

For decades, the NDP's constant claim of moral superiority came from depicting themselves as having higher standards of integrity and honesty than their opponents who are usually portrayed as less moral, always with a hidden agenda and even being dishonest or crooked. Of course, this is part of the NDP mythology—their party and its supporters are no better or worse than anyone else in public life. But, in the early 1990s, the NDP hit the motherlode of all self-righteousness when some of their opponents actually turned out to be corrupt.

Just before the 1991 election, which defeated the Grant Devine Progressive Conservatives and swept in the Roy Romanow NDP, the RCMP began investigating questionable transactions inside the Conservative government caucus office. By the time the dust settled on "Operation Fiddle" several years later, 12 former Tory MLAs and two staff members had either been convicted or pleaded guilty to fraud offences related to the misuse of communications and expense allowances.

In 1992, just as the NDP was hiring Ann Lord, the political buzz was intensifying around the Legislature as staff gossiped about the RCMP investigating the Tories—Mounties were interviewing former MLAs and asking tough questions; bank records and safety deposit boxes revealed strange transactions involving Tory staff and $1,000 bills; and the Legislature's financial services office was untangling a confusing web of fraudulent transactions.

This was the climate—a political fraud scandal was enveloping the former government of the NDP's arch enemy Grant Devine and all the NDP had to do was stand back and watch the explosion.

But as bad luck would have it, the NDP had a fraud of its own going on with Ann Lord forging cheques, ripping off the party and skipping town. With the focus on their opponents, the NDP seemingly didn't want their

"Oh, what a tangled web we weave when first we practice to deceive."

Sir Walter Scott (the novelist and poet,
not our first Premier)

own dirty laundry aired. So, the theft was concealed from the police and the media was lied to.

With hindsight, the NDP's mistake in hiring a thief and the relatively small theft of $6,000 of public money paled in comparison to the scandal sweeping up the Devine Tories, which ultimately involved over $800,000 of taxpayers' money.

But for reasons of timing—not to mention pride in being the noble, virtuous and self-righteous party—NDP apparatchik and lifetime loyalist Jim Fodey and others in the party couldn't let it be known that their party had ever been involved in fraud or theft. But like most deceptions, the harder and longer someone tries to conceal them, the more they hurt when they surface, as they inevitably do.

When the SaskParty went public in April, 2007 with the leaked documents, a firestorm of controversy threatened to consume what was left of the Calvert government's public credibility. Just weeks earlier, the government had been mercilessly pounded over agreeing to pay out Murdoch Carriere $275,000 and a published public opinion poll had the NDP more than 20 points behind the SaskParty. And now this.

Most damning in the police reports was the revelation that Fodey in 1992 led the police to believe that there were no financial problems in the Caucus office following Lord's departure. And, a police report from 1994 revealed that NDP MLA Pat Lorje had gone to the police to talk about the Lord case two years later and, in the words of the police incident report, "Lorje advised that it was the intention of caucus to conceal the fact that Lord had committed the fraud."

There was no explanation by the Regina Police Service why charges were not later pursued against Lord—presumably as she had already been extradited to the U.S. to face 85 federal charges in the American courts, there was likely no point. The police also never explained, either in their files or subsequently, if steps were taken to investigate Fodey or anyone else on suspicion of obstruction of justice for misleading the police in 1992.

As the scandal consumed the Saskatchewan Legislature, the opposition kept hammering on several fronts: why hadn't charges been laid against Ann Lord; why wasn't Fodey, who had misled the police and media (and was still in 2007 the NDP's caucus chief of staff) criminally charged or at least fired; what role had Glenn Hagel—caucus chair in 1992 and still in Cabinet in 2007—played in the cover-up; and, the seminal question in every cover-up scandal "who knew what, when?"

Compounding this, questions swirled over Lorje's 1994 statement about the "intention of caucus to conceal." As 12 members of Calvert's caucus, including him, had also been in the 1992 caucus, allegations flew. Then the demands began for a public inquiry and a police investigation. In spin and timing, the Calvert government had lost any opportunity to control this scandal. And when that happens, a scandal tends to take on a life of its own.

A flustered Hagel told the Legislature that Lord's confession letter had been turned over to the police in 1992. The next day, Regina Chief of Police Cal Johnston called a news conference to say that wasn't true. The NDP's chief of staff, Fodey, then resigned and Hagel made a statement "clarifying" that he had based his comments on what Fodey told him. Under siege from the opposition to fire Hagel from Cabinet, Calvert refused. But he did refer the matter to the Legislature's conflict of interest commissioner to investigate, which meant that nothing would be received or publicly re-played until after an election which Calvert was expected to call within six months.

As the daily grilling moved into a second week, several seasoned NDP veterans well acquainted with attack politics launched a counter-offensive to try turning the scandal back on the SaskParty. The NDP accused the critics of being opportunists by holding on to the leaked files for a year before going public. Perhaps, but it didn't make the NDP fraud cover-up any less serious. The NDP's Pat Atkinson bloviated that the opposition members with the police files were guilty of possessing stolen property and were breaking the law. Debatable—but it didn't change what was in the files.

By mid-May, three weeks into the scandal, the Regina Police Service announced it had asked the RCMP to investigate the entire matter because questions had been raised about the adequacy of the original RPS investigations in the early 1990s and the RCMP would bring "independent oversight". With this, Hagel finally announced he was resigning from Cabinet, saying that because "important matters of integrity and honesty" were being investigated, he would step aside while the investigation was proceeding.

Like the report of the conflicts commissioner, nothing would be known about the RCMP investigation until after the 2007 election, which resulted in the defeat of the Calvert government. Glenn Hagel lost his Moose Jaw seat in the election but wouldn't stay away from public life for long—he was elected as Mayor of Moose Jaw in 2009.

Jim Fodey—the disgraced NDP insider caught lying to the media and misleading the police—was paid an undisclosed severance settlement by the NDP for his "resignation" in the midst of the scandal. Only later, it would be discovered that Fodey's payout was $130,000, not of NDP donors' funds but of taxpayers' money.

Today, Fodey continues to be actively involved in Saskatchewan politics as an enthusiastic supporter of NDP leader Dwain Lingenfelter and a scathing critic of both the Brad Wall and Stephen Harper governments. Fodey operates in relative anonymity on the Internet, using the pseudonym "Leftdog" and frequently posting comments on political blogs.

In early 2008, after being sent by the RCMP for an independent review by Alberta prosecutors, the recommendation was made not to criminally charge anyone involved in either the NDP caucus fraud or its cover-up—not Fodey, Hagel or even Ann Lord whose detailed confession letter would make a conviction a slam dunk. By this time, with nearly 16 years having elapsed and witnesses' recollections foggy and Lord long gone, the case did not meet what's known as the "prosecutorial standard" of whether charges would be in the public interest and whether a conviction would be likely.

Later in 2008, the final chapter was written by Saskatchewan Conflict Commissioner Gerald Gerrand, whose 50-page report carefully reconstructed the facts of the case. The report was critical of Fodey and concluded that Hagel "played no active role" in the deception but did cause the Legislature to be misled when he said the Lord letter had been turned over the police in 1992 when it had not.

Gerrand put it well in his conclusion that this "sad tale of theft would have been long forgotten if those that learned of it had dealt with it in an honest, straightforward and transparent matter. No one was to blame for the theft except Ann Lord. Regrettably, those that first learned of it chose to deceive and mislead others about the theft for misguided political objectives."

The Tradition Continues

The NDP was not the first government in Saskatchewan to be rocked by scandal but it certainly was the most scandal-prone in history, with nearly a dozen major scandals tarnishing the government in less than a decade. Other governments have had significant scandals but no government in Saskatchewan history has equalled the sheer number of scandals during the Calvert years.

In virtually every case, a mistake was made that was not fatal had the government moved quickly to correct the error, come clean and set the record straight. But with the Romanow and later Calvert NDP, there was a hard-wired resistance to admit wrongdoing, which then led to delays, cover-ups and attempts to deny, minimize and deflect both the problem and responsibility for it. Laced with a good dose of arrogance, many of the NDP scandals involved public figures either incapable or unwilling to admit their mistakes. And it is telling how these NDP politicos viewed the important trust relationship with voters.

In 2009, just weeks before the NDP leadership convention to replace Calvert, staff at NDP headquarters noticed that 1,100 memberships submitted by the campaign of Dwain Lingenfelter looked irregular—they were in similar handwriting and many had the same mailing address. It was discovered that these memberships, which had been filled out in the names of people who were unaware of what was happening, originated from two First Nations in the Meadow Lake area.

Claiming no personal knowledge and attributing it to an "overzealous" campaign volunteer, Lingenfelter and his campaign team deflected responsibility. Later, the campaign volunteer, Ernie Morin, a former president of the Saskatchewan Aboriginal New Democrats was criminally charged with fraud. At least one high ranking New Democrat, Deb McDonald, who was the NDP's provincial secretary at the time, believes that Morin did not act alone and that those with knowledge of the fraud will be revealed.

Lessons learned from a generation of earlier scandals? It seems not.

Chapter 8

THE SANCTION OF THE VICTIM: COURAGE, CAPITULATION AND SOME WEASELS IN SASKATCHEWAN BUSINESS

"I saw that there comes a point, in the defeat of any man of virtue, when his own consent is needed for evil to win—and that no manner of injury done to him by others can succeed if he chooses to withhold his consent. I saw that I could put an end to your outrages by pronouncing a single word in my mind.

I pronounced it.

The word was 'No'."

Ayn Rand, Atlas Shrugged

For a political movement like the NDP to have flourished for more than 80 years, it needs a strong, organized and positive base, which it's always had in its supporters. But never far beneath the surface, there's a negative aspect that keeps the NDP well entrenched—businesspeople, those most apt to be victimized by socialism, are generally unwilling to do anything to stop their own oppression.

In my hometown, we had the same NDP MLA for nearly 30 years—a large, loud and imposing figure who won seven straight elections. Eiling Kramer began life as a farm boy and paid CCF organizer in the 1940s, started a small auction business and then became an MLA and later multi-millionaire whose auctioneering company flourished. A big guy with an imposing presence and a huge cowboy hat, he'd walk down the street sounding like Foghorn Leghorn on Bugs Bunny—"I say, I say, boy." And he never forgot a name.

A particular trick of Kramer's—especially when the NDP was under siege and voters were becoming angry—was to visit local businesspeople who'd decided to take a stand against the government. He'd remind them that he controlled 2,000 unionized workers at a nearby mental hospital and if local NDP-friendly civil servants and unions caught wind of what was going on, "they might just put you out of business." That usually quelled dissent pretty quickly.

The occasional businessman—back in those days most were "men" — would tell the bullying Kramer where he could stick his unions and NDP. Oddly, these people flourished. But in my town they were brave and few.

The true irony occurred to me while in high school when I was starting to figure out politics. As Kramer's popular auction business grew, right-wing-ers and pro-businesspeople would flock to his farm sales by the thousands. I wondered aloud that if everyone who didn't vote NDP (at least half the population) decided to vote with their feet and chose to stay away from Kramer's auctions and told everyone else to, sale attendance would drop, farmers would stop using him and he would soon be put out of business. But I was told "we don't do things that way here." Hey, I was just a kid. What did I know about politics anyway?

If you are in business you may want to put this book down, now. Or jump ahead, because I'm about to offend you. The most mysterious and frustrating aspect of Saskatchewan politics— incomprehensible, really—is how the same self-reliant, courageous and smart people in business can be so naïve, clueless and obtuse when it comes to politics. And that bothers me because I truly like everything about business people—even when they behave like idiots.

Most business people I know are innovative and hardworking, resilient and adaptive. Their businesses are their lives. Everything is on the line, including their life savings, their home and their car. And they get paid only after all their employees, bills and taxes are paid. There's freedom and independence but also bone-wearying work and the fear of not making it. Saskatchewan businesses, large and small, donate millions of dollars to charity every month, countless hours to improving communities and generate millions of dollars in taxes and economic activity that ultimately benefits government.

But Saskatchewan, under generations of NDP governments, has been the one Canadian province that historically creates tax policy, labour laws, business regulations and government policy to make it really tough to succeed in business. Even more oddly, time after time, when years become generations, businesspeople have consistently permitted the NDP to victimize them, actually allowing an anti-business political party to pass laws that make doing business more difficult.

The NDP knows who its friends are and, in good strategic fashion, always plays to its strengths: trade unions, social activists, Crown employees and the so-called MUSH sector—municipalities, universities, schools and hospitals. People in business are not typically NDP supporters.

Inside the NDP and in the inner narrative of modern socialism there's a clear view of private business: it exploits people in the pursuit of profits and business is all about greed. Even a cursory glance at the NDP's *Commonwealth* magazine offers up plenty of this. And, still on the NDP website today, is the party's founding document, the *Regina Manifesto*, which promises to "eradicate capitalism". (I've always wondered how you do this without eradicating *capitalists*.)

The NDP View of Business & Business People
If you're in business you probably:

(a) Exploit workers;

(b) Greedily pursue profits;

(c) Do not pay enough taxes

(d) Hurt or at least ignore the poor and marginalized; and

(e) Need to be controlled and managed by government because,
if unsupervised, you will cause more harm.

During the 2003 election, a letter from Premier Lorne Calvert to every NDP member in the province implored them to donate money and stop the Saskatchewan Party from allowing the business community "to take over the most profitable part of the Saskatchewan economy."

Back in the early 1980s, I worked with a guy active in Saskatchewan's Young New Democrats (SYND). His big brother was a well known union lawyer and NDP advisor since appointed a Provincial court judge. My buddy came back from a SYND meeting, giddy about a speech by Roy Romanow, who'd lost his seat a year earlier in the Grant Devine sweep. Mocking Devine's "open for business slogan," Romanow called it "bend over for business." The left-wing kids loved it. And this was the same Romanow that many business people still fawningly refer to as the "business-friendly NDPer."

If business people are systematically singled out for criticism by NDP partisans and governments, why don't they push back? Or at least, why don't they stop giving the sanction of the victim to their own oppression? Because many of them are chickens, that's why. Worse, still, some are weasels.

Businesspeople should consider this scenario: if someone regularly insulted you, your beliefs and your family members, how would you deal with them? Would you face them, challenge them and tell them to change their behaviour? Or, would you sit, helpless like a prisoner silently staring at your feet, hoping your jailer won't return and do worse things?

There are generally four reasons that Saskatchewan business people are reluctant to stand up. First, they directly rely on the government for business —and as the NDP is usually in government —best not offend those who govern; second, they've been threatened that if they want government business in future they'd best tow the party line or at least stay silent with their heads down; third, they fear NDP customers will stop shopping with them; and fourth, they fear political interference in certain government regulations or laws they must follow. There's a lot of fear going on here—largely baseless fear, but the kind of stuff that makes many people chicken.

It is rare when the business community rises up as one, which it did in 2004 when the NDP proclaimed the Most Available Hours law. Finally, the proposal was yanked entirely when the Calvert government faced scalding anger and all-out resistance from the business community. But Calvert had merely proclaimed a law passed 10 years earlier by Premier Romanow and Deputy Premier Dwain Lingenfelter. Where were the demonstrations on the streets then?

Yet in Saskatchewan—unlike any other place in Canada I've ever seen or lived in—many business people, afraid to stare down those acting against their interests and insulting them, dutifully line up to plunk down money to buy NDP dinner and golf tournament tickets, so the NDP can raise more money to continue belittling business.

I've seen the enemy and it is us. The cost of capitulation by business is to reward the negative behaviour of the bully, which gives him permission to continue pushing people around. It also allows hard-core NDP partisans to think they're keeping business in line. And it reinforces the belief inside the NDP brain trust that businesspeople are chumps who can be easily controlled.

For some in the business community who have put up with this for years it is a demeaning ritual like domestic violence—a cycle of abuse built on power and control, forgiveness, apology, the make-up, but then the inevitable repetition, co-dependency, enabling and the cycle repeats itself. The only way to stop the cycle is to stop the abuser. For good.

Rolling Over for Socialism: Business People Who Just Don't Get It

From chambers of commerce to various industry groups, there are many dedicated and smart people with hearts and heads in the right place advocating for business. But others in business leadership—pontificating on philosophy, writing windy position papers and secure in the lofty sense that they're being taken seriously by NDP governments—are humoured, condescended to and even chuckled at behind closed doors by mainstream NDP politicians and campaign strategists who listen attentively and then do whatever they please, usually not in the best interests of business.

For many on the left, the words "chamber of commerce" are code for greedy and simplistic business boosters who just don't get it—pejoratively chucked out the same way right-wingers refer to radical socialists as the "Birkenstock Crowd."

Remember the "WWJD" bracelets, the ones asking "what would Jesus do?" Businesspeople trying to get their message out should always think "WWLD" – what would labour do? The Saskatchewan Federation of Labour (SFL) and its hundreds of affiliated union locals stands for nothing more than always advancing the cause of trade unions. Sure, the SFL sometimes gets loopy on far left causes and can be downright rude and disrespectful to those who disagree with it, but generally labour has been the most effective lobbying force in the history of Saskatchewan.

Unions look out for their own pro-labour causes. But they also let it be known that consequences follow. Union dues, in the millions of dollars, are funneled to provincial and local NDP campaigns; unions send in full-time paid staff from Saskatchewan and around Canada to run local NDP election campaigns; union members take paid training in political organizing; and, during elections, unions run parallel information and disinformation campaigns designed to help the NDP and undermine their opponents.

This is not to suggest that business should be allied with the SaskParty or any political party. Nor should it be officially opposed, hostile or as openly abusive to the NDP as labour is to non-NDP governments. But standing up, in a tough and uncompromising way, for the principles of business is just common sense. So is backing policy choices that encourage investment and allow jobs and businesses to flourish. It is also simple survival to steer clear of political philosophies that can hurt you. And if they're destructive enough, it makes sense to stop them.

For business, it should be simple to never tolerate or accept political parties that do not accommodate you—actively support the party that supports you and furthers your agenda. Yet business lobby groups take great pride, in fact they fall over themselves, proclaiming that they are "fair" and "non-partisan."

In this respect, they are victims of their own generosity and naiveté. The modern left often leverages our virtues against us. Many businesspeople were raised to be tolerant, inclusive and fair. And this is used against them, with a vengeance by the NDP and proxies of the left.

Business groups say they welcome members of all political stripes. Fine. But do these business groups have a set of non-negotiable core values they stand for? And do these values define their membership, even to the point of making people of "some political stripes" understandably uncomfortable? When active members of the left and the NDP sign up in business groups, preying on business' sense of fair play, they should get a message, conveyed clearly and respectfully: you are welcome here but if you come from a philosophic or partisan world that approves of taxing, over-regulating and insulting business, you're not going to feel very comfortable with us.

Principled and committed organizations should not be about appeasing the fringes of their membership; these groups must commit to serving their objectives and goals.

> "It's a truism of life that any organization that is not genuinely defined by a clear set values and principles—from churches to senior citizens groups—will ultimately be taken over by left-wing loons."
>
> *Ann Coulter, American Conservative commentator*

Going back to "what would labour do," I challenge businesspeople to imagine the scenario of a young woman in her first job, a unionized position, and she gets elected to the local union executive because she wants to be active in workplace issues. But she comes from a family that owns a business; she is pro-free enterprise and a young capitalist.

She attends her first union local executive meeting and hears about the evils of capitalism, the inequities of wealth creation, the dishonesty and greed of businesspeople, the exploitation of the vulnerable by business and the "fact" that management is only out to screw every employee. To top it off, the union executive is passing resolutions confirming these views and sending them off to a regional union conference and to city hall to object to new businesses setting up in a big box centre.

As a member of the executive that passes these resolutions—our young friend objects or abstains—she is then asked to sign her name to the resolutions because they are the "view of the union executive." As she drives home from that first meeting, the young woman thinks "Wow, I'm not welcome here—better look for something else to get involved in." I challenge any business group to ask if this is how some of their members from the political left feel after a meeting where pro-business objectives are being discussed.

Recently, a group of young Saskatchewan professionals and business people, 600 strong, who are often dismissed publicly by the NDP as a shill for the SaskParty, elected to their board of directors a partisan NDP university professor, quite open with his radical left-wing views and his support for the NDP. Some members of this business organization thought it was "fair" to put him on the board. It would show they were balanced. Then he began suggesting projects unrelated to the founding principles of the group and even had some ideas to start going after the Wall government. Then, as some of the business club members began to question what went wrong, I wondered is naiveté contagious in business these days?

There are a few in the business community, not socialists by any measure, who get ugly fast when non-NDP governments are elected because these business types have prospered under the NDP and expect to continue running the show. While fairly clever and versed in business, these people become big fish fast in the tiny NDP business pond because they wield great influence in governments run by union leaders, teachers, ex-civil servants and United Church ministers. When a more pro-business government arrives and brings in professionals and advisors from boardrooms and large consulting companies, these NDP-linked Saskatchewan business sorts are no longer the prettiest girl at the dance. And they get nasty, especially when the new government doesn't do exactly what they demand.

One well-known Regina businessman comes immediately to mind, after pouting within weeks of the Wall government being elected because the premier and his staff weren't making time for this egomaniac to have personal audiences with Wall to "explain" things to the new premier. Upset that the new government undid certain of his pet NDP projects, this whining quisling holds court for all within earshot to deride Wall, his advisors and anyone associated with the government. As the NDP's designated little pet capitalist, this guy won't rest until the NDP is back—at least they return his calls and fawn over him.

For some business people in Saskatchewan—having spent generations under the thumb of NDP governments and living in fear of angering the NDP ruling class—they have turned into Stockholm Syndrome sufferers who have grown quite fond of the people holding them hostage. At the lowest end of the scale, some businesspeople and their organizations have even become duplicitous weasels contributing to the problem.

A business group in Saskatoon called the North Saskatoon Business Association (NSBA) took weasel-ness to new heights in recent years. Just months after moving to Alberta to become a junior executive and lobbyist in an oil company, former NDP Deputy Premier Dwain Lingenfelter was invited by the NSBA to participate in a roast. Mocking "lefties" and describing Premier Calvert and NDP MLA Pat Atkinson as "redder than a baboon's ass," Lingenfelter portrayed himself as the newfound Alberta right-winger. A few years later, he spoke again to the NSBA, talking up free enterprise, passionately supporting nuclear power and again joking about the left-wingers in the Saskatchewan NDP.

From Lingenfelter's performance came a gushing comment from a businessman in the crowd who cooed "gee, Dwain, you should come back and be our premier," which was exactly what Lingenfelter was planning, as his leadership ambitions were never exactly a well kept secret. At this, reasonable people could be forgiven for asking "is this the same Lingenfelter who supported and still defends the NDP's expropriation of the potash industry in the 1970s, agreed with the land bank program, regrets that SaskOil was ever privatized and was involved in both the Channel Lake and Spudco scandals? And a business person wants this guy as premier?

Ironically, NSBA—which was established in the 1980s as a breakaway group from the Saskatoon Chamber of Commerce, which it regarded as too timid, self-absorbed and unprepared to push government—wasn't finished with Lingenfelter yet. The NSBA's Shirley Ryan—a delightful woman who is a scrappy and outspoken advocate of all things pro-business and claims privately to be a right-winger—developed an odd affection for Lingenfelter and had him back for a third speaking engagement following the election of the SaskParty Wall government.

As Lingenfelter was to speak on "powering up Saskatchewan," I pointed out his long pedigree of radical left-wing and interventionist NDP policies. And I wondered how this 1970s-era socialist had become the darling of the ever-gullible business community. I also questioned if somewhere in the uranium capital of North America (Saskatoon) there might actually exist someone with direct knowledge of nuclear power development, something Lingenfelter notably lacked. I suggested, with Lingenfelter chomping at the bit for a return to NDP politics, that the NSBA and its business members didn't have to be rude; they just had to be principled and take a pass on this wannabe left-wing politician.

Later, an NSBA board member—a guy I've known since childhood who has grown a huge and successful business—dismissed my criticism, saying "having Lingenfelter speak means the SaskParty will have good competition. It makes everyone in politics better if we have strong parties, including a stronger NDP." This struck me as odd. The NDP has never had a problem with not being strong, least of all when it comes to smacking around business. And, just seven months after the NDP had been defeated; here was a businessman on the board of a business advocacy group doing his best to prop up the NDP. It told me all I needed to know about the sad state of the NSBA.

It should be pointed out, in fairness, that the guy lecturing me on politics was not Greg Trew, who also sat on the NSBA board of directors. A private industrial relations consultant, for years Trew was a hard-core NDP supporter who worked for SEIU, the powerful international health care union which is one of the NDP's strongest proxies. His cousin is NDP MLA Kim Trew. He seems to fit in so well in the NSBA and its values.

How Politics Works for Business

The concepts of "support" and "not support" often have to be explained to business people, who are otherwise pretty bright but when it comes to politics, not so much.

Supporting does not mean merely giving a cheque to a party or saying "I'll vote for you." And, of course, many businesspeople do the notorious "I can't really work for you but I'll be an advisor and phone you with advice and ideas." Oh, great—phoning with "advice" is cheap, lazy and actually makes you a pest, not an advisor. And none of these things wins elections.

Nor does "not support" mean merely not voting for someone.

Let's play a game. Think of a party that denigrates business and makes policy decisions hostile to their interests. Let's call them the NDP. Then, imagine a party more supportive of business principles and creates a better environment for business. Let's call them the SaskParty.

Using the model of organized labour, businesspeople would not give the NDP a free pass and would, in fact, up the ante. A unified and cohesive force from business would dramatically outspend those who support the NDP, like organized labour.

Employees of businesses would be freed up—with pay—during elections to work on local SaskParty campaigns, in campaign offices, on the streets knocking doors, on sign crews, on phone banks and working computer data systems for voter tracking and ID. The business owners themselves who couldn't do this kind of "hands-on" work (after all, they have a business to run) would help recruit and pay for out-of-province political consultants and campaign workers to come into individual ridings and to work in the provincial war-room. Some of these hired political strategists and workers—paid by businesses—would shore up vulnerable SaskParty campaigns. Others would be sent into NDP seats to specifically target sitting NDP MLAs and Cabinet ministers who are not accommodating business. This is simply all that labour has done for years in Saskatchewan as standard operating procedure.

Yet, many in the business community express great surprise when this is explained to them. They believe, as their grandparents did in the 1960s, that dutifully cutting a cheque to a candidate and paying chamber of commerce dues will actually get business the political respect and the results it deserves. It won't.

When it comes to the hands-on political strategy used by organized labour, virtually every business advocacy group recoils in horror "we can't get directly involved in elections. We have members from every political party—we don't do campaigns."

This is not to suggest that chambers of commerce start waging campaign wars but there are ways that business people and their groups can become involved in separate, politically active organizations that actually insert themselves into election campaigns. But the high-minded and naïve people who typically run business advocacy groups think this is "icky stuff," beneath them and not their "job." Fine. But don't complain when things don't work out to the benefit of business and, as usual with the NDP, organized labour gets its agenda answered because it actually affects the outcomes of elections while businesspeople don't.

For years in Saskatchewan, arguably the most effective and outspoken business lobby group—and the one that initiated the province-wide resistance to the NDP's Most Available Hours law—is the Canadian Federation of Independent Business (CFIB). Staunchly pro-free enterprise and not prepared to back down from NDP governments, this group has often been alone in using labour-like focus on maintaining the objectives and goals of small business.

Recently the Saskatchewan Chamber of Commerce became more involved at an activist level on tax policy, deregulation and nuclear power. But, even as it initiated a strong and convincing campaign to promote nuclear development, the chamber and its own business members were completely out flanked by anti-nukes who raised Hell on coffee row and at public meetings while chamber people stayed home.

When nuclear power was shelved, as I predicted it would be, part of the reason was the perception that 80% of Saskatchewan people were strongly opposed to nuclear development. Of course this is not correct— usually about 60% of people favour nuclear power. But 80% of all public feedback was passionately and loudly opposed to nuclear development because anti-nukes work harder than those who support the industry.

Inexplicably, the nuclear industry itself sat on its hands as did the organized business community which thinks that filing a brief and appearing at a hearing is what it takes. Business organizations and their members were nowhere to be seen or heard in letters to the editor, calls to talk shows and playing a noisy and direct role in shaping public opinion, as the anti-nukes did. Even as public hearings began, with the same travelling groups of anti-nukes attending every meeting, I desperately searched for the flash teams of business people using hired students and proxies reiterating at every meeting the same points they had the night before. Nothing. In Saskatchewan, it always seems to happen this way.

Just like the business community's weak understanding of how election campaigns work, an odd dichotomy exists in how some businesspeople deal with governments that are on their side. They often behave badly.

Almost as if to atone for their appeasement and collaboration with NDP governments which play on their fears and intimidate them, many Saskatchewan businesspeople do the opposite with pro-business governments. Brimming with confidence, comfort and high expectations, within weeks of the election of a new government, some in the business community waste little time in publicly criticizing the government they supported for not going far enough to sell-off Crown corporations, fire civil servants en masse and do things that moderate free enterprise governments aren't going to do.

Because, under NDP governments, business people are usually playing defense—reacting, deflecting and minimizing harm—their standard approach toward government tends to be negative and critical. But when a government more sympathetic to them arrives, they demand, expect and have little appreciation for how the process of government works, how legislation is made, how regulations are promulgated and how gradual change moves throughout the civil service and into practice.

Business people are notoriously bad at politics for the same reason they're good at business. Politics takes patience, team work, slowly advancing new concepts, gradually telling everyone the plan and incrementally introducing change through dozens of people who must eventually buy-in for the success of the project. Self-employed business owners, on the other hand, are decisive, fast, and flexible and always want to be the boss—what they say goes. These skills are great for moving a small business into a larger one; they don't work in government—never have and never will.

Knowing this, and having seen it in my short federal political career, I bumped into a highly placed political advisor in the Brad Wall government just weeks after their election and asked how it was going. As he explained the transition (proceeding as expected), he shrugged and said, "it's our friends that are killing us—they complain, they're demanding, they want stuff, they're impatient and they don't understand that this ship doesn't turn on a dime." I felt sorry for him but it's an age-old Achilles' heel of business people—not knowing how to get effective results from friendly governments.

It wouldn't hurt business people to remember how they live their own lives: you don't discipline an employee in front of others. Nor do you publicly chide those you get along with. Generally, criticism of a friend is better done in private. Even though you have issues, you're still friends.

> "The person who agrees with you 80 percent of the time is a friend and ally—not a 20 percent traitor."
>
> *Former U.S. President Ronald Reagan*

It's so rare that Saskatchewan elects business-friendly, non-NDP governments that neither a new government nor the business community knows the dance steps. As the business community ratchets up the complaining, the government gets defensive and this filters down to average citizens. A sharp and aggressive NDP opposition usually takes business complaining and puts out the message that if the government can't even do the right thing for its friends in the "chamber of commerce" (remember the NDP code), then clearly it's a government that cannot do right by the average Saskatchewanian.

Hey, Buddy, Can You Spare a Job?

So, where is the best place for NDPers to work when they're done with politics? Most elected people, particularly those with Cabinet experience, are well qualified to give advice on government relations, lobbying and—if they're reasonably sagacious—strategy and planning. But can they, in good conscience being socialists, take a dollar—or usually a whole bunch of them—from capitalists?

Logically, given the non-business background of most NDPers and their skepticism if not open hostility to business and profit, there are areas well suited to them—jobs in unions, churches, community organizations, in the health and education sectors and in left-wing think tanks.

Universities are always fertile ground for socialists: Premier Calvert, with two bachelor's degrees, rates a principalship at St. Andrews College at the University of Saskatchewan. Another United Church minister and defeated NDP Cabinet minister, Mark Wartman, was hired by the U of S as a fundraiser in the college of agriculture.

But for reasons that confound, some Saskatchewan business people actually reach out to socialists and offer them jobs. Sure, the money is way better in capitalism. But if you believe, as I do, that life's choices have consequences, obviously a consequence of being a socialist who criticizes free enterprise is that you won't eventually end up collecting a pay cheque from a free-enterprise business. In cases where NDP governments are in power, high-ranking former NDPers can help open doors. But when the NDP is out of office, it's difficult to understand the appeal of a socialist in business.

A good example is Eric Cline, a Romanow and Calvert-era Cabinet minister, who is a lawyer by training and a clever and affable guy but an often hyper-partisan NDPer in public debate during his political career. In the Legislature, Cline was strongly critical of attempts by the business community to bring balance to Saskatchewan's notoriously pro-union labour laws. In 2003, he suggested that changes would remove protection of employees from unfair treatment; take away health and safety provisions; scrap overtime; and even lower the minimum wage. All scary, reactionary and entirely made up stuff.

So after leaving NDP politics, Cline was hired as vice-president corporate affairs with Shore Gold, a mining company controlled by one of Saskatchewan's most pro-free enterprise and right-wing families that has been extremely critical of the harm that socialism has wreaked on the province's economy and reputation. Go figure.

Even in local politics, one of Saskatoon's most left-wing city councillors, Darren Hill, is executive director of Junior Achievement, a group funded by business to promote entrepreneurship and leadership. When Hill, during a heated debate on condo conversions in 2008, suggested that business people could dishonestly manipulate the law to make a profit, it was incongruous to hear the integrity of business people and capitalism being besmirched by the same guy paid to promote and represent business values.

But, so typical of the naiveté of some in business, the scion of one of Saskatoon's wealthiest business families and a promoter of JA defended Hill's comments as being made "under the auspices of a councillor" and not as head of JA. And he chalked this up to "freedom of speech."

Just imagine if the director of a labour studies program for high school students—funded by unions—started riffing publicly and questioning the morality of the trade union movement. Anyone who thinks that unions would give a free pass for free speech is even more clueless than a business community that remains its own worst enemy at advancing its political agenda.

This has never been a problem shared by organized labour and the political left.

Chapter 9

DANCING PARTNERS FOREVER: UNIONS AND THE NDP

Unions and the NDP have a formal alliance that began in 1961 when the CCF and the Canadian Labour Congress formed the "New" Democratic Party. Tommy Douglas, who became the first leader of the new federal NDP, wasn't opposed to the merger but moved slowly and vacillated on hooking up organized labour to his base of farmers and small town prairie socialists who shared his fear, loathing and envy of big business and capitalism. Even Douglas' Saskatchewan CCF —the party on which he put his personal stamp—did not change its name to NDP until 1967, five years after the federal party had.

Douglas eventually convinced farmers and unions that they needed each other: labour, so it could actually get candidates elected; and farmers, so they could expand to an urban base with union money and a new source of committed and indefatigable party workers.

Like any alliance, some people on each side had understandable misgivings but, in time, they would be overcome. But not for everyone —think sore loser.

"The NDP has now become the tool of a small labour clique and is effectively under their domination and control. The NDP has come more and more under the control of a few labour leaders, mainly within a few large and powerful international unions."

Hazen Argue, 1962, after losing the federal NDP leadership to Tommy Douglas and joining the Liberals. In 1966, Argue would be named to the Senate by the Liberals.

Argue's warning seems prescient today at those times when labour hijacks the NDP—like convincing the Calvert government to nearly destroy itself by proclaiming the unpopular Most Available Hours of Work law or "the job-killing monster" as it became known.

Both the NDP and labour have richly benefited from their alliance. Historically, with about 36% of the workforce belonging to unions, Saskatchewan has Canada's highest overall unionization rate. This is largely because of the high proportion of civil servants and Crown employees in Saskatchewan—and they're highly unionized. While a reasonable and balanced union environment promotes worker rights and productivity, it's not uncharitable to point out that historically in Saskatchewan unionized workers behave and produce differently than non-unionized people. Just check the productivity numbers, sick days, absenteeism rates and the cost of union grievance arbitration and government regulations.

Recently, as Saskatchewan's population has grown, along with the non-government economy, unionization rates have started to slip into the 33% range.

"In the NDP, unions play a structural role in the decision-making processes of the party. In addition to contributing significant amounts to the NDP war chest, unions and union locals affiliated with the NDP send their own delegates to party conventions, including leadership races. By being able to vote in the delegate selection process for riding associations and affiliated unions, the views of these members are overrepresented in the councils of the NDP."

Chris Baker, political consultant and former
New Brunswick Deputy Minister, Toronto Star, June 2010

Much of the NDP's strength as the natural governing party is due to its disciplined and dynamic relationship with labour. As the official voice of unions, the NDP gets money every year from individual union locals and provincial chapters that use a portion of their members' union dues to fund NDP campaigns. Depending on the year, the donations range from tens of thousands of dollars to several hundred thousand dollars. In the 2003 election, unions contributed $300,000 to 56 NDP candidates and approximately $90,000 to the central NDP campaign. In 2007, unions formally donated $281,000 to 43 NDP candidates. This does not include individual donations made by union members who, like business supporters, kick in their own money and hours of volunteer time committed by unions to NDP campaigns.

What the Political Parties Get in Donations								
Party	2001	2002	2003	2004	2005	2006	2007	2008
NDP	$877,000	$1 million	$1.2 million	$856,000	$1.02 million	$1.01 million	$1.5 million	$692,000
SP	$723,000	$933,000	$2.7 mil	$816,000	$878,000	$1.1 million	$4.02 million	$1.3 million

Like armies that travel on their stomachs, political campaigns need to be well funded. But money, alone, does not win elections. If it did, the 2003 campaign, when the SaskParty collected more than double the NDP donations, would have been a big SaskParty win.

The key to campaigning is having the right people in place, not just in the "war-room" which coordinates the overall election, but in each one of the 58 campaigns being waged simultaneously around the province. And this is where the labour-NDP relationship is magical. Unions send in paid staff from their head offices to campaign, even recruiting union members and paying them to work in local campaigns.

> "The National union is looking for people to help out in the provincial election and is willing to pay any and all expenses up to $100 per day. If you're interested please contact me at the office."
>
> *Ron Rucks, CEP Local 1120, Prince Albert, October, 2007*

Calling All Sisters and Brothers

While organized labour has always supported the NDP, it's gone one step further—making sure its members are the NDP, joining local and provincial party executives and even getting elected as MLAs.

During the job-killing monster debacle of 2004, I saw copies of letters written by unions imploring the NDP to hold firm and go ahead with the Most Available Hours law, which was strongly opposed by nearly everyone but labour. Replying to a union letter, one Cabinet minister addressed her letter to "Dear Brother so-and-so," the preferred term of endearment inside the union world when referring to a fellow union member. The minister didn't actually have a union background but was obviously trying to curry favour with her labour supporters.

But in the Calvert Cabinet and caucus, there was no shortage of "brothers and sisters" that came by the union tag honestly—and I don't mean people like me who brag about having paid dues to two different unions because I was forced to.

At least eight NDP MLAs are union first and union always.

NDP MLAs and their union affiliations before becoming politicians:

1. **Judy Junor** Resigned as president of Saskatchewan Union of Nurses (SUN) to run for the NDP

2. **Deb Higgins** Safeway cashier; first female president of Saskatchewan Council of United Food and Commercial Workers International Union (UFCW)

3. **Kevin Yates** Corrections worker: SGEU provincial bargaining representative

4. **Kim Trew** Safety officer: bargaining committee member Grain Services Union (GSU) organizer

5. **David Forbes** Teacher: Executive member Saskatchewan Teachers Federation (STF)

6. **Warren McCall** Self-described "labour activist"

7. **Sandra Morin** Safeway cashier; head UFCW shop steward representing 600 staff

8. **Andy Iwanchuk** Full-time employee of Canadian Union of Public Employees (CUPE)

With all eight of these MLAs being re-elected in 2007, the hard-core labour faction now comprises 40% of the 20-member NDP caucus in the Legislature.

What You Get for What You Give: Union Payback

The strength of the NDP-labour relationship is also based on what unions get from government in exchange for their dedicated support. When businesses, individuals and corporations donate money, their interests are diverse. Some want a better investment climate—and that's a complex set of variables—others a more positive attitude. Some have specific agendas like certain tax policies, regulations or things that governments do or don't do; yet others just want "change." And the interests of these groups, while supporting the same party, are often in conflict—what one group wants, another doesn't. But it's not this way with organized labour.

With unions, the agenda is cohesive and unified regardless of which labour group is stepping up to donate money and volunteers: provide a labour relations climate that keeps unions in charge. And this is not negotiable. It's done by making it easier to unionize a workplace and more difficult to de-certify. It is carried out by ensuring labour laws and government policy do not diminish the role, power and wealth of unions—pretty simple, regardless of what union you're running.

To be clear, most reasonable people, including me, see the value of unions to ensure collective bargaining, to advance employees' interests and to provide checks and balances against unreasonable employers. But reasonableness is the key. And under the NDP, very little about Saskatchewan labour laws was reasonable.

87% of businesspeople believe NDP labour laws were too pro-union

8% of businesspeople believe NDP labour laws were "reasonably fair"

0% of businesspeople believe NDP labour laws were too pro-business

Canadian Federation of Independent Business
"Future of Saskatchewan Survey", 2007

Under the NDP, Saskatchewan unions demanded and got a "card check" system where no secret ballot was held among employees to determine if they wanted a union at their workplace—instead a union would be automatically imposed where 50% percent plus one of the people at work merely signed union cards. During a union organizing drive, the NDP prevented an employer from communicating with employees. At the same time, union organizers could stake out an employee's house or hit them up anywhere and anytime with pamphlets, a sales job and the squeeze to sign a union card.

Saskatchewan also remained the only place in the industrialized world where the law actually permits unionized workers to be fined by their union for crossing picket lines. And, under the NDP, the government-appointed Saskatchewan Labour Relations Board (SLRB) rarely ruled against unions.

Some of the NDP's concessions to labour were absurd—and even dangerous. In 2008, after several murderers tunneled out of the Regina Provincial Correctional Centre in the plain view of 87 different jail guards over four months, an inquiry found low morale among staff. It also revealed that the NDP's minister of corrections instituted a policy where SGEU shop stewards at the jail could bypass management and go directly to him. The minister was former jail guard and ex- SGEU shop steward Kevin Yates.

With policies and practices like this, Saskatchewan under the NDP became Canada's most labour-dominated province with little if any balance between the interests of unions and the interests of employers.

Shortly after being elected, the SaskParty changed the most obvious and blatantly unfair aspects of Saskatchewan's labour laws, allowing secret ballot union certification votes once 45% of the employees have signed cards and permitting limited employer communication with staff during a union organizing drive.

In addition to passing laws that unions wanted, many pro-NDP labour leaders and their supporters were rewarded with important jobs and influence inside NDP governments. Some, like former SaskTel union boss, Bill Hyde, were involved with the Romanow transition team in 1991. Hyde was later appointed by the NDP as a vice president of SaskPower. Before this, he had no experience as an executive of a large corporation.

CUPE major domo Jim Fergusson, whose wife Angie is an NDP campaign manager and was responsible for Calvert's Saskatoon Cabinet office, was hired by the NDP to manage labour relations in the Saskatoon Health Region. It was more than ironic that a former high ranking, lifetime union player was put in charge of representing management in negotiations with labour. Fergusson, with strong NDP ties and absolutely no previous health care management experience, was then promoted by the NDP to President and CEO of Saskatoon's health region, the largest in the province.

Terry Stevens, a long time NDP organizer and head of the United Steel Workers of America was a Crown corporation board member, executive on the Saskatchewan Federation of Labour (SFL) and, in the years before he retired, was hired by the NDP to run the department of labour's conciliation and mediation branch, the government office that would hold discussions between parties involved in labour disputes. One of our listeners—a business owner—tells of being in a meeting with Stevens when he entered the room, warmly greeted everyone and then turned to the union representative, gave him a "homie-handshake" and called him "Brother." Our listener started to get that turkey-at-Thanksgiving feeling.

The NDP has always ensured that the department of labour is well stacked, not only with strongly pro-union supporters but also with loyal New Democrats. The political pedigree in Labour is long with names of deputy labour ministers like Bob Sass, Don Ching, Bob Mitchell, Gary Simons—all loyal NDP supporters and advisers. In the Calvert government, Labour's deputy minister was Bill Craik, a former union lawyer who became embroiled in one of the government's uncomfortable embarrassments when a SLRB member was pushed out for being too fair!

What's With Wally?

Wally Matkowski, a lawyer, mediator and arbitrator, was an NDP-appointed vice chair of the SLRB. Known for being neither pro-labour nor pro-business, Matkowski was a respected labour law expert who had authored over 300 decisions, none of which was ever quashed by the courts.

The SLRB is similar to a court, known as a quasi-judicial tribunal whose job is to impartially make rulings under the *Trade Union Act* and several other statutes. And under the NDP governments of both Roy Romanow and Lorne Calvert, the SLRB had become controversial, viewed by many businesses inside and outside Saskatchewan as a pro-union tribunal that would rarely give business a fair hearing. Impartial labour boards elsewhere, such as Manitoba or Alberta, at least had reputations where fairness dictated that labour would win some and business would win some. But not so in Saskatchewan.

In 2005, the SFL began targeting Matkowski in its monthly newsletters, writing that his decisions were "misguided, entirely wrongheaded, and contrary to the spirit and letter of the law." And several powerful unions that had lost certain decisions at the SLRB—a rather rare occurrence at the best of times—began to mention Matkowski by name in newsletters with the heading "what's with Wally?"

After one of these union attacks, Matkowski said that he was approached by Deputy Labour Minister Bill Craik and told that he would not be reappointed when his term expired and, if he would step down immediately, he would receive full pay until his term was finished. When he declined, he was no longer scheduled to conduct any hearings.

When Matkowski went public with this complaint and appeared on my radio show, the NDP and Craik denied any interference in the SLRB. But a powerful Saskatchewan union boss said that Matkowski was responsible for his own demise. Bert Royer, a staunch NDPer, executive with the Iron Workers and president of the Saskatchewan Building Trades Council said when his union did not succeed in certain cases, "Matkowski picked on us and we…retaliated…"

So, in the Saskatchewan union world of the NDP, when certain unions didn't get their way in front of the SLRB and lost decisions, they thought they were being "picked on." For the sake of us not turning into Iraq, let's hope people who don't like the outcome of court cases don't start "retaliating" against judges!

As Matkowski sat in my studio—a careful, quiet, bookish and diligent man—he teased me off the air about my frequent and relentless bashing of the SLRB by saying that if he'd been punted by upset unions, then the board was obviously much fairer than I'd described it. My reply was, "No, Wally, it's just you who's fair. That's why the NDP and big unions dumped you!"

Matkowski would eventually settle his lawsuit out of court several years later with the provincial government, by this time the new SaskParty government. Matkowski was paid an undisclosed amount of money and given a job in government as an arbitrator, adjudicating disputes in a provincial agency.

One day while practicing labour law in Alberta in the 1990s, I was chatting on the phone with a Saskatchewan lawyer friend representing an employer in a SLRB hearing. Exasperated, my friend told of how the high ranking member of the SLRB chairing the hearing had a slip of the tongue and instead of using the pronoun "you" to describe the labour movement, had said "we" and then quickly mumbled a correction. My buddy laughed that this Freudian slip showed the true face of Saskatchewan's Labour Board—little more than a pro-union outfit advancing the cause of organized labour.

For many years in Saskatchewan, employers who become involved in a dispute with a trade union had a choice when the SLRB became involved—avoid the board at all costs, surrender early and beg the union for mercy; or appear before the board, lose your case, get publicly humiliated and then beg the union for mercy.

If this perception had stayed only in Saskatchewan it would have been bad enough. But, as a former management labour lawyer in Alberta in the 1990s, I still feel sheepish—though not apologetic—for my advice to employers considering Saskatchewan. I would tell them that between the SLRB and the province's dogmatically pro-union regulatory environment, they should avoid Saskatchewan at all costs—set up in Alberta, B.C. or even Manitoba. "Anywhere but in Saskatchewan," because it made doing business a challenge.

For much of the Calvert NDP term, many businesses did avoid Saskatchewan, as evidenced by the NDP's weak performance in attracting jobs, businesses and population to the province.

....

"A dispassionate observer could well conclude that the impartiality of the Saskatchewan Labour Relations Board has been compromised by the manner in which it has permitted the UFCW to conduct and direct the hearing process. It appears that the role of the Board was often restricted to enforcing the demands made by UFCW and that it, rather than the Board, was controlling the course the hearing took."

Saskatchewan Queens Bench Justice George Baynton, 2004

....

In many SLRB dealings there was always that niggling sense that something was going on behind the curtain—that faint "sproing, sproing" sound a kangaroo makes when it's heading to court. In 2004, Queens

Bench Justice George Baynton ruled that there was a perception of bias in the Board's behavior. This pulled back the curtain for a moment to reveal what was going on inside the SLRB. Baynton's decision—later reversed by the Court of Appeal—involved the SLRB case of the United Food and Commercial Workers International Union (UFCW) trying to organize Wal-Mart and having a dispute over documents that were being requested by the union. When every single union request was granted by the SLRB and every single Wal-Mart application was denied, the judge noted that "seldom is a dispute so one-sided."

The SLRB has always defended itself that it is has an equal number of appointed union and business nominees. This is correct. Hearings usually have a panel of three board members—the panel is headed up by the chair or one of two vice-chairs of the SLRB and then there is one representative from each of labour and business. But the chair and vice-chairs are hand-picked by the NDP. So, more often than not in the Calvert years, when the Board would rule against businesses or prevent employees from leaving unions when trying to de-certify, it would be the chair or vice-chair (NDP appointed) plus the union nominee (hard-core union/NDP supporter) outvoting the business side in a 2-1 vote.

"Union laws have always been a hill to die on for this NDP government. Too bad that a bunch of businesses and jobs have to die as well."

Gormley ranting, July, 2004

Let's Get Ready to Rumble: Unions Enter the Election Ring

Most Saskatchewan unions and their senior staff are officially allied with the NDP—they have resolutions on their books to support, fund and volunteer for the NDP. From the Canadian Union of Public Employees (CUPE) to the Service Employees International Union (SEIU), the many building trades, the Canadian Office and Professional Employees (COPE), the food service unions like UFCW or Retail Wholesales and Department Store Union (RWDSU), Communications Energy and Paperworkers (CEP), United Steelworkers (USW), Grain Services Union (GSU) and dozens of other unions—they're all firmly behind the NDP.

The Saskatchewan Union of Nurses (SUN) has a long NDP history, headed by Rosalee Longmoore, a committed social activist and NDP supporter. Her predecessor, Judy Junor, quit SUN to successfully run for the NDP in Saskatoon, encouraged by the Saskatchewan Federation of Labour (SFL) which sent a note to its entire membership, on SFL letterhead, urging "let's do everything we can to get Sister Judy elected."

Unions are most effective in Saskatchewan when they're campaigning in elections. During the 2007 campaign, dozens of unions and their locals pulled out all the stops and blanketed workplaces and their members' homes with newsletters and pamphlets supporting the NDP and attacking the SaskParty.

A very entertaining political blog called "NDP Boogeyman" followed each day of the campaign and displayed scanned copies of several union politicking efforts:

CUPE Saskatchewan pamphlet delivered to hundreds of nursing homes, long term care facilities and hospitals across the province: "Is it Time for a Change? Welcome to Sask-Alberta: Brad Wall doesn't want you to have three weeks of vacation a year, doesn't want you to enjoy Family Day, and doesn't want Minimum Wage laws. You will pay Alberta-style bills for car insurance and utilities"

UFCW 1400: "Help avoid four years of bad luck...you have the ability to ensure Saskatchewan has four more years of good luck instead. The NDP is a party that is pro-labour, pro-family and pro-Saskatchewan."

CEP 1-S, SaskTel: "There have been recent statements by certain politicians with regard to the possible sale of Saskatchewan's Crown Corporations."

CEP two pamphlets: "While CEP would never be so presumptuous as to tell you how to vote..." one newsletter questions how much at risk SaskTel would be if the SaskParty privatized it and, in the other pamphlet the NDP universal drug plan is explained as "fair, secure and cheaper" and "the SaskParty opposes this."

SGEU "Privatize Liquor Stores —Why Risk It?"

CEP 1120, Ron Rucks: questions why Brad Wall will not honour "the agreement" to re-open the PA pulp mill and asks for people to "help out in the election" and be paid for doing it by CEP.

SEIU International office Toronto: Sandy Weyland, Sharleen Stewart and Christine Miller: "Let's hope that Saskatchewan workers are going to vote for the party that stands on the side of working families—the NDP have well laid out plans."

CUPE Health Care Workers: "The SaskParty has not committed to publicly delivered health care."

SEIU pamphlet: "Whose Health Care Plan Includes My Job?" lays out the party positions and provides the answer—the NDP's plan.

CEP, Don MacNeil, Western region vice-president: "Brad Wall will gut the Saskatchewan Trade Union Act. The NDP's proposed universal drug plan is an opportunity that should not be missed."

CUPE 5111, Brian Manegre: "We believe a SaskParty government will privatize many health care services [including] long term care. The Sask-Party sings to the tune of big business and large corporations."

Two questions arise when reading such patently politicized pamphlets aimed at influencing an election: first, what do decent and hard working union members think of their union dues being hijacked for NDP propaganda? And, second, what would the effect be on legal campaign spending limits if the NDP campaign had to declare the thousands of dollars in printing and distribution costs of the union pamphlets which are obviously part of an orchestrated campaign in support of the NDP?

SGEU: Canada's Most Political Non-Partisan Union

Of the many unions officially allied with the NDP, the notable exception is the SGEU which represents government employees, who are supposed to be professional, apolitical and capable of carrying out their duties regardless of the party in government. So the SGEU will not formally support any particular party. This, of course, sounds good in principle. But in practice, most SGEU shop stewards, bargaining committee members and executive members are so deep inside the NDP gravity well that they're little more than NDP hard partisans who go to work every day in government to religiously spread the NDP gospel.

Like many large labour organizations, SGEU is challenged by a new generation of employees who wonder if unions are obsolete and any longer relevant. The speaking notes given to SGEU shop stewards coach them how to explain that unions can negotiate for staff; that unions are stronger than one employee alone, and that unions balance an employer's power— all fair enough. But the notes point out a warning to staff that "employers still want to cut wages and increase workloads like they did 150 years ago when unions first started."

Before the Industrial Revolution calls and wants its talking points back, the union also urges advising the skeptical that "unions fight for good things for all Canadians like Medicare, unemployment insurance and maternity leave." Exactly—60 years ago unions fought for these.

In the early 2000s, the SGEU secretly persuaded the NDP to reclassify hundreds of middle managers who were "out of scope" and not represented by a union. The government forced the managers to become SGEU members alongside the same people they were supposed to be supervising. By expanding the SGEU membership base, the NDP was playing into the big three objectives of organized labour: government always needs to be hiring more employees; the size of the civil service cannot ever be reduced—including by cutbacks, contracting out work or by privatization—and government employees should regularly be paid more.

For the people employed in government these are obviously good things. But they're even better for the SGEU which has a good sized piece of the action when you follow the money.

The SGEU has 22,000 members who are forced to pay dues of 1.5% of their salary to the union every pay day. Assume an average salary of $40,000 and this means the SGEU's revenue every year will be at least $13 million. Philosophy, ideals and politics are all fine. But money's finer—and it can buy a lot of influence, power and control. The SGEU has over 13 million reasons to keep the civil service growing.

For obvious reasons, the SGEU is one of Saskatchewan's most ardent critics of any government work being done by someone who is not a government employee paying SGEU union dues. The union's anti-privatization fight defines its existence, from warning of the perils of private liquor and wine stores to resisting any contracting out of the government work.

In 2003, the SGEU became embroiled in what we called the "Marigold Affair" when senior citizens and cottagers in a provincial park planted flowers to beautify their neighbourhood. SGEU members employed in the park came along and dug up the flowers because the volunteers had "done union work" and, intoned an SGEU spokesman, today it might be flowers, tomorrow sewer services.

With no apology and even less insight, SGEU came off looking like the governor in the movie Blazing Saddles who shrieks "Gentlemen, we've got to protect our phony baloney jobs!" The deeper irony for SGEU executives was that they didn't seem to get that most taxpayers —politically left, right or otherwise—don't wake up every morning thanking their lucky stars that civil servants are tending flowers in a provincial park. We just don't care. We look for results and outcomes at a reasonable cost.

Highly qualified experts who safeguard our lives are to be valued, whether in the private or government sectors, whether unionized or not. And these experts should be well paid and empowered. But (while this may come as a horrible surprise to union true believers who drink the same philosophic Kool Aid), no one has a constitutional right to a government job. And your job security means nothing to the rest of us. We just don't care. Suck it up and get used to it.

The SGEU has 35 staff of its own. And, in the "what's good for the goose is good for the gander" category, these staff members have been on a "defined benefit" pension for years, just like the gold-plated civil service pensions that SGEU negotiated with the government. Defined benefit means that regardless of how little money the employee puts in and the employer matches, the employee gets a defined amount on retirement, like 70% of their best five years.

Because these pensions are not based on the money actually put into the plan, today the Saskatchewan government—as the employer who must issue pension cheques every month—holds an unfunded pension liability in the billions of dollars. As a result, in the 1990s, many governments and employers began switching pensions to "defined contribution" where the amount put into the pension is known at retirement and then buys an annuity which produces a pension income.

Inside the SGEU its staff never made the switch to a defined contribution plan and remains on the expensive and unsustainable defined benefit plan. As a result, this huge union—in this case, an employer—is seeing its pension plan running out of money. Unlike government, which has taxpayers who will be forced to backstop the civil service pensions, in this case the SGEU is learning what it's like to reap the consequences of bad decisions.

So, SGEU's staff asks, "Is the boss going to step up and help out the employees?" The SGEU answer, in trying to restore the pension balance, was to make its staff members pay 20% of their salaries toward pension in late 2009. When SGEU, effective 2010, tried ordering the employees to pay a staggering 54% of their salaries to pension—over half their pay— the staff got a court injunction to stop the plan. The response of SGEU president Bob Bymoen was to say "we fully appreciate that this sucks." Yes, Bob, it does.

In early 2007, the SGEU made an irresponsible decision that resulted in a public relations disaster. And it also eventually led to Saskatchewan passing an essential services law that allows certain unionized jobs to be deemed essential and prevented from striking.

Armed with a strike vote in January 2007, the SGEU decided not to send over 12,000 of its members on strike but instead to pull snow plow operators off the roads during the same week a blizzard warning was in effect. While clearly a tactic to hold the public hostage, the general view on my radio show was that this union had sunk to new depths—putting public safety at risk. Worse than immoral, it was obscene.

The only defenders of the snowplow strike were hard-core union support- ers lamely trotting out the union mantra that it was the government's fault that snowplows weren't running. But no one was buying it—it was the SGEU's decision alone to abandon work, leave snow plows idle and threaten the lives of thousands of people who rely on our highways for school bus travel, work and medically necessary trips.

SGEU boss Bymoen would never forgive me when I tore a strip off him during a radio interview, saying he'd be held personally responsible if a single person was injured or worse and he'd have "blood on his hands" as a result of his reckless union gambit. He tried shooting back that they pulled the snow plows only after receiving assurances from the government that an emergency plan was in place for 100 highways department supervisors to do the work of 425 operators.

I pointed out that no one has ever accused either Bymoen or his union brass of being very bright, but even they might figure out that snow plows operating at 25% effectiveness in the middle of a dangerous Saskatchewan winter was not acceptable.

Sixty-three hours later, public outrage forced SGEU to turn tail, surrender and send the striking snow plow operators out to keep Saskatchewan highways safe. But neither the union executive nor any SGEU member ever apologized, conceded or even expressed regret for endangering the public.

"The fact that SGEU's snow plow drivers' dangerous strike wasn't stopped once it started speaks volumes of this hapless government's fear of offending the powerful union bosses that prop it up. And here's what else we learned in the 2 1/2 day game of union Russian roulette: we now know what the SGEU thinks of us and our safety. We know what the government thinks, too.

Gormley, still ranting, January, 2007

This dangerous maneuver by SGEU strikers would be remembered 10 months later in October, 2007 when CUPE members at the University of Saskatchewan launched a widespread strike on the first day of the provincial election campaign. As the strike by support workers dragged on, it turned out that some of these CUPE members were also responsible for booking certain medical appointments through the College of Medicine—as a result, dozens of patients were having their appointments cancelled each week of the strike. In the same Saskatchewan already notorious for health care waiting lists, this was unforgivable and was evidence that Saskatchewan needed some form of essential services regulation during strikes.

Long opposed by the NDP, as an appeasement to their trade union base, essential services strike laws were in place in every province of Canada except Saskatchewan. Thanks to the SGEU snow plow debacle and the effects of the CUPE strike on patients, one of the Wall government's first and long overdue measures after being elected in 2007 was to enact an essential services law. It still has broad public support in Saskatchewan today.

Larry…You Never Call, You Never Write

Labour's Big Kahuna is the powerful Saskatchewan Federation of Labour (SFL), the umbrella group that represents 95,000 union members, 37 unions and 700 locals. It's funded by union dues paid by working men and women to their unions who, in turn, kick money upstairs to the SFL. One of Saskatchewan's most radical left-wing organizations, the SFL is committed to what it calls "social unionism" and, through its "political action fund" it consistently supports the NDP in election campaigns.

Between elections, the SFL conducts workshops and conferences that teach activism, collective bargaining, how to promote and manage conflict, labour law, counseling and even how to "face management"—all things that well organized unions should do. The SFL workshops also include political issues where union members are taught voter ID/GOTV principles, strategic planning, "volunteer recruitment, campaign organizing and voter contact," all put into use on NDP election campaigns.

The SFL is headed by Larry Hubich, a former Wheat Pool employee, whose politics incline toward Marxism. Responding to the Obama administration's auto bailout, Hubich suggested that "auto CEOs, who carted off wheel barrels of money last year as their industry swirled the toilet bowl, should be thrown in jail and their workers should run the business." This prompted newspaper columnist Murray Mandryk—not usually a staunch critic of big labour—to call this "idiotic, self-aggrandizing rhetoric that makes no sense to anyone."

Hubich is at the highest echelon of the NDP. Earlier in 2010, at the NDP annual convention, he formally nominated Dwain Lingenfelter to continue on as party leader. Paving the way for the NDP, which would later follow him, Hubich decided in 2007 to boycott my radio show when he didn't like some things I said about organized labour and his leadership.

He says that while I am up front and fair when I interview and debate him, later when he is not on the air with me it is unfair of me to criticize what he says because he is not there to respond. Using Hubich's logic that I can only disagree with him or criticize his often wacky politics when he is in the same room with me, I'd have to hire him as a co-host.

Ever the union boss, Hubich wants to bargain, saying he will only come back on the radio show when our company agrees to a "code of conduct" that he will negotiate with us. Responsible broadcasters don't do business this way—we have enough industry codes of conduct that we're legally required to follow. And so far, with no dent in either the talk show ratings or the heat of the debate, Hubich's boycott has only bounced back on him. In the intervening years he has been joined in boycotting me by other radical leftists like the SGEU's Bob Bymoen, Lingenfelter and CUPE.

There are other more forward looking union leaders who regularly come on the talk show with me. But, as I thought about Hubich's boycott it struck me that it must be a coincidence that the union leaders and politicians most prone to pushing people around don't seem to like butting heads with me. I have this weird, almost pathological urge to beat up on bullies. Can't explain it.

Hubich's other disappointment in recent years came in 2005 when he was named in a dispute with a longtime SFL staffer after a "severe confrontation." Garnet Dishaw, a career labour advisor, was involved in an altercation with Hubich that involved verbal abuse, insults, bad language and finally so much "contempt and hostility" that Hubich fired Dishaw.

I'd heard about this at the time and tried getting Dishaw on my radio show but evidently pro-labour/anti-Gormley to the end, Dishaw wouldn't even return my calls. It was only later—after the SaskParty became government—that Dishaw went to the Labour Relations Board alleging that his union, COPE, had failed to properly represent him and was more interested in protecting the image and reputation of the SFL's Hubich than in representing him.

None of this I doubt—but Dishaw showed bad judgment in waiting for a new SLRB and government. Unlike the NDP days when the SLRB was regularly used to settle scores, a newly appointed vice-chair of the SLRB heard Dishaw's application and properly ruled that the case had been brought too late after the firing.

Too bad—it would have been interesting to watch Hubich's behaviour and management style get a public review. And, by the way, Garnet—there's no limitation period on *John Gormley Live*. You're welcome to come on the show anytime and tell us what kind of boss Larry Hubich was and how he treated an employee in the workplace.

Cast Off the Chains That Bind

"Workers of the world unite—you have nothing to lose but your cottages and your motor homes!"

"John Gormley Live" anonymous caller, October, 2003

During the 2003 election when a caller phoned with the twist on Karl Marx's "workers of the world unite, you have nothing to lose but your chains," it made me laugh. He explained it well—the old, exploited union member of the class struggle has entered the 21st century. Unions today are rich and powerful, wages are good—in some cases obscenely so—and the only thing at stake if unions decline is the excellent quality of life enjoyed by many union members.

In fairness to unions, their efforts led to conditions we now take for granted—and which are in the mainstream and enshrined in law—a 40-hour work week (or less), overtime, benefits, statutory holidays, sick leave, and the list goes on. But why do unions still have to play to the negative and keep class warfare going?

It is about survival. If union members accept the gains they've made and the continual progress of working people—and they start backing away from active union participation—it will spell the end of the hard-core Marxists and political zealots who trade in class struggle, conflict and confrontation. It will also mean an end to the benefits flowing to some of these union bosses from the large and wealthy unions funded by union dues in the tens of millions of dollars.

At the local level, unions are the ultimate democracy. Every unhappy, left-wing and angry shop steward gets elected by someone. Most people in the complacent majority don't vote. They let the disenchanted pick the local executive members who ultimately move up the chain until the management of modern unions in no way reflects the values and aspirations of the reasonable and moderate people whose union dues pay for extreme causes and even more radical union leaders.

Many union members have no problem with labour laws that allow a secret ballot vote or essential services legislation to set rules for strikes in certain sectors. But in 2008, when the SFL delegates began howling and shouting down Saskatchewan's Labour Minister Rob Norris and standing at the back of the room singing "Solidarity forever" who looked childish and rude? Not the politician.

Then, a year later when the SFL's Hubich publicly "un-invited" Norris because "we've got better things to do," yet another message was sent. And, again, it wasn't the politician who looked bad.

In some parts of the world—certainly not Saskatchewan—some unions advocate and collectively bargain and represent values like productivity, work place safety and professionalism on the job. These unions may be involved in the political process as activists for the union and serious, mature, respected and trusted stakeholders. But not here.

In federal politics, the NDP has encountered serious organizational difficulties in the 2000s, stemming in part from the 2004 federal election financing law which limits union and corporate donations. The NDP's other national problem comes from a break in the usually rigid and laser-like party discipline with union leaders, occasioned by Buzz Hargrove of the Canadian Auto Workers suggesting strategic voting that would involve voting Liberal in some cases. This resulted in a major falling out between the NDP and Hargrove and his supporters in the CAW.

But in Saskatchewan provincial politics, there has been no similar shrinking of either money or support between labour and the NDP. The relationship remains strong and committed. More dedicated than ever to the NDP, and prepared to use their members' union dues, organized labour is tightly aligned with the NewDems. The partners are doing all the right dance steps, just like they learned so long ago.

Chapter 10

The final countdown: 2007 election

The Brad Wall Run Down

In the province known for growing the world's toughest hockey players, Saskatchewan politics has always had high elbows and cheap shots. But, like the "code of the road" or a bad hangover after a night of regrets, no one talks much about the nasty edge of our politics—hoping that if we just clam up and forget, maybe it didn't really happen the way we remember. Or, better still, hopefully it won't happen again. But it always does. Politics as a blood sport is a fact of life in Saskatchewan, particularly against an opponent as experienced and ruthless as the NDP.

In the run-up to the expected 2007 election, SaskParty leader Brad Wall was the charmed child of Saskatchewan politics, coasting through high polling numbers and showing off his skills as an eloquent and compelling speaker. Bright, personable and good looking, Wall was tapping into a general desire for change and living under a lucky star. But that was going to change if the NDP had any say in the matter.

In 2006, as the SaskParty hammered the NDP on dozens of thefts in the civil service that had resulted in over $2 million of stolen public money, Wall was hitting hard on trust, competence and the NDP's seeming inability to manage even the basics of government. For a party long accustomed to governing and being morally superior to its opponents, this could not stand.

One afternoon, Wall got a foreshadowing of what the next year's election would bring. Like something from the hockey parody "Slapshot," Premier Calvert and Finance Minister Andrew Thomson came over the boards—like the Hanson Brothers with hockey hair flying in the wind and taped-up glasses—and laid the lumber to Wall at centre ice. Whether rehearsed or just great improv—we'll never know—but Wall was taught a lesson.

Nearly 20 years earlier, in the late 1980s, Wall had worked as a junior assistant to several Cabinet ministers in the Tory government of Grant Devine. One of Wall's ministers, John Gerich, was among a group of Conservative politicians later convicted and jailed for fraud. In the years Wall worked at the Legislature, an auditor's report on the Saskatchewan Liquor Board confirmed "complimentary" booze being sent to Cabinet ministers offices which, presumably as an employee, Wall consumed at some point.

According to Thomson, arranging and drinking free booze for his boss made Wall a party to fraud and Wall's criticism of thieving civil servants amounted to hypocrisy.

Character assassination inside the legislative chamber has been done for years by NDP politicians when they go on the attack. It is protected under parliamentary privilege which grants absolute immunity to the person speaking. But some of Thomson's claims were being re-spun outside of the chamber.

Just before defamation lawyers were called in to referee, the premier and finance minister quickly hopped back in the players' box and took pains to "clarify" that they weren't actually accusing Wall of fraud, nor was the liquor delivery necessarily "fraudulent." But, Calvert, taking one last poke, observed that "Mr. Wall was employed in the office of Mr. Gerich, was employed for many years in the government of Grant Devine and surely at that level would have observed at least what was happening within that building and within that government."

If the NDP—and Calvert in particular—were going to do guilt by association based on what someone should have observed at the Legislature, wasn't this the same Calvert who had been an NDP insider and caucus member since 1986 in the same government responsible for the NDP fraud cover-up scandal, Channel Lake, Spudco and the Murdoch Carriere debacle?

For the first time—and I've known Wall since he was a kid in university—the SaskParty leader looked flustered and hurt. As he awkwardly stammered a reply to the NDP attack, it was a good learning experience for Wall: the NDP are never down and out—struggling, perhaps, but always capable of grabbing one last personal attack on character. Wall was never again lost for words and it readied him for what would come in the 2007 election campaign.

As 2007 arrived, the economy was strong and improving by the month but population still lagged. I lamented to a political friend—one of my NDP-schooled buddies—that the Calvert government's greatest sin was its lack of a strategy to deal with growth. There was no agenda with specific objectives and measurable targets to grow Saskatchewan's population and increase investment and jobs. My friend, who is more plugged in than I am to NDP governments, pointed out that Calvert's problems were a lot bigger than a lack of a growth plan.

He played reverse word association with me, challenging me to quickly name one big, positive thing delivered by Calvert that had not been a reaction to something. I thought about it. There wasn't much.

In any event, the mounting scandals had overwhelmed anything that was positive—and to Calvert's credit —he had cut royalties on new oil exploration, finally lowered Saskatchewan's nation-leading high taxes (though not to Alberta or BC levels but at least competitive) abolished front license plates, permitted out-of-province people to buy farmland and gave us an extra day off work for "Family Day." More than six years had passed and Calvert's positives could be named on one hand. And not one of them was a defining "big plan." The problem wasn't a lack of a growth agenda: it was the absence of any sort of agenda, beyond reacting to often external events outside the control of Calvert and his NDP.

By this time, the opposition SaskParty was prefacing every comment about the Calvert government with the slogan "old and tired," words which were increasingly showing up on blogs and in editorial and media commentaries on the government.

In Saskatchewan, autumn has become the preferred time for elections. As summer came in 2007 and seven veteran MLAs announced their retirements —including Cabinet ministers Eric Cline, Clay Serby, Eldon

Lautermilch, Joanne Crofford and Andrew Thomson—Calvert made one more Cabinet shuffle. If there wasn't already the sense of inevitability that the NDP was past its "best before date," the Cabinet changes might have been greeted with outrage.

Long time minister Pat Atkinson was given the powerful finance portfolio. Very bright, but one of the most left-wing members of any NDP Cabinet since the 1970s, Atkinson was now being handed the keys to Saskatchewan's financial and economic future. This could have been really scary.

Combining Atkinson's rising star with new ministers Warren McCall, a labour activist whose professional experience was being an assistant to former NDP MP Lorne Nystrom, and former Safeway union shop steward Sandra Morin, gave the Cabinet a distinct leftward tilt. Then, the return to Cabinet of the SGEU's querulous Kevin Yates and ex-SUN boss Judy Junor brought the labour factor way up. With visions of Atkinson, Morin, McCall, Yates, and Junor alongside labour's Kim Trew and ex-UFCW boss Deb Higgins was enough to conjure up thoughts of a virtual Karl Marx-style workers paradise under construction in Saskatchewan. But the new Cabinet wouldn't have enough time to do any damage.

Setting the Table for the Election

Like the run-up to the 2003 election when the NDP spent over $5 million within months on the Wide Open Future campaign —half of it secretly financed by Crown corporations —another feel-good campaign was in the offing before the 2007 election. Actually, there were a few of them.

After spending over $340,000 worth of taxpayers' dollars to try whipping up support for Saskatchewan's equalization position, the government spent another $300,000 in 2006 for the "Imagine" campaign which asked people to imagine what we could do with $800 million, the amount the NDP argued we were entitled from Ottawa under equalization. Then in 2007, before the election call, a blizzard of government dollars blanketed the media—$2.7 million in advertising the budget, the "Opportunities" and "Real Careers/Real Life" campaigns and spending from the Departments of Health and Education to promote a brighter future.

The Media Weighs in on NDP Government Public Relations Campaigns

"A clear case of waste."

Re: Equalization campaign, Regina Leader Post,
March 26, 2004

"Hard to imagine a bigger waste of money."

Re: Imagine campaign, Regina Leader Post,
October 13, 2006

"Advertising that's little more than thinly-veiled propaganda designed more for the benefit of the governing party's re-election chances than the benefit of the public."

Re: Health and Learning ad campaigns, columnist Murray Mandryk,
September 15, 2007.

But no single campaign would match the NDP's funding of Canada's most expensive exclamation. At a cost of $1.5 million, the NDP unveiled a new and dynamic Saskatchewan "word-mark." It was the word "Saskatchewan"—but with an exclamation mark. So, it was "Saskatchewan!" instead of "Saskatchewan."

To be used on government advertising, highway signs and other displays, "Saskatchewan!" would convey the message that "Saskatchewan is the best place in Canada for young people to live, work and raise a family." It was not made clear that if a civil servant forgot to insert the "!" would this mean that Saskatchewan might be less a great place?

The stern message, in a book of guidelines for government staff, made it clear that "Saskatchewan!" was to be used only for optimistic messages and not for gloomy things like coroners' inquests, forest fires or West Nile virus outbreaks. Because the "!" campaign —including TV ads —was to be focused inside the borders of Saskatchewan, it was rightly dismissed as pre-election hype.

Warming Up the Campaign Machine

Well-oiled political machines like the NDP —even ones 20 points behind in the polls —know the eternal rules for effective election campaigns. In addition to local voter ID and "get out the vote," the overall provincial NDP campaign is built around winning at all costs. And no one is better at this than the NDP.

This singular focus on winning requires finely tempered discipline, putting the party above all else, "never saying never" and staying on message. As Saskatchewan's natural governing party, the only issue for Calvert and his campaign advisors was developing what the campaign message would be.

"The SaskParty craves power for its own sake. If elected, they would undo all the good work our NDP government has done by privatizing Crown corporations and carrying out a visionless regime of tax cuts and debt reduction. Don't let this happen."

Lorne Calvert, NDP fundraising letter, April 2007

Like its 2003 shock-and-awe campaign on Crown corporations against a hapless SaskParty election team, the campaign of 2007 would need something to take voters' minds off Calvert's weak leadership and his scandal-ridden government's faltering performance. Some campaigns, like 2003, need only a simple wedge issue—my opponent will do "x," which is his hidden agenda, and I will save you from "x." If done right, this also incorporates trustworthiness and fear of the unknown.

In 2007, a more complicated formula was devised, in part because the SaskParty had been unequivocal in its support for Crown corporations. So a campaign message was developed involving three prongs—a negative, a wedge and a vote buying platform.

The negative issue:

Change is bad. Change is not needed, especially when it's unknown. It will mean Brad Wall—unknown, inexperienced and a guy with a hidden agenda —will change what you have become accustomed to. And it won't be good. In addition, Wall is a scary right-wing Tory from the Devine government. The Devine issue had been so effective in the past—why stop now?

The wedge issue:

Only Lorne Calvert will fight for Saskatchewan against Ottawa over equalization. Brad Wall is afraid to offend Stephen Harper and won't stand up for us.

The vote buying issue:

The NDP will give "free" prescription drugs to every man, woman and child in Saskatchewan and Brad Wall won't. This is because (see Negative issue) Wall is an untrustworthy right-winger who doesn't care for people and is opposed to universal health care. He'll say it's too expensive but that's just an excuse.

Who's Afraid of the Big Brad Wolf—in Sheep's Clothing

The NDP launched its negative issue early, before the election campaign began, with a media blitz called "Wolf in Sheep's Clothing," suggesting the SaskParty and Wall were the Tories of old taking on a new guise and tricking people into voting for them.

Actually it wasn't the NDP that launched the ad; it was the SaskParty that got out in front early with a leaked version of the NDP campaign. Because the wolf disguised as a sheep in the NDP ad looked a great deal like a Siberian husky, the SaskParty diffused the impact of the attack ad by dubbing it "Lamb Chop, the Dog-Faced Sheep." When the NDP got around to unveiling its actual ads, the wolf face had been made more malevolent.

"Mr. Wall is a pretty good looking guy. This ad is about a guy who looks like he's friendly, warm and cuddly but the reality is he's not even close to that image. That's how sheep get enticed by friendly wolves."

NDP Deputy Premier Clay Serby, September, 2007

Just like Serby's peculiar understanding of how wolves run down sheep —they don't entice them; they usually sneak up on them and rip them to shreds—the NDP ad then ran into the law of unintended consequences. If there was a wolf named Brad Wall sneaking around dressed in sheep's clothing, then who were the sheep? Were the NDP calling the people of Saskatchewan "sheep"?

The ad also claimed that one of Wall's hidden agendas was to "make us more like Alberta." Beyond the traditional NDP hatred and envy of Alberta, it seemed to elude the NDP brain trust that the hottest economy on the continent and home to thousands of Saskatchewan youth —Alberta— wasn't such a bad place. Perish the thought that Wall's hidden agenda would be to "make us a carbon copy of Alberta." Logically, this would involve paying down the provincial debt, delivering the lowest taxes in the country, eliminating sales taxes, creating thousands of jobs and well funded social programs, and building the nation's best roads. The Alberta threat didn't exactly strike widespread panic among Saskatchewan citizens.

And the NDP TV ad tried too hard to be cute; as the word "privatization" faded from view the distinct grouping of the letters "p o r n" filtered across the screen. While I'm as sexually enlightened as the next person —put the word "porn" in the same picture as sheep and I'm outta here.

The SaskParty answered the NDP attack ads with a telegenic Brad Wall wearing a tee shirt and tossing a football in the air as he watched his son's football team. Looking at the camera, Wall joked that the NDP was trying to say he was scary, if he was elected winters would be longer or that he was even a secret Calgary Stampeders' fan. With just the right note of good natured dismissiveness, Wall's ad put lie to the NDP's hysteria over a menacing wolf in sheep's clothing.

It's a truism of politics and psychology that attack ads only work when they seize on something that is inherently believable, usually a fact or truth coupled with a claim that is credible or likely to be believed. The people of Saskatchewan never believed the hysterical claims of Brad Wall as a wolf in sheep's clothing. And for an ad to fail, that's all that is needed.

Four years earlier, Calvert said that when people explain in politics they're losing. This time, his NDP was trying to explain and defend its bizarre TV ad. And their opponents were laughing.

Just days before Premier Calvert called the election for November 7th, rumors swirled that the NDP's master strategist Dale Schmeichel was unhappy with the party's campaign strategy. Schmeichel denied this but confirmed that he would not be "co-chairing" the NDP campaign. He explained that he simply did not have the time to dedicate "150%" to the job.

Two thoughts came immediately to mind —first, what could occupy Schmeichel's time more than a political campaign? Schmeichel not being involved in an NDP campaign was like the sun refusing to rise or the laws of gravity being suspended—some things just never happen. The second thought was who in their right mind would ask Schmeichel to "co-chair" or share in the management of an election campaign? Renowned as tireless, hard driving, tough, ruthless and always in charge, Schmeichel "co-campaigning" was inconceivable—it would reduce his effectiveness.

The actual hands-on campaign management usually done by Schmeichel fell to Doug Still, the party's provincial secretary, a retired school teacher from Humboldt and doctrinaire socialist. Obviously trusted by Calvert for his dogged loyalty, Doug Still lacked one of the gifts of natural campaign gurus like Schmeichel and my friend, the late Ed Tchorzewski, who'd helped Schmeichel salvage the 2003 campaign.

Schmeichel and Eddie the Torch could humour the party faithful— with their hype and partisan hatred of Wall —and look down Main Street to see which issues resonated emotionally with average people. Sometimes, the issues that had maximum impact weren't the same inside baseball issues that pre-occupied the true believers like Doug Still and his campaign team of hard partisans.

Even today, many dedicated NDPers still believe that every word of the wolf in sheep's clothing pitch was true—it was just that the unwashed masses didn't "get" the ad. The people understood it all right —they just didn't buy it. The ad was a failure. And it ended up saying more about the NDP than their opponents.

"Only in Saskatchewan can the phrase "quality of life" be synonymous with both "moral superiority" and "lower standard of living."

Internationally renowned Saskatchewan blogger
Kate McMillan, www.Smalldeadanimals.com, October, 2007

The Election Issues Emerge: Equalize This

As Calvert called the election, it didn't take long to realize that equalization was a non-starter and would be replaced by an aggressive anti-change message.

Like the Blakeney NDP's incomprehensible and disastrous campaign in 1982, which challenged Grant Devine for his lack of support of the federal Crowsnest Pass Freight Rate for moving grain, equalization was equally abstruse. Who understood it? Who cared?

And to the extent that Calvert tried arguing that Saskatchewan was "entitled" to $800 million from Ottawa and the feds should not have capped Saskatchewan's future payments, an unlikely skeptic stepped forward and deftly shot down the arguments mounted by Calvert. Former NDP Finance Minister Janice MacKinnon, well respected in academe and by federal and provincial politics watchers alike, made it clear that Premier Calvert and Finance Minister Andrew Thomson had blown the equalization deal with Ottawa by ineffective bargaining.

Unlike other provinces that opened with hard positions and then negotiated, Calvert had refused to back down or move to an alternative stance. And Saskatchewan's intransigent "take it or leave it" position resulted in us getting less than we could have, argued MacKinnon. Although Stephen Harper let Saskatchewan keep all of our resource revenues as promised, his cap of $226 million for the following year was not part of the deal. But, according to MacKinnon, the cap was both necessary and sensible because it protected the principle that provinces paying money into equalization should not be worse off than the provinces getting the money. And, argued MacKinnon, Saskatchewan could have ended up with a higher cap, if Calvert's NDP had been prepared to negotiate instead of being obstinate.

As MacKinnon talked of the need for the equalization debate to move on, it began to overshadow Calvert politically and reflect poorly. As a low-key, old style "keep things small" socialist, he was being broadsided by the edges of MacKinnon's message: Saskatchewan could either show the world—because we're a "have" province like Alberta, B.C. and Ontario —that we'd become progressive, successful and a good place to be. Or, Saskatchewan could continue to be oppositional, claiming hardship, demanding hand-outs and sending the message that we're an under-developed province not living up to our potential.

By the time MacKinnon was done —and this didn't sound like Saskatchewan's typical old style socialism—she was appealing to a new

Saskatchewinner attitude where we could seize the future. Or, looking backwards like Saskatchewhiners, we could promote the creed of the underachiever, whining about entitlement and the way things "used to be." Calvert stopped talking about equalization.

Change is Bad. Scary. Don't Touch It.

On the opening night of the campaign kickoff, both Calvert and the Sask-Party's Wall spoke of change.

"With Saskatchewan booming like never before; with Saskatchewan families benefitting like never before, the question tonight is simple. Is it really time to put all of this at risk, for the sake of change? Is change for the sake of change worth the risk? Should we go forward or should we go back?

Lorne Calvert, October 10, 2007

As Calvert warned of change —risky, unknown and fearsome change —he hinted at a broad and universal drug plan he called "the boldest new social program in Canada." Within a day, he would unveil a fully universal drug plan to apply to every Saskatchewan citizen, regardless of financial means. No price tag was immediately offered.

The SaskParty's Wall spoke of change from a tired and underperforming government and promised a post-secondary tuition rebate of up to $20,000 per student, designed to encourage young people to stay in Saskatchewan. Wall's promise was priced at up to $90 million over four years.

In the politics of emotion —and campaign politics are designed to appeal to emotions —this wasn't about prescription drugs or students. It was about money in pockets, personal well-being and the security of children and families. Typically in Saskatchewan elections, the core values break down to "security" issues versus "opportunity" issues. And the NDP is masterful at owning security —that's why change is unknown and bad and we need the NDP to protect us and our way of life. It was no coincidence that Wall's SaskParty named its platform "Securing the Future."

Generally, people's strongest feelings and emotions center on money, family and jobs. In 2003, when the NDP took down the SaskParty's Hermanson on the sell-off of Crown corporations, the emotional issue wasn't about Crowns—it was about changing our way of life, people losing their jobs and their sense of personal security being threatened. And it was fear of change and the unknown.

On the change-resistance pitch, the NDP was in safe territory—this theme has been woven into nearly every NDP campaign since the 1950s. In 2007, as they had in four elections previously, the NDP also tied risky and unknown change to their old nemesis Grant Devine, the last person who had defeated an NDP government and brought political change to Saskatchewan 25 years earlier.

The anti-change issue is fundamental to the NDP core vote of senior citizens, social activists and the MUSH sector of municipalities, universities, schools and hospitals. This is not a fertile place for opportunity voting. It's all about security and preserving the status quo.

Many seniors do not like the new or different; why change when things have always been done the same way? And, for public sector employees and those receiving government benefits, political change-resistance is always strong. This is also propped up by large government and Crown employee unions that are officially affiliated with the NDP and staunchly resistant to institutional change.

Whether it was Janice MacKinnon's intention to torpedo her old party, or whether it just worked out that way, after undermining the premier on equalization, the former finance minister wasn't done with Calvert yet. As the election campaign began, MacKinnon would return to pop the NDP's balloon on the party's most expensive election promise in a generation.

Calvert's centerpiece campaign issue was to take the seniors' drug plan, which capped every prescription at $15, and extend it to a fully universal prescription drug plan for every man, woman and child in Saskatchewan. The NDP estimated this to cost $150 million a year or $600 million over a four year term of office. But based on the cost of the seniors' drug plan, which was climbing at 13% a year and still rising, this would have pushed the NDP universal plan to nearly $750 million—or three-quarters of a billion dollars—by the end of its first four years. And, with an aging population and prescription drug costs escalating at double-digit rates, the cost of Calvert's drug plan would only increase.

In several media appearances and op-ed pieces, MacKinnon would question both the need and the cost of such an expensive and ambitious expansion of universal Medicare.

"If this were implemented, some government in the future during an economic downturn would either have to curtail this program, cut spending in some other area or raise taxes to finance it."

Janice MacKinnon, October, 2007

The NDP's costly and controversial universal drug scheme had another problem—it was seen as vote buying and diverting precious money away from the existing Medicare system which already consumes 43 cents of every single dollar spent by the Saskatchewan government. And, in case voters needed reminding, this was the same Medicare system plagued by long waiting lists for specialists' appointments, diagnostics and surgeries. And with doctor and nurse shortages, ER overcrowding and public anger— the NDP answer appeared to be setting up something new to pay for when they couldn't get the basics right.

"Given what we know about universal programs—the coverage of rich and poor alike, the duplication of existing benefits, the inducement to increased consumption—we should think twice before launching yet another universal health care program.

"Any drug plan should be targeted, affordable and based on need, but it should also protect the public against cata-strophic drug costs. The NDP plan doesn't meet this test".

Bruce Johnstone, Leader Post Financial Editor, October, 2007

The NDP Boycott Begins

In the weeks running up to the election, Premier Calvert's increasingly choleric press secretary, Jay Branch, was being testy with my talk show producer, claiming that Calvert and other senior NDP ministers were too busy to appear on the radio show. In the past, agree or disagree with me, the NDP would always put up ministers and spokespeople to defend the government.

By two weeks into the campaign, the NDP boycott was underway—no leader, no ministers, not even candidates when we offered them free air time. This meant little to me—if people don't want to appear on my radio show, I can't make them. The best I can do is to extend the invitation. But it doesn't mean that we will stop talking about issues or people just because they're boycotting us.

The only inconvenience was that during election campaigns we are required by broadcasting laws to provide equal time to the major parties and ensure that issues are balanced in the allotment of time and the presentation of diverse opinions. Ironically—and a rather odd coinci-dence I later thought—just as the NDP boycott began, we started getting complaints from certain NDP-supportive callers that I was being unfair and breaking the law by denying the NDP radio time. Whether this was a deliberate and clumsy strategy by the NDP campaign to target the talk show we'll never know, but it did require us to put clearly on the public record that it wasn't us turning down or denying the NDP; the party had been offered air time but declined. And, like the laws of gravity, no broadcasting laws are going to save a party that wants to jump off a cliff.

. . . .

"Is the NDP refusing to appear because they don't agree with Gormley's conservative politics or are they punishing Gormley for not towing the NDP line of "everything's fine, don't change it"? My guess is the latter.

This tactic, over the next 14 days, will not only raise the ire of Gormley but the ire of a large segment of the electorate, left, right or centre, that rely on Gormley for information, opinion and debate.

The desired effect that Calvert is trying to accomplish will be the opposite of what he believes."

www.NDPBoogeyman.blogspot.com, October, 2007

. . . .

In fairness to several NDP MLAs, there were usually a few prepared to ignore the boycott, including justice minister Frank Quennell and ex-finance minister Harry Van Mulligen. The NDP boycott continued not only for the rest of the campaign but thereafter. In 2009, with the ascension of Dwain Lingenfelter as leader, his trusted right hand man, former 1970s CBC reporter and ex-Romanow staffer Garry Aldridge hissed to my producer "we'll never come on Gormley's show." Later, Lingenfelter's communications director inadvertently confirmed in an e-mail that a "caucus policy" existed that no NDP MLAs would appear on *John Gormley Live*.

C'est la vie.

Political Children on Facebook & Grant Devine's Last Stand

Ever since Saskatchewan's first election in 1905 when political parties erected placards and campaign signs, they have inevitably been torn down —usually by over-zealous opponents or by bored kids looking for fun. The destruction of campaign signs is nothing new. It happens in every campaign and is against the law, both under the Elections Act and the criminal law.

But in 2007's Saskatchewan campaign, a Canadian first occurred —the social networking site, Facebook, became the forum for high school kids who also happened to be politically connected, supporting the vandalism of campaign signs. Six Saskatoon high school students set up a Facebook group called the "New Saskatchewan Sign Kickers Party," encouraging kids to kick down political signs and, particularly, "we find it unfair that the SaskParty has three times the funding of any other party so they get all the big signs—we seek to even this out."

The site—complete with a picture of one of the teens kicking down a SaskParty lawn sign and identifying himself in the photo caption—got the phone lines jumping when I brought it up on the radio show and read the names of the kids and others who had joined the group and posted pictures. One of the founders of the site was the nephew of disgraced NDP former Chief of staff Jim Fodey. Another was the nephew of longtime NDP MLA Peter Prebble and younger brother of the rabidly left-wing editor of the U of S campus newspaper The Sheaf.

As expected, when we outed the kids they stopped what they were doing and apologized. But these baby New Democrats weren't exactly Rhodes Scholars in waiting. After identifying themselves committing criminal acts, and getting caught, they sent a shot my way by setting up a Facebook group called "John Gormley Should Go F**k Himself". On the site, which stayed up for only several hours, these geniuses attached a picture of John Gormley, with an obscene caption across the face. But it wasn't me. It was John Gormley, the leader of the Irish Green Party.

As the days of October 2007 slipped away and the November 7th Election Day approached, the SaskParty's strength in the public opinion polls held and the NDP grew increasingly desperate. Having successfully branded the words "Grant Devine" to mean everything negative and bad about non-NDP politics in Saskatchewan, the "Devine Effect" was all the NDP had left. So they pulled out all the stops and diverted campaign ad spending away from wolves and sheep to a series of ads comparing Brad Wall to Grant Devine. Some, with bouncing heads through a meadow, were reminiscent of Monty Python's Flying Circus circa 1972. Others grimly warned that a vote for Wall meant the end of Medicare and Crown corporations.

For Doug Still and the hard partisans in his NDP campaign war-room, Devine was a touchstone, a mantra. These were lifetime, middle-aged and ideological New Democrats who had foot soldiered in every election from the 1970s. But for thousands of voters not even born over 25 years earlier when Devine was elected —and in grade school when Devine was defeated in 1991 —it was like running a campaign against faux singers Milli Vanilli. Nobody knew what the hell the NDP was talking about when they kept invoking Devine's name and picture.

Why the NDP Lost

"Hope beats fear."

Brad Wall, Election Night, November 7, 2007

Undeterred and not frightened by the NDP campaign, on Election Day the voters overwhelmingly supported Brad Wall and the SaskParty. With 51% of the popular vote, Wall won 38 seats —the NDP polled 37% and won 20 ridings. Having picked up five urban seats from the NDP in Saskatoon and Regina and one each in Prince Albert, Moose Jaw and Yorkton, the old "rural-urban split" of earlier elections had disappeared.

"We ran a good campaign. We campaigned on our principles and our values…Friends, tonight we leave government, but we leave with heads held high. I would not have changed a great deal about the campaign itself."

Lorne Calvert, November 7, 2007

Calvert did not run a good campaign. He ran a disastrous one which will be remembered for its dishonesty. Telling lies and fabricating stuff about people isn't the Saskatchewan way and ultimately this made voters angry. And it actually drove some of them to the SaskParty.

For all the left-right divide that has defined Saskatchewan politics since becoming the Petri dish of democratic socialism in 1944, our people are pragmatic. As one blogger commented on election night, "They like honest people. They like decent people. And they have an inherent sense of fairness."

The NDP had not recognized that their win four years earlier in 2003 had been conditional. After their vulgar beat down on Elwin Hermanson, a decent guy with an awkward name and manner that bred mistrust, Calvert's NDP was given a chance to redeem themselves by turning around not just their timid and weak style of governing but also their nasty style of politics. The campaign of 2007 was not the election in which to tell lies, spread fear and try to kick another opponent to the curb.

The seeds were sown for Calvert's loss four years earlier. Within weeks of the 2003 election he raised the PST with the explanation that talking about tax hikes during elections isn't popular. This was followed by four more years of thinking small, staying safe and trying to pick a fight with Ottawa over equalization as an election wedge issue. As an economic boom began sweeping Saskatchewan, it seemed to be happening in spite of the Calvert government not because of it. And the NDP appeared incapable of getting out in front and leading—doing something positive, upbeat and forward looking.

The NDP had eventually grown old, tired and arrogant. In part, they fell victim to what former Premier Allan Blakeney used to describe as the backpack of politics —a new government starts with an empty backpack into which every day someone puts a stone until eventually the load is overwhelming.

As the 2007 election dawned, there was no NDP campaign built on positives which attempted to harness and develop Saskatchewan's excellence—that job was left to Brad Wall and the SaskParty. The only upbeat message by the NDP was trying to advance an irresponsible and costly universal drug plan that was the answer to a question that no one had asked in the first place.

When the drug plan issue failed to get traction, the NDP operators' manual was pulled out and the best Calvert could come up with was another attempt at fear-mongering, name calling and manufacturing stories about his opponent. In the "old Saskatchewan" this might have worked. But it was not consistent with the emerging positive, can-do attitude of Saskatchewan and our people.

Chapter 11

THE LAST WORD AND
THE ROAD AHEAD

What Hit the NDP?

One has to be either naïve or cynical to think that Saskatchewan's NDP did not receive a clear message from the people that night in November, 2007. But how the party deals with that message will determine the future of not only the NDP, but of Saskatchewan politics.

The NDP doesn't lose its grip on government very often—only three times in the last 65 years. As a result, a couple of things happen. First, because there is an ingrained belief by many of its supporters that the NDP actually owns the politics and government of Saskatchewan, the party responds bitterly to loss. The last time the NDP had a stint in opposition, in the 1980s, one union leader promised that "we, in concert with the NDP, will work to make this province ungovernable." And they did. Procedural delays, days of extended sittings of the Legislature, acrimonious sessions and NDP MLAs storming out of the Assembly saw the most poisoned legislative environment in Saskatchewan history.

When the NDP is in opposition, its *modus operandi* is clear—do nothing to cooperate with the people who usurped power and "stole" government from the NDP. The strategy is to make governing for the new people as difficult as possible by being uncooperative, obstructive and even vicious and personal in attacking individuals on the government side of the Assembly.

Now, just three years after its election defeat, the NDP is again playing true to form, refusing even to agree to the traditional parliamentary procedure where, by mutual consent, the parties allocate certain hours of debate for certain issues. The NDP continues to angrily resist doing anything that might allow the people who denied them power to govern, although the SaskParty won the right to form government by winning more seats than the NDP. Ironically, Dwain Lingenfelter, who in the '80s led the "ungovernable campaign" as the NDP opposition House leader is now the party's leader.

The second aspect of the NDP in defeat is a remarkable capacity to move on after an election loss as if nothing ever happened. Like the lawyer on TV's Ally McBeal who'd say "bygones" every time he offended someone, the party simply picks up and keeps all eyes directed forward to the next election: the best way to deal with the past is not to talk about it. On my radio show just days after the 2007 election, an irate caller responded to my criticism of the defeated Calvert government by saying "it's been two days, let it go." Then, later that week an anonymous handwritten note arrived in the mail, urging me to "stop talking about our NDP"…quick closure for 16 years of political rule.

Obviously somewhere there's a reasonable period of time after which the faults of defeated governments should be let go. I'm guessing it is something more than the three days "forgive and forget" policy of Calvert supporters and somewhat less than the 29 years the NDP has milked Grant Devine who still, even today, features prominently in NDP election campaigns, party newsletters and attacks on the SaskParty government.

Finding the Iconic Negative

This raises another aspect of NDP losses—how the party that defeats an NDP government chooses to position itself. A new government should always ask "what would the NDP do if it were in our position?" which is not an admission of anything beyond intelligent strategy —there are reasons the NDP is Saskatchewan's natural governing party.

I don't know how the Ross Thatcher Liberals of the 1960s launched their government—I was working hard on graduating from kindergarten at the time. But the Devine Tories of the 1980s made an early political mistake after their 1982 election victory that came back to punish them. Some inside Brad Wall's SaskParty political brain trust are determined to repeat the Devine mistake—only time will tell if they are clever enough not to doom themselves.

Here's the mistake: new governments—full of optimism and brimming with change —quickly move forward, send a positive message, wipe the slate clean and sell Saskatchewan people on their "brand new" approach but fail to link their agenda back to the government they just defeated. That's what separates the NDP from the parties that occasionally knock them off.

After every big election win that restores them to power, the NDP aggressively implements its campaign promises. But on every issue it tackles and frames in its own image, the NDP always reiterates why it's making the changes. It's not because the NDP is a party of nice people doing nice things. It is to repair the damage caused by the last government or to fill a need created by the last government's negligence, carelessness or incompetence. The NDP avoids doing the "new, shiny government" thing and gets down to business, implementing change but always from the perspective as being a savior from a fundamentally bad government that shall never be forgotten or forgiven for its sins.

Although the NDP sells the message of positive new change, which is important, it also reinforces what I call the "iconic negative"—the constant reminder for voters of why they dumped a government they wanted to be rid of. In the hands of NDP tacticians the iconic negative is sustained and even grown into a type of boogeyman of which tales are told and from which the NDP will always save us.

The iconic negative also comes in handy as a measuring stick for the new government. Moving forward, why compare yourself to your own record when it's far easier to compare everything you do to the evil thing you vanquished? This regular looking backwards can also be used to remind voters what might await them in future if they're not careful to keep the boogeyman away.

Frequency and consistency are critical in political messaging. Voters have to be repeatedly reminded of why they did the right thing in electing a new party to government. But they also have to be reminded just as frequently of what it was that made them mad enough to vote out the previous government on Election Day.

Some people in the SaskParty's highest echelons are bright and well-intentioned but more naïve than strategic—after all, they've never been in government before—and they seem to think that their premier, party and policies are so attractive and positive that they will carry the government forward. They will —but not alone and not for long.

As the positives must be reinforced and reminded, at the same time there must be a regular re-telling of the last decade of the NDP—mistakes, arrogance, incompetence and scandals. Swept up in this should be the population crisis, Canada's longest hospital wait lists, highways that were a laughingstock, the most expensive government scandal in history or the shameful abuse of vulnerable women in the Murdoch Carriere debacle and subsequent cover-up.

Whether everyone in the SaskParty brain trust really understands this, colour me dubious.

Watching this internal tension within the SaskParty between wanting to be positive agents of change—without reinforcing what voters wanted change from —brings me back to an earlier time. For reasons never apparent to me, shortly after Grant Devine's government was elected — maybe it was because I hosted a radio show at the time —the new minister of finance, a guy named Bob Andrew, took me to lunch. When he asked what I thought his early priority should be, I asked him if he was going to explain in his first budget that the government books he'd inherited from the NDP were dramatically different than they appeared.

From the full depth of my 24-year-old wisdom I queried the new finance minister on whether he would set out for the public two sets of actual raw numbers that would show a stark contrast. One set would be the figures used just months earlier by the NDP that showed neatly balanced budgets. The other set of numbers, I suggested, would be the actual summary financial statements of government that showed how massive borrowing and deficits hidden inside Crown corporations had driven the provincial debt to its highest level in years and had been used to get the NDP through the 1981 recession. Andrew condescendingly explained that "we don't do things that way and we're going to be a positive, forward-looking government." I thought he was a naïve know-it-all.

The NDP will bounce back —they always do. But whether they get a free pass on the negative part of their legacy will be up to the SaskParty.

Fixing the NDP

The more difficult question for New Democrats is whether the party will pause for some self-examination or continue chugging ahead as if the 2007 election loss was an aberration, a fluke where the NDP was simply sent to its room for a time-out.

"All left-wing parties have lost a lot of that fire in the belly. They used to be about changing the world. In part it's because they succeeded—we have Medicare and universal education system. But they've been unable to respond to a resurgent right-wing in the past 20 years...As well, they've abandoned their own economic model—which may or may not have been working—which leaves them to work with the economic status quo, and not creating an alternative."

Prof. Howard Leeson, former NDP senior advisor, August, 2008

Far be it from me to offer solutions for an NDP fix, even if the party truly believes that it needs to be put up on the hoist. From its coming to power in 1991 until its defeat 16 years later at the hands of Brad Wall, the NDP never faced a challenge from another strong political party engaging it in a clash of ideas and policy. As a result, it has not always re-invented itself enough to adapt or even ask itself the tough questions.

Whatever brand its socialism is to take, the NDP will have to find room to be more positive, more outward-looking and to banish the class struggle rhetoric. The NDP should re-evaluate its "fear, loathing and envy" paradigm that has worked well in the past with certain negative "take away" voters but has done so much damage over the decades to Saskatchewan's self-image and our national reputation. Can a social democratic, left-wing party in the most prosperous part of the world sell itself without tearing down success and without using the politics of fear to trump hope and truth?

My radio show has spanned four distinct NDP governments: the end of the 1995 Romanow era; the 1999 minority marriage with the Liberals; the transition to Lorne Calvert; and then the 2003 Calvert comeback that saved the NDP until its defeat in 2007.

Toward the end of the Romanow years, the NDP embarked on a plan to monitor 16 benchmarks of Saskatchewan life. It was helpful, as a periodic check-up, but lacked the roadmap that identified a specific "where" we were going or how we would get there. By the Calvert years, there seemed to be no plan at all—a penchant for studying but not taking action; reacting and following developments rather than leading.

In the fall of 2005, after Saskatchewan officially turned 100 years old, the NDP embarked on our second century with the proclamation that we were "a province where no one is left behind on the path to opportunity, a province with an unbreakable social fabric, built on the foundation of diverse and growing communities and a green and prosperous economy." What the hell did that mean? With a plummeting population at the time and expectations continually being tamped down by the NDP, was the "path" of opportunity actually going to lead somewhere for once? Where would it lead and when?

Now in opposition, the NDP seems to have defined itself by being "not Brad Wall" and bringing a "throw everything and hope it sticks" approach which is distinctively personal and excoriatingly negative—not to mention continually talking down Saskatchewan's prospects. For the NDP to regain a foothold on relevance, it will have to do better than this and offer a responsible, alternative commentary that sets out a clear vision and specific policies that can be benchmarked not just against the SaskParty but against earlier NDP governments which let us know how little they thought of us.

In the summer of 2009, the National Post's Kelly McParland prescribed several steps to save Jack Layton's federal NDP. His solutions apply equally to the Saskatchewan provincial version.

Simple Steps to Save the NDP

Cut the union yoke: You don't need these guys: everything they're in, they're in for themselves and loyalty is a concept they understand only in terms of what it can do for their next contract.

Set free the crazies: The Conservatives suffered for years over the occasional eruptions of the right-wing fringe. Stephen Harper put a muzzle on those he can influence, and built a firewall between the party and those he can't. The NDP should do the same, starting with the Israeli apartheid crowd and progressing from there. The fringers have nowhere else to go anyway.

Drop the conceit: Canada is a wealthy and generous country that has one of the world's most liberal social policies. Quit pretending the NDP alone cares about social policy and craft some proposals that fit the Canada that exists and that consist of something other than a willing-ness to write big cheques.

Read a book on economics: Canada depends on trade, on resources and its ability to compete with bigger and more populous industrial economies. Railing about the need to make Canada a more expensive place to do business is wrong-headed, short-sighted and self-defeat-ing. Hire someone with a bit of credibility to write new policies that suit the country rather than party ideology.

Kelly McParland, National Post, August, 2009

The last time Saskatchewan's NDP truly looked itself and its policies in the face was in the late 1960s. After the 1964 loss to the Thatcher Liberals and a second defeat in 1967, the NDP went through the Waffle crisis and deposed its leader, Woodrow Lloyd, who was sympathetic to the new left. In 1970, rejecting the young Roy Romanow and others in the so-called "right-wing" of the NDP, the party chose Allan Blakeney who was clearly a left-winger but more grounded and strategic than the dogmatic Marxists in the Waffle. Blakeney was elected in 1971 and shaped the next decade by promoting increased government intervention in the economy, an expan-sion of the welfare state and the creation of new Crown corporations.

After the Devine years of the 1980s, although the NDP carried out a significant policy review, the party did not robustly debate its direction or concretely change any policies when acclaiming Romanow as leader in

1987 with no one running against him. Although Romanow's time governing during the 1990s was mainly marked by restraint and restructuring government, there wasn't a peep of policy discussion when Calvert triumphed over six other candidates in 2001, as the choice of the party establishment. Clearly to the left of Romanow, Calvert was a weaker and less decisive leader and the party seemed directionless on policy.

Following Calvert's retirement, in 2009 the party mainstream chose 60-year-old Dwain Lingenfelter, who had left Saskatchewan nine years earlier and moved away to Alberta after quitting the NDP. Although a policy review was announced after Lingenfelter became leader, there was no debate, policy conflict or serious clash of ideas during the leadership that caused the party to re-examine itself.

Never once during the NDP leadership or since has anyone in the party publicly explained or apologized for the scandals, arrogance and loss of touch with the people that so discredited Saskatchewan politics in the early 2000s.

The Lingenfelter Effect

Beyond farming and being a customs officer on the U.S. border, there isn't much about Dwain Lingenfelter's life that isn't politics. A career politician, he was first elected as an NDP MLA in 1978 and retired from politics in 2000, leaving Saskatchewan and moving to Calgary, though he still owned the family farm and vast tracts of land near Shaunavon and throughout Southwest Saskatchewan. Returning to Saskatchewan in 2009 he was elected NDP leader.

When Lingenfelter moved to Calgary, it was to take a job at Nexen as a "GR guy," a government relations junior vice president, which included lobbying politicians. Just three years earlier, when Lingenfelter sat in Romanow's Cabinet, the NDP sold to Nexen—then known as CanOxy —the Saskatchewan government's remaining shares in Wascana Energy, the former Crown corporation once called SaskOil, which was privatized in the mid-1980s and, in 1997 the NDP completed the privatization by selling the government's shares to Nexen.

Lingenfelter had supported selling the shares to the company that would later employ him. But after taking the Nexen job and working with them for nine years, he told NDP delegates that "the privatization of SaskOil was a big mistake for the province" and he promised that should he ever become premier he would set up a government-owned energy company "that does our own drilling and exploration for gas in this province. I'm committed to do that if I'm the premier."

Wealthy, married three times, charming and a close talker, Lingenfelter is very effective one-on-one as he sidles up to people, locks eyes and speaks in a low, lilting cadence that is quite persuasive, I've always thought. Some women tell me they find it creepy.

From a policy perspective, Lingenfelter has been flexible in a Gumby/Pokey bend any way you need to be flexible. Since returning to Saskatchewan, he has supported nuclear power. Now, he does not. After strongly supporting left-wing and interventionist government policies in the past, Lingenfelter now assures business audiences of his right-wing bona fides. At the same time, Lingenfelter is strongly supported by the Saskatchewan Federation of Labour, which will work with him—should he become premier—to repeal changes made to labour laws by the SaskParty government which have leveled the playing field between unions and businesses.

Lingenfelter has an Achilles' heel, and it's not policy. It is his congenital need to go negative and personal against his political opponents. He is seemingly unable to distinguish between disagreeing with positions and attacking the people who hold them.

Moments after becoming NDP leader, Lingenfelter—in a province-wide, live interview on our radio network—demanded an apology from Premier Wall because "Brad," according to Lingenfelter, had apparently deceived Calgary oilmen into thinking that Wall's background was in the oil business. Exactly how the premier did this was not made clear, but it was vintage Lingenfelter—impugn motives, attack character and then demand your prey "come clean."

Several months earlier, before returning to politics, Lingenfelter crankily reacted to a newspaper column I'd written laying out his involvement in many unpopular and left-wing measures of NDP governments that he was part of. Rather than challenging me as being incorrect, mistaken or even mischievous, Lingenfelter swung for the upper deck, suggesting that I was deliberately lying about his record. "John should know it's a lie. John is lying about that. And he knows that. And he's disingenuous."

In the same interview he observed that I was "the kind of individual who is ingenuous about these kinds of issues." I think he meant "disingenuous." However, when you're me, "ingenuous" is good and I'll take it. But, in an odd Lingenfelter affectation, ever notice that when he's smearing people he often calls them by their first name? It's almost like sliding the knife into someone is more acceptable when the victim's first name is used.

On the same day he did his disingenuous/ingenuous tirade, Lingenfelter had a go at me during a business speech when he opened his remarks by mocking me for being a failed politician, among other things. When you dish out as much stuff as I do in life, clearly I expect to take a few shots now and then, even probably deserve some of them. It goes with the territory when you're a talk show host. But Lingenfelter made a mistake that day. Moving from ridiculing me, he made an incorrect and libelous statement about my law practice (I remain a lawyer in both Saskatchewan and Alberta). This is where I make part of my living. So, a day later I hired a lawyer and put Lingenfelter on notice of my intention to sue him should he ever repeat his words. I think he got the message.

The old NDP warrior Lingenfelter has recently been tripped up in an increasingly viral video world which demands consistent statements and positions from public figures. The morning after his by-election win, he was caught on tape saying that Premier Wall was trying to play down the by-election loss by the SaskParty "because that's what losers do." Two months later, Lingenfelter denied this, saying "I didn't say 'a' loser." Then, just 12 days later—seeming to forget that everything's recorded these days—he said "when I refer to a loser, I'm not talking about anyone but Brad Wall."

In an attempt to play counter-stereotype, six months after becoming NDP leader, Lingenfelter told a reporter that he came from the "corporate world where there's a politeness between executives" and mentioned how difficult it was for him to adopt the negativity associated with being an opposition leader. He assured the interviewer that he was now different than he was in the 1990s. This came just days after he'd publicly called a SaskParty backbencher a "dummy," reiterated his "Brad's a loser" line and was being repeatedly warned about his disruptive behaviour in the Legislative Assembly.

For a guy renowned for his toughness and personal attacks, Lingenfelter can be surprisingly fragile. During the NDP leadership campaign, miffed at me mocking him on the radio show, one day he singled out a young female news reporter from our company, belittling her in front of other reporters and refusing to answer her questions because "Rawlco and John Gormley are nothing more than the Fox News Channel of Saskatchewan." When senior members of the legislative press gallery intervened and scolded Lingenfelter over his unacceptable behaviour, he relented.

While he is free to avoid me—and assiduously does—Lingenfelter seems unaware that Fox News, which has higher ratings than CNN and all cable news channels combined, has two distinct branches. On one hand, there are opinionated talk show hosts like me; on the other, there are professional, well-regarded journalists, just like in our company, who cover the same stories as other news organizations do. While some of Fox's talk show hosts intimidate and scare away left-wing politicians who tend to avoid them—like I seem to frighten off certain people—there is a clear distinction between talk show hosts and the professional news-gathering side of the operation.

Besides, verbally abusing a young woman in front of other people is nothing more than bullying. I'm clearly what bothers Lingenfelter. Yet he's never tried that with me. Perhaps he knows how it would end and he wouldn't like it.

Days after Lingenfelter's win, I checked in with an NDP insider friend, whose advice I've come to value over the years. His prescription was blunt: "The NDP shot itself cleanly and squarely through its collective foot. Link will not win against Wall next time out. Link will not relinquish leadership after one loss. As a result, NDP will be led by 66 year-old Link in his second attempt.

Unless the SaskParty makes the same type of 2nd term errors Devine made, Link will prove unsuccessful yet again. But he will still not relinquish. Even if he is convinced to shuffle out, his Garry Aldridge-led squad will have strangled the party sufficiently to ensure an 'orderly transition' to more of the same. The NDP has just caused itself to become frozen in time for at least the next 10 years. If I was Wall et al, I would be quite pleased."

My friend observed that Ryan Meili, who finished second to Lingenfelter with 45% of the vote, would have stood no chance of defeating the Sask-Party "but the next four to six years would have allowed the party to sort itself out and move on to someone electable. Where were the real alternatives to Lingenfelter? If Meili could get nearly one-half of the votes, couldn't someone electable have actually won it? Poor Deb Higgins." As usual, my NDP pal was right on the money.

The NDP could not have chosen a tougher and more experienced campaigner than Lingenfelter. But, with more baggage than Air Canada, he is a lightning rod for anyone disaffected with a generation of failed NDP policies. Representing a three-decade menu of NDP hits and misses, Lingenfelter wears anything that people found offensive about the 1970s-era NDP. He was in the Blakeney Cabinet after being elected in 1978.

In the '80s, when Lingenfelter was part of an extremist opposition during the Devine years, many observers have never forgotten how toxic our politics became. Or in the early '90s, when Lingenfelter smirked "there'll probably never be water" in the Rafferty-Alameda Dam (there is now —a full lake of it) or when Saskatchewan's crumbling highways were a national embarrassment, Lingenfelter was there, too.

In the unpopular Romanow-era decisions to close hospitals and pass (but never proclaim) the "job-killing monster" law, Lingenfelter was in Cabinet. He was also there for the raising of the PST to 9%, the Channel Lake scandal and the $35 million Spudco debacle.

There have been some remarkable political transformations in life, where prepared and lucky politicians shed their past, morph into something new and successfully re-invent themselves as Lingenfelter is trying to do. But often the road ahead is measured by the bridges that have been burned behind.

With some staff and former senior NDP advisors grumbling about a fractious and divided office and caucus environment under Lingenfelter, the NDP leader faces an important personal issue about the image he conveys. Genuine warmth, sincerity and trust are critical in politics. And, like the intangible negative impression that NDP pollsters discovered about former SaskParty leader Elwin Hermanson, Lingenfelter is dogged by an indescribable "ick" factor for many voters —a manner that is off-putting.

Lingenfelter is in stark contrast to Tommy Douglas, who used the strength of his personality and character to convert people into lifelong cheerleaders. The late Ed Whelan, five term CCF/NDP MLA, authored with his wife Pemrose, "Touched by Tommy," a book which chronicled the stories of hope and humour from the people who lives intersected Douglas'. It's difficult, when viewing Lingenfelter, to imagine a book called "Touched by Dwain." Wouldn't be much of a page-turner.

Zeroes & Heroes: NDPers I Like… and Some Not So Much

Listeners often say, "I hear you criticize the NDP but what do you really think of the people inside the party?" It's a good question.

Like most things worth doing in life, politics is an intensely human affair grounded in people's perceptions and aspirations. In trying to do their best, some people just don't know what "best" is because they don't get out much and that's been a problem in the past for many in Saskatchewan politics. Others in politics lapse into a cynical and arrogant sense of entitlement.

But, by far, most people in public life work hard and believe they are doing what's best for their community. Because people are as inspiring as they are disappointing and ultimately we're all fallible, there is a broad range of personality shapes and sizes —smart, kind, sincere, well-meaning, selfish, stupid, petty and mean. I've met them all in politics and in every political party.

While the NDP's philosophy of fear, thinking small and resisting change has held back my province for generations—which has often been so frustrating—there are notable New Democrats that I respect and like.

NDPers I Like*

Frank Quennell	**Deb McDonald**
Deb Higgins	**Chris Axworthy**
John Nilson	**Ryan Meili**

*this is not an exhaustive list —there are others

Frank Quennell, with a meek and unassuming appearance, looks like the "before" picture in the old comic book bodybuilding ads. A clever, funny, tough and self-deprecating man, Quennell is one of my favourites. He deservedly took heat during the Klassen malicious prosecution scandal for his delay in apologizing on behalf of the government and for the way he backed a disgraced Crown prosecutor. But he was not acting with malice, rather the belief —mistaken, in my view—that he was seen as standing up for his justice department lawyers as their minister. There were other ways he could still have given support to his staff but appeared more sympathetic and accommodating to the victims of the malicious prosecution.

Quennell's quiet dignity, class and his ability to disagree without being disagreeable have always struck me as what the word "honourable" should mean in politics. And unbeknownst to most people was Frank's unswerving support for his own son, a young reservist serving with the Canadian military in Afghanistan. As one who is humbled by the courage of brave military families, I often said a silent prayer for Frank and his family and all the moms and dads like him who nurture and grow such remarkable young Canadian heroes.

Deb Higgins is an unabashedly left-wing union leader—approachable, open to debate and someone for whom my respect grew every time I met her. Even in the midst of the "job-killing monster" debacle, she never backed down or took the debate personally. Though we sharply disagreed, I always had the sense around Deb that she would be open to at least talking about how we could improve the lives of Saskatchewan people, her way or maybe even mine! Bonus: as an avid golfer who hits a nice ball and is so pleasant to be around, a golf game with Deb is a good walk made better.

John Nilson is probably the Romanow and Calvert Cabinet minister I knew least well. He had a hyper-partisan staffer who kept him at arm's length from my show long before it became fashionable in NDP circles to boycott me. But the few times we did chat on the radio or socially, Nilson's grace, good humour, generosity and intelligence made for enjoyable conversation. And although some who don't understand politics whine about lawyers in public office—although their numbers have dropped precipitously in recent years—lawyers like Nilson understand that good debate and sharp repartee can be had with enough civility and respect that there will always be another day.

Deb McDonald is a career NDP strategist and party worker who has done it all since the 1970s—campaign volunteer, paid party senior staffer, campaign manager, NDP bureaucrat, Cabinet advisor and deputy minister.

But like most political operatives I respect, she understands the rules of politics well and is able to rise above the petty hate sessions. I may, however, have gotten her fired. After I referred to her in glowing terms during the 2009 NDP leadership convention and commended her consummate professionalism, she was fired as one of the first acts of the new NDP leader Lingenfelter. Sorry!

When Chris Axworthy, law professor and NDP MP, quit federal politics to join the Romanow Cabinet in 1999, and was elected shortly after in a by-election in a safe NDP seat, it looked like a scripted play that he would become the next premier, post-Romanow. It didn't work. Axworthy lost to Lorne Calvert on the final ballot of the 2001 NDP leadership. Of dubious partisan purity it turned out—Axworthy's last two campaigns were as a federal Liberal—he is a rakish guy, clever, with an often irreverent sense of humour and the ability to bluntly concede that things might not be going as well as others in the NDP were trying to portray them.

And, the oddest of all my NDP favourites is a guy I likely have the least in common with philosophically. Ryan Meili, a Saskatoon physician, is as pure socialist as I am not. He's a collectivist with grave reservations about capitalism, the market economy, international trade and globalization. I can't think of what we'd talk about over dinner but we would have a good conversation. With sincerity, respectfulness and transparency I found refreshing in his run for the NDP leadership in 2009, Meili was not only the most left-leaning candidate but the most prepared to engage in debate. I found myself respecting and liking the guy.

It's pretty clear from the radio show and my always subtle opinions that some NDPers really bug me: they're petty and vindictive bullies accustomed to getting their own way. And they don't play well with others they disagree with. But rather than make a list, which would be long and might leave someone out, it's better to talk generically about the type of people in the political left who would rather run over their opponents and critics instead of thinking about a position, confidently and intelligently asserting it, debating it, agreeing to disagree and then selling their argument in the public marketplace of ideas and free speech.

For some prominent NDP MLAs, party staff and consultants over the years, I was never sure if they lacked the intellectual horsepower and defaulted instead to behaving like thugs or if they got some sort of satisfaction from pushing people around. Others, like the parable of the scorpion riding across the pond on a frog, just can't help themselves —they have to sting and kill the frog, even it means drowning themselves because, hey, they're scorpions and that's what they're supposed to do. It's these people that heap scorn on their critics and seem to be hardwired to go personal in their attacks against their political enemies.

It is probably a character flaw of mine but, like a moth drawn to the light, I just couldn't seem to stay away from certain NDP staff, MLAs and their union boss proxies who had pushed Saskatchewan people around unchallenged for far too long. Fortunately, some of these have since retired, others have moved away, but some of these intimidators —who are usually found taking on anyone weaker than them —are still around. But they tend to boycott my talk show.

At least on the boycott issue, Lingenfelter is consistent. Adamant that he will not talk to me on the radio, it was surprising to recently discover that he now can't even look at me. During the live broadcast of the provincial budget in 2010, which I've done from the Rotunda of the Legislature twelve years running, the NDP leader took such pains to avoid making eye contact with me that he stood with his back toward our broadcast booth, shuffling with backwards baby steps across the marble floor of the Legislature to be interviewed by our reporters but never facing me. Staring at Lingenfelter's bald spot, I had this urge to play the "ostrich game"—the well-known teasing we've all done with two-year-olds— "Where did you go? Where are you? If you can't see me, I can't see you…" But I didn't. Someone had to be the grown-up.

The Road Ahead

While I'm often critical of the NDP's long history of holding back the greatest province in Canada —our Saskatchewan—and driving our kids away by the thousands, you may have inferred my respect, even begrudging admiration, for how effectively the NDP has so tenaciously clung to power for all but 19 years during the last seven decades. Both times in the last 25 years that NDP governments were defeated, 1982 and 2007, their hopeful critics talked about changing the face of Saskatchewan by squeezing out socialism and diminishing the NDP as the natural governing party.

History suggests this likely will not happen. Or at least it will not happen without a concerted and unified effort by non-NDPers to take the principles and behaviour of the NDP and hold them up to public scrutiny. The challenge is then for the NDP to demonstrate an alternative to the 1950s and 1970s socialism that is no longer relevant to a Saskatchewan that has become a hopeful, upbeat, optimistic place that is embracing the world and its people like never before.

The strength of the NDP is its ability to get elected at all costs. This comes from finding its own center—not a politically philosophic center —but a place in the NDP that embraces stakeholders like unions, social activists and the left and keeps them cohesive enough to rally around a certain set of seminal principles which endure and never change. The NDP core principles include: avoiding raised public expectations; promoting fear of change, of new things, of the unknown; perpetuating "fear, loathing and envy" toward people who do not conform to the lowest common denominator; warning that any alternative position always has a hidden agenda that will hurt the most vulnerable, even if the most vulnerable people don't think so; maintaining the mantra that life is always made better for Saskatchewan people by the NDP (without explaining how); and, promoting enough social disharmony to keep negative and unhappy voters—particularly poor and systemically disadvantaged—inside the NDP tent.

In observing the NDP for years—and reading more NDP speeches, campaign platforms, political books and Hansard than any non-NDP human being should be subjected to—there is one last point that unifies the NDP core: brilliant execution. From instituting policy to winning elections and even setting up a target for a smear campaign, few political parties are better at carrying out a plan than the NDP. On every issue, a need is identified, publicized, then "third party" supporters come forward (often choreographed by NDP strategists) the issue is studied, critics are isolated, wedged, sometimes politically marginalized or attacked, and then policy is launched, promoted and driven home hard and quickly.

Unfortunately for Saskatchewan's place in recent history, many NDP policies and government strategies were neither sophisticated nor even particularly smart. But, as clumsily crafted as they were and lacking originality and best practices, these policies were effectively pulled off with the support of NDP stakeholders in academia and inside various proxy groups.

Looking back on the Calvert government and other periods in the history of NDP governments in Saskatchewan, there has been an unwillingness by voters to challenge the natural governing party, to expect—no, demand—higher standards and expectations and to refuse to settle for mediocrity or falling short of the greatness that we can achieve.

For generations in Saskatchewan there has been a type of deference to government, an expectation that they knew "the Saskatchewan way." They didn't. Many NDP governments lost their way and took Saskatchewan with them.

Like many great political dynasties built on personality and the branding of a party through its policies, the NDP's best days are behind them. The imprints of Douglas and Blakeney on Saskatchewan life and politics were significant and set a solid foundation for the political left. Romanow was less a defining political force than he was the guy caught by history to look back to the NDP glory days of the 1970s while fixing the province's finances in the 1990s. By the time Calvert arrived, it was his fate to preside over a shallow talent pool within his own party and to witness the emergence of a cohesive and unified opposition in the SaskParty.

Arrogance is an inevitable byproduct of governing. Stick around long enough and political actors—both inside government and the bureaucracy—become arrogant and detached from reality. In part, this comes from what passes for life in the artificial world under the dome of the Saskatchewan Legislature. Another part of it happens when weak people start power-tripping. Every government gets arrogant and the ones that don't deal with it get defeated.

The Calvert government —with some vestiges of the Romanow-era before it—had MLAs, bureaucrats and political staff whose arrogance had disconnected them from real Saskatchewan people, just as the earlier governments of Devine and Blakeney had grown insufferably arrogant before they collapsed.

Brad Wall's SaskParty government will grow arrogant, too. Trust me on this. If they're smart, they'll stay hyper-vigilant to forestall arrogance for as long as possible. And a lot of the best arrogance prevention comes from a well-grounded premier and a small cadre of advisors who can see life beyond the Legislature's dome. Like the premier, who lives in Swift Current and commutes to Regina several days a week, Wall has a couple of trusted advisors who also don't live in Regina. The longer the premier keeps far away from the political cannibalism, incest and pettiness of the Legislature, the longer he will keep an unjaundiced view of how his team is keeping connected with the people and avoiding arrogance.

At the staff level, the premier's deputy minister must control the civil service; his chief of staff must ruthlessly cycle through senior advisors and ministers' staffers, changing them often to keep them fresh, dynamic, humble and focused on results rather than place, position and arrogance.

Many leaders fall into two traps. First, they are surrounded by "yes" people who keep them insulated from reality and tell them what they want to hear. Second, leaders weaken in the ability to thank someone for their service and then get rid of them, helping advisors and political staff alight back into private life and the worlds of business, professions, academia, think tanks, whatever. There is a tendency in politics—and it was endemic in both the Devine and Calvert governments—to see people well beyond their "best before dates" not being removed from government but being shuffled from Cabinet advisors to government departments, back to the party, Crowns and government agencies and commissions.

The Last Word

I'm the luckiest guy in the world. I like what I do and am fortunate to work with wonderful people and an employer, Gordon Rawlinson, who is a true class act committed to great broadcasting and a stronger, better Saskatchewan.

Every day on the radio is a new and exciting adventure. And, after a dozen years, it's still as satisfying, exhilarating and scary today as the first day we went on the air. For a political junkie I've got the best seat in the house.

In today's Saskatchewan there is an energy, buzz and feel on the street like Alberta in the early 1970s. One of my NDP friends compares Brad Wall to Alberta's Conservative Premier Peter Lougheed who broke 36 consecutive years of Social Credit rule in 1971. With an expanding economy, an aura of personal energy and appeal, an attractive vision and a high personal trust factor, Wall is off to a promising start. Provided that he governs moderately and —most critical—competently, he may be the first political leader in two generations to challenge the NDP to re-evaluate its policies and core values.

No party in Saskatchewan history that has defeated the NDP has ever won a third election. The 1960s Liberals and 1980s Tories knocked off the NDP and won only one subsequent election. If Wall were to win next year in 2011 and again in 2015 he would become the only non-New Democrat since Saskatchewan's first premier, Walter Scott from 1905 to 1916, to have been elected to government three times.

Very few parties in a democracy can govern continuously for decades without constantly re-inventing themselves, moving across the political spectrum and staying closely aligned with changing values, social and economic mores and expectations of the voters. In Saskatchewan, the NDP has done this more than any other party, which explains its electoral successes. But this book has profiled how the NDP "big tent" has become smaller, along with the party's perspective and attitude of low expectations, thinking small and settling for second best.

Among his supporters, there are high hopes that Brad Wall may have the capacity to hug the dynamic political center and bank on strong personal appeal to keep his party closely aligned with voter expectations longer than others have. I don't have a crystal ball—part of me sees Wall as a modern day Tommy Douglas who will be a game changer; another more jaded part sees a guy who will flame out, as every non-NDP leader has, because his party and natural constituency of business people will not have the discipline it takes to stay in the game and understand how complex and subtle governing is.

At this point, with Saskatchewan's future ahead of us, it is easy to look back to those early years, a century ago, of exploding population, boundless hope and a "can do" attitude that required dreaming big and then living it. In those days, Saskatchewan mattered and stood proud, secure in the knowledge that one day there would be millions of people choosing this remarkable place. Saskatchewan excelled, our people expected and got results and still had the enduring optimism for greater things. Most importantly we had a sense of place, second to none in Canada and the belief that there would be better days because we deserved them.

But somewhere we lost our way. We were left out by the people who governed us and left behind by the rest of Canada. We abandoned our high expectations and personal bests in favour of an attitude that accepted mediocrity.

My message is that Saskatchewan does not have to be left out ever again. And we won't be if we look ahead, not backwards, embrace change and deliberately reinforce higher standards of ourselves and those fortunate enough to govern us.

In our politics, it comes down to expecting excellence and the consequences that come from hard work and smart policy. Politics also requires that each one of us empower ourselves as voters, no longer bystanders. And we must accept that political parties —whether new like the SaskParty or decades old like the NDP—must evolve to keep up with the new Saskatchewan rather than justifying the old ways of insularity, building walls and trying to keep the rest of the world out.

Each of us will determine the fate and future of our home and of how it will look for future generations. And it is up to every one of us whether we allow Saskatchewan to ever be left out again.

Bibliography

Barnhart, Gordon (ed.). Saskatchewan Premiers of the Twentieth Century. Regina: CPRC, 2004.

Brown, Lorne, Joseph Brown and John Warnock. Saskatchewan Politics From Left to Right '44 – '99. Regina: Hinterland Publications, 1999.

Bryson, Bill. A Short History of Nearly Everything, New York: Black Swan, 2004.

Crowley, Brian Lee, Jason Clemens and Niels Veldhuis. The Canadian Century: Moving Out of America's Shadow. Toronto: Key Porter, 2010.

Eisler, Dale. False Expectations: Politics and the Pursuit of the Saskatchewan Myth. Regina: CPRC, 2006.

Gergen, David. Eyewitness to Power. New York: Simon and Shuster, 2000.

Goldberg, Bernard. Crazies to the Left of Me, Wimps to the Right: How One Side Lost its Mind and the Other Lost its Nerve. New York: Harper Collins, 2007.

Jones, Gerry. SaskScandal: The Death of Political Idealism in Saskatchewan. Calgary: Fifth House, 2000.

McCourt, Edward. Saskatchewan. Toronto: Macmillan, 1968.

McLeod, Thomas and Ian McLeod. Tommy Douglas: The Road to Jerusalem. Calgary: Fifth House, 2004.

Moon, Robert. This is Saskatchewan. Toronto: Ryerson, 1953.

Moore, James and Wayne Slater. Bush's Brain: How Karl Rove Made George W. Bush Presidential. New York: Wiley, 2003.

Pitsula, James and Ken Rasmussen. Privatizing a Province: The New Right in Saskatchewan. Vancouver: New Star, 1990.

Porter, Jene. Perspectives of Saskatchewan. Winnipeg: University of Manitoba Press, 2009.

Rand, Ayn. Atlas Shrugged. New York: Random House, 1957.

Safire, William. Safire's Political Dictionary. Toronto: Oxford University Press, 2008.

Leeson, Howard (Ed.). Saskatchewan Politics: Crowding the Centre. Regina: CPRC, 2008.

Leeson, Howard (Ed). Saskatchewan Politics: Into the Twenty First Century. Regina: CPRC, 2001.

Siggins, Maggie. Love and Hate: A Canadian Tragedy. Toronto: McClelland & Stewart, 1985.

Simmie, Lois. The Secret Lives of Sgt. John Wilson: A True Story of Love and Murder. Saskatoon: Greystone Books, 2003.

Slayton, Phillip. Lawyers Gone Bad: Money, Sex and Madness in Canada's Legal Profession. Toronto: Viking Canada, 2007.

Spencer, Dick. Singing the Blues: The Conservatives in Saskatchewan. Regina: CPRC, 2007.

Stewart, Walter. The Life and Political Times of Tommy Douglas. Toronto: McArthur & Company, 2003.

Stobbe, Mark and Lesley Biggs, eds. Devine Rule in Saskatchewan: A Decade of Hope and Hardship. Saskatoon: Fifth House Publishers, 1991.

Waiser, Bill. Everett Baker's Saskatchewan Portraits of an Era. Calgary: Fifth House, 2007.

Waiser, Bill. Saskatchewan: A New History. Toronto: Fitzhenry and Whiteside, 2005.

Warren, Jim, and Kathleen Carlisle. On the Side of the People: A History of Labour in Saskatchewan. Regina: Coteau Books, 2005.

Westen, Drew. The Political Brain: The Role of Emotion in Deciding the Fate of the Nation. New York: Public Affairs, 2007.

Wilson, Barry. The Politics of Defeat: The Decline of the Liberal Party in Saskatchewan. Saskatoon: Western Producer Prairie Books, 1980.

Index

About the Author

Opinionated, informed and entertaining,
John Gormley takes no prisoners as
host of Saskatchewan's top-rated radio
talk show. John Gormley Live is heard
weekday mornings on Rawlco Radio's
News Talk 650 CKOM in Saskatoon and
on News Talk 980 CJME in Regina.

A lawyer, John is a former Saskatchewan
Member of Parliament and a graduate
of the University of Saskatchewan College of Law. He writes a popular
weekly newspaper column in the Saskatoon Star Phoenix and has been
recognized by Saskatchewan Business Magazine as one of Saskatchewan's
most influential people. Gormley has been a lecturer in Political Studies
at the U of S and is a sought after convention speaker on a range of
subjects from politics to pop culture.